LOVE AND THE EXPANSION OF SELF

Understanding Attraction and Satisfaction

Arthur Aron
Elaine N. Aron
University of Santa Clara
Santa Clara, California

HEMISPHERE PUBLISHING CORPORATION
A Subsidiary of Harper & Row, Publishers, Inc.
Washington   New York   London

DISTRIBUTION OUTSIDE THE UNITED STATES
McGRAW-HILL INTERNATIONAL BOOK COMPANY

Auckland	Bogotá	Guatemala	Hamburg	Johannesburg
Lisbon	London	Madrid	Mexico	Montreal
New Delhi	Panama	Paris	San Juan	São Paulo
Singapore	Sydney	Tokyo	Toronto	

LOVE AND THE EXPANSION OF SELF: Understanding
Attraction and Satisfaction

1 2 3 4 5 6 7 8 9 0   E B E B   8 9 8 7 6 5

*This book was set in Press Roman by Hemisphere Publishing Corporation.
The editors were Amy Whitmer and Christine Flint; the production
supervisor was Miriam Gonzalez; and the typesetter was Rita Shapiro.
Edwards Brothers, Inc. was the printer and binder.*

Library of Congress Cataloging in Publication Data

Aron, Arthur.
    Love and the expansion of self.   SB 2771 /16 . 4.91

    Bibliography: p.
    Includes index.
    1. Love. 2. Self. 3. Interpersonal relations.
I. Aron, Elaine, II. Title.
BF575.L8A825   1985   158'.2   85-13970
ISBN 0-89116-394-8 (hard cover)
ISBN 0-89116-459-6 (soft cover)

SM 2771. INF
(Aro)

16.00

LOVE
AND THE EXPANSION
OF SELF

Contents

Preface   *ix*

I
THE MEANING OF SELF-EXPANSION

1   **Background**   3
      Introduction   3
      Study of Love in the West   3
      Vedic Psychology   6
      Main Vedic Psychology Concepts Used in This Book   7

2   **"Self"**   9
      Introduction   9
      Self-Concept   9
      Self versus Self-Concept   10
      Self Itself or "Actual Self"   11
      Components of the Actual Self: "I" and "Me"   11
      Eastern View of the Self   13
      A More Comprehensive Understanding of the Self   17

3   **"Expansion" and "Including Others in the Self"**   19
      Introduction   19
      Motivation to Expand the Self   19
      "Incorporating Aspects of an Other into the Self"   27

II
IMPLICATIONS FOR ATTRACTION

4   **Predicting Attraction**   33
        Introduction   33
        Definitions of Attraction   33
        Research   34

5   **Understanding Attraction**
        Introduction   41
        General Theoretical Perspectives   41
        Attraction as Self-Expansion   45
        Definition of Attraction Reconsidered   52

6   **Strong Attractions**   55
        Introduction   55
        Types of Attraction   55
        Causes of Strong Attractions   61

III
MAINTAINING RELATIONSHIPS

7   **Theoretical Perspectives**   71
        Introduction   71
        Prevalence of Maintained Relationships   71
        Major In-Depth Study   72
        Theoretical Perspectives   73
        Social Exchange Theory   73
        Role Theory/Symbolic Interactionism   77
        Psychodynamic Theories   79
        General Systems Theory   81
        Comparison of the Four Approaches   83
        Self-Expansion and the Maintenance of Relationships   85
        Does Expansion of the Self Imply Losing the Self?   88

8   **Getting Tired of the Other**   91
        Introduction   91
        The Scope of the Problem   91
        Theoretical Explanations   92
        Current Proposed Solutions   94
        Marital Happiness and Boredom in Light of Self-Expansion   96
        Pure Consciousness Experience as a Facilitator of Solutions
            to Getting Tired of the Other   102

9   **Obstacles to Expansion**   109
        Introduction   109
        Ineffective Communication and Problem Solving
            or Other Skill Deficits   110
        Incompatibility   114
        Difficulty Coping with Change   117
        The Other's Poor Mental or Physical Health   122
        Social Stressors   123
        Alternatives to the Relationship   124

10   **Optimal Relationships**   129
        Introduction   129
        Studies of Optimal Relationships   129
        Comparisons on One Variable   131
        Theories   134
        Optimal Relationships and Self-Expansion   136

References   139
Author Index   157
Subject Index   165

Preface

This book explores a single theme—that the emotions, cognitions, and behaviors of love can be understood in terms of a basic motivation to expand the self. It also provides a broad overview of the literature on interpersonal attraction and on the maintenance of close relationships—not only romantic relationships, but friendship, sibling, and parent-child relationships as well. The book's main purpose, however, is to stimulate thinking by offering a new approach to unifying this wealth of data, using the idea of self-expansion, and to illustrate this idea's theoretical and practical implications.

This unifying proposition—taken from Eastern thinking—is radically different from the ways love usually has been understood by the social sciences as developed in the West, where love has been explained with one of the following motivations: hedonism, tension reduction, normative expectations, reduction of uncertainty or cognitive disorder, resolution of unconscious conflicts, or attainment of mastery or power. These are all such successful, long-standing approaches to understanding behavior that one tends to doubt that there could be any others. Thus a fresh perspective from our planet's other hemisphere is bound to be at least thought provoking.

Using its own systematic theories, research methods, and evaluation of the effects of practical applications, the East has studied the psyche for thousands of years (if one accepts the idea that science can take a form that is not identical in its surface details to the form Western science has taken). From this Eastern psychology—specifically, its oldest "school," the Vedic tradition—we have taken this book's central idea: *Another way of understanding the motivation for loving thoughts and behaviors would be to see them as attempts to expand the self as fully as possible.*

Approaching a psychological phenomenon from such a new perspective—Eastern—presents difficulties for both authors and readers. It is easy for us, as authors, to assume that our readers will understand ideas that are obvious to us, but entirely new to them. We have tried our best to explain these ideas in several contexts and to relate them to familiar theories. It is also easy for readers to hold preconceptions that are very difficult for authors to overcome. For example, in this case, that a person who discusses an Eastern viewpoint, especially a particular school of Eastern thought, probably holds that viewpoint as a matter of faith, or accepts its ideas on the basis of authority.

All we can say to help our readers overcome this preconception is that we have chosen our use of Eastern ideas only on the basis of their empirical support and their usefulness in understanding and organizing the data on love. We have tried to be very clear about what we think is fairly well proven, and what we regard as merely possible implications that seem worth testing.

Now a word about the scope of this book. It considers the literature on both initial attractions and ongoing, close relationships of all types. The book's focus, however, is primarily on the individual, as its principle theme implies, rather than on the relationship. Although we feel that the study of relationship variables is an excellent approach to understanding love, it is not the one emphasized here.

As for the book's authors, we are two psychologists—one social, one clinical; the intended readers are our colleagues in psychology, sociology, marriage and family counseling, communications, psychiatry, ethology, and other fields, who are researching and/or trying to facilitate loving relationships. We also hope that the book will be useful for students in graduate or advanced undergraduate courses studying close relationships.

The book is divided into three parts. Part I explores the central theme of love as self-expansion. It begins with some background on the history of love research in the West, and introduces Vedic psychology. Then it analyzes in detail our use of the terms "self" and "expansion."

Part II considers the implications of love as self-expansion for the research on attraction—first generally, and then for strong attractions.

Part III considers the implications of the book's central idea for maintaining love relationships. It begins with some additional aspects of expansion of the self that require consideration when the idea is applied to ongoing relationships. Then it discusses the motivations to stay in relationships and the motivations and problems that lead to a relationship dissolution. Finally, we review opinions about future navigation in the field—the issue of optimal relationships. While Part II's concern was with falling in love, Part III's is with staying in love. The latter, apparently tougher to manage, has inspired far more applied research. Thus this part takes on a more practical tone than Part II.

This book has been a labor of love for many besides ourselves. In particular, we thank Professors E. Berscheid, M. Dermer, W. Grazziano, and A. Tesser for their thoughtful comments on the seed paper for this book. We are especially grateful to Professors M. C. Dillbeck, D. G. Dutton, J. B. Gilmore, and two anonymous reviewers for their very helpful responses to the entire manuscript. We also wish to thank our mothers, who first taught us the meaning of love.

Arthur Aron
Elaine N. Aron

I

The Meaning of Self-Expansion

1

Background

INTRODUCTION

Our basic proposition is that an individual seeks to expand his or her self. Each does so in many ways, one of which is through relationships with others. People enter and maintain close, loving relationships in order to enjoy expansion through the incorporation of aspects of the other into the self.

So far as we know, this is a new approach to the Western scientific understanding of personal relationships. Further, its source—Eastern, and specifically, Vedic psychology—has been outside the Western scientific tradition. Therefore, before plunging into what is new, we would like to review the history of the study of love in the West. Then we will discuss in an introductory way Eastern psychology and, in particular, its Vedic tradition.

STUDY OF LOVE IN THE WEST

In 1970, one of us audaciously set out to construct and experimentally test a theory of love for a doctoral dissertation. We made an intensive search of the scholarly literature and uncovered fewer than twenty books (and less than a dozen research articles) directly on the topic of love (Aron, 1970). Of course, throughout history, most great thinkers have at least commented on the topic—but mainly in passing, and rarely in a systematic way.

The first major treatment was in Plato's *Symposium,* which characterized love as serving a human desire for immortality and union. This theme, or variations on it, pervaded nearly everything else written on love in the succeeding 2500 years, inside and outside of philosophy.

Other major contributions came mainly from literary figures, most notably the French novelist Stendhal. His classic *On Love* puts in essay form a discussion of the usual literary emphasis on passion and "falling in love" (which he described in terms of a "crystallization").

Then, around the beginning of this century, the historian-anthropologists took an interest in love, yielding such classics as Westermarck's *History of Human Marriage*. Writers in this tradition typically took a Darwinian approach to love, showing in a variety of cultural contexts how it functions to promote reproduction.

However, the major figures in the quest during the first half of this century were psychiatrists and clinical psychologists. The classical Freudians emphasized libido, cathexis, parent images, and the like, while the "revisionists" offered alternative explanations that were, however, still in the psychoanalytic tradition of unconscious determinants of behavior. Theodore Reik's conceptualization of love as vicarious fulfillment of the ego ideal and Carl Jung's theory of anima and animus archetypes are probably the two best known theories from that era.

By the 1950s there was a growing interest in love among sociologists studying marriage and family. The most cited results were studies of "mate-selection," "marital satisfaction," and "attachment" in child rearing. The favored methodology was large questionnaire studies, with the hope that certain simple, molar variables would predict important differences (e.g., a mother's positive self-regard predicting her child's marital happiness in adulthood).

At the same time, the emerging post-Lewinian experimental social psychology, while mainly focused on "group dynamics" and "attitudes," was showing a small interest in a variety of topics which bordered on the psychology of love: "need for affiliation," "the acquaintance process," "interpersonal exchange," "group cohesion," and even "positive attitudes" towards objects that happened to be persons!

In the early and mid-1960s, a few more sociologists, clinicians, and social psychologists took an interest in the topic of love. In sociology, Winch's (1958) theory of need-complementarity in mate selection was widely influential. Clinical psychology and psychiatry showed a growing interest in marital and family therapy, family communications, and family systems. And in mainstream social psychology, studies of "interpersonal attraction" were in good repute, especially following the seminal work on the effects of attitude similarity on attraction conducted by Donn Byrne and his students. All of these will be considered in more depth in coming chapters.

In the late 1960s, social psychology finally took a real interest in attractions of a bit more intensity than a slightly positive first impression. Byrne began to study interpersonal attraction between men and women (sometimes in ongoing relationships), and Hatfield (then Walster), Berscheid, and their associates carried out the first of what are now classic studies of "romantic liking" and "dating behavior."

Again, their findings will receive considerable attention in this book. But for now we simply wish to give a picture of what a shelf of books and articles on love might have contained by 1970. Clearly the shelf was not empty. But on the other hand, if you opened the two most popular social psychology texts of the 1960s (Krech et al.'s *The Individual in Society* and Roger Brown's *Social Psychology*), you would not have even found the word "love" in their indexes!

Moreover, the fledgling research area was meeting resistance both in and out of social psychology. Most of the books and articles written at this time began with stories of how difficult it was to study love scientifically, or how the authors' academic colleagues looked down on the topic. Indeed, Hatfield (Walster, 1971) commented that it seemed to be one of those topics that inspired researchers to conduct one study, early in their career, before turning to more "serious" topics. No doubt the best example of resistance was Senator Proxmire's strong attack on the awarding of federal research funds to Berscheid and Hatfield for the study of love.

Nevertheless, the study of love *did* survive, and in the 1970s it became a major topic in social psychology. Of all articles published in the *Journal of Personality and Social Psychology,* articles on "attraction" constituted 0% in 1944, 1949, and 1954; about 2% in 1964; nearly 6% by 1969; and in 1973 they were more than 10% of all articles (Lamberth, 1980).

Social psychology's research on love in the 1970s mainly followed the method-ological and theoretical fashions of the 1960s. The method was laboratory experi-ments, and the theoretical approaches were cognitive balance and dissonance theories; exchange, equity, and reward theories; cognitive labeling of emotions and attribution theories; reactance theory; and the like. This body of research provides one of the major sources of empirical data cited in this book.

However, by the end of the 1970s some serious limitations to the typical experi-mental-social-psychology approach to love were being voiced. A "crisis" in social psychology had been announced in the early 1970s, from a widespread feeling that the field had stagnated and was failing to produce any practical results. As a result, there arose a new emphasis on "external generalizability" and on the study of issues having practical, social importance. By the late 1970s this new emphasis had finally caught up with the researchers working on the social psychology of love. Suddenly it seemed obvious that insights from "attraction" generated in the laboratory might not be very applicable to the strong or long-term emotions of love felt in the rest of the world.

Moreover, it was finally recognized that there is more to a relationship than initial attraction, and that "romantic" love is not the only important close human relationship. Thus in the 1980s there is talk of "passionate" versus "compassion-ate" love; of "systems properties" and of the general nature of "close relationships" and "intimacy"; of "commitment" to, "maintenance" of, and "dissolution" of relationships; and of the nature of friendship, parent-child, sibling, and other non-"romantic" love relationships. Above all, emotions are re-entering social psychology generally, after a very cognitive couple of decades, so that the emotional aspect of love is finally getting some attention.

As the study of love has become less tied to experimental social psychology of the 1960s, it has also opened up to a more interdisciplinary perspective. The First International Conference on Personal Relationships (held in the summer of 1982) was mainly organized by social psychologists, but they were a minority of the attendees. Others present included psychologists in the developmental, industrial, and clinical areas, and researchers from departments of sociology, ethology, and communications. Both the meeting and the citations in current research articles show that a real interdisciplinary research interest has developed. There is even a growing acknowledgment by researchers that those on the "front lines"—counse-lors and consultants in the areas of marriage, parent-child, family, and work rela-tionships—have much to contribute.

As for this book, it follows very much in the tradition just described: Its roots are in the earlier work in social psychology, in the still earlier work in clinical psychology and sociology, and in the thoughtful proposals of the philosophers and other thinkers who preceded the social sciences.

At the same time, this book looks outside these traditional sources, because there is a growing feeling that the study of love still sorely needs some kind of unifying conceptual framework. With this book we hope to help achieve this goal, by introducing an idea—the motive of self-expansion—which is crucial to Eastern psychology's understanding of love, but thus far only peripheral to the West's. As Hall and Lindzey (1978) point out in their chapter on Eastern psychology, "Other peoples have developed theories of personality as sophisticated and as well grounded in empirical observation as our own" (p. 347). Thus it seems not only appropriate but prudent to take advantage of some of these theories and data, especially when we are searching for new ideas.

VEDIC PSYCHOLOGY

Eastern psychology and its Western siblings are similar in at least one respect: They are rich with competing traditions, each with their "eminent researchers" and acceptable research methodologies. However, almost all Eastern traditions originate from one core, much as almost all Western psychology springs from a commitment to Baconian-style science. That core is the Vedic literature, said to be the oldest continuous body of knowledge about the workings of the human mind (Basham, 1959).

The familiar varieties of Eastern psychology (e.g., Buddhism, Vedanta, Hatha Yoga) all arise from differing interpretations of that Vedic core, or major reformations in the course of the Vedic tradition's evolution. And whether the practical implications of a particular approach suggest one should improve behavior, follow certain physical practices, meditate, study the *Bhagavad-Gita* (a small but crucial part of the Vedic literature), or whatever—these techniques are all discussed somewhere in the Vedic literature.

In approaching Eastern psychology, we have chosen to rely mainly on the very cogent descriptions of Eastern thinking in the "Vedic psychology" developed by Maharishi Mahesh Yogi (e.g., 1969, 1972, in the form of the "science of creative intelligence") and those working with him (e.g., Orme-Johnson et al., in press). Although a well-known Vedic scholar, Maharishi is of course best known in the West as the developer of the Transcendental Meditation and TM-Sidhi program. But while Vedic psychology emphasizes meditation as the Vedas' most important contribution to *applied* psychology, its diccussions of the Vedic literature itself, in relation to both theoretical and applied psychology, tend to be very inclusive, rather than focused on one aspect of the Vedas.

Three other characteristics of Vedic psychology make it a particularly useful point of entry for Western social scientists into Eastern theories:

1. Clear parallels have been made between Eastern and Western concepts, often by translating the former into the latter's equivalent terms. This task has been tried by Westerners dipping into Eastern literature (e.g., Carl Jung and Alan Watts), but clearly something useful would be added when an expert from the East, who is also fluent in Western concepts (Maharishi has a degree in physics), does the boundary crossing.

2. There is already a substantial body of research and operationalization in other areas of social science (besides relationships) based on Vedic psychology concepts and applications (e.g., Kanellakos, 1978; Orme-Johnson & Farrow, 1977; Truch, 1977).

3. This approach makes the assumption that whatever is worthwhile in the Vedic literature can eventually be operationalized and subjected to empirical test—that nothing in this domain is mystical or inherently beyond the reach of intellectual understanding and experimental test.

MAIN VEDIC PSYCHOLOGY CONCEPTS USED IN THIS BOOK

Of course, the aspects of psychology emphasized by the East, like those emphasized in the West, traditionally have not included much on the nature of love relationships. Indeed, in the East the main theorists have very often been monks and recluses, and thus perhaps even less inclined than Western psychologists to focus on this very "worldly" topic. Accordingly, there is relatively little written specifically on friendship, family, or romantic relationships in traditional Eastern texts. But as with Western psychology, what little there is, is very provocative. In particular, the perspective presented in this book comes mainly from two short but very rich sources.

The first is a passage in the Vedic *Upanishads (Brihadaranyaka Upanishad* 4.V.1). "The [wife's] love of the husband is not for the sake of the husband but for the sake of the self; the [husband's] love of the wife is not for the sake of the wife but for the sake of the self." and so on, eventually including love of children, wealth, and every other conceivable affection.

The second is a videotaped 1970 lecture by Maharishi, which is apparently an elaboration of the same point. It is titled "The Source, Course and Goal of Love," and in it he says, for example, "All love is directed to the self. . . . The purpose of love is the expansion of the self. . . ."

In both these quotations, the motivation for loving behavior is said to be the enhancement or expansion of the self. The full text of these and other Vedic passages makes clear that the motivation not only for love but for all behavior is seen to be self-expansion. Love is apparently emphasized in these passages because love is especially likely to be thought of as "selfless."* In the Vedic context, self and self-expansion have very specific meanings, which are discussed in the next two chapters.

In addition to what Vedic psychology has to say specifically about love, this book will refer extensively to one concept of Vedic psychology which is closely related to the idea of self-expansion—the experience of *pure consciousness.* According to Vedic psychology, the self in its truest, most expanded sense is known only through this experience, which is described as a state of alert awareness—without thoughts, feelings, or perceptions, but simply awareness by itself (Farrow & Hebert, 1982).

There is much, much more to Vedic psychology than this book can discuss. Nevertheless, besides our central purpose, in this book we also attempt to introduce from the East this sometimes very different way of looking at human behavior.

---

*For most readers, the idea of love not being "selfless" is already familiar from current approaches to close relationships, such as exchange theory. But for other readers—perhaps justly proud of our long ethical tradition of at least trying, lovingly, to put others first—this view of love as self-expansion or self-anything may sound like a backwards step in our social evolution! However, in the end we think the self-expansion approach actually substantiates the possibility of "selfless" love very well.

2

"Self"

INTRODUCTION

In this chapter we explore the first of the two crucial components of what we mean by "self-expansion." First we consider current research findings and conceptualizations relevant to the self, then the view of the self which has developed in the East. Finally, we give the conception of the self used in this book, which integrates Eastern and Western descriptions.

SELF-CONCEPT

"Self" is used in many ways by psychologists and other social scientists. Those who have written on the topic typically distinguish between (a) *what I perceive myself to be* and (b) *the actual self to which my self-perceptions refer.*

The first—one's perception of oneself—is generally called the "self-concept" and has generated a considerable body of research literature and techniques of measurement (reviewed in Wylie, 1974, 1979).

This self-concept, or self as an object constructed from perceptions, plays a central role in modern symbolic interactionist approaches to social psychology (e.g., Gergen, 1977; Kinch, 1963; McCall, 1977). These in turn follow from the early work of Cooley (1902) and Mead (1934). In symbolic interaction theories the self is a highly changeable construction based on one's current perceptions of how others see one.

Personality psychologists (see Hall & Lindzey, 1970), on the other hand, mainly emphasize the issue of how one evaluates the self one perceives—the esteem or approval one holds for one's self, the control one feels the self has over the outcome of events. They also usually describe this concept as difficult to alter very much after childhood (although sometimes therapeutically it may be essential to try to make such an alteration).

Recent experimental social psychology focuses mainly on how an individual maintains or restores a particular self-view despite conflicting information (e.g., Gollwitzer et al., 1982; Greenwald, 1980; Swann & Read, 1981), and on how one's "self-schemata" affect the processing of self-relevant information (e.g., Markus, 1977). (Self-schemata are self-relevant cognitive structures, such as thinking of oneself as an independent person, which, when all are taken together, could be considered a kind of self-concept.) Two influential earlier papers related to the self-schemata approach are Sarbin's (1952) view of the self as a cross section of the entire cognitive structure at a given point in time, and Epstein's (1973) argument that the self-concept is constructed by individuals in much the same way that scientists construct theories.

Psychologists take considerable interest in the self-concept issue, as illustrated by a series of major papers of the last 30 years in the *American Psychologist, Psychological Review,* and *Psychological Bulletin.* These include at least two American Psychological Association presidential addresses on the topic (Hilgard, 1949; Smith, 1978). Overall, it seems that most psychologists hold the self-concept to be an integrating conceptual structure one maintains about oneself, playing an important role in mediating behavior and perception.

SELF VERSUS SELF-CONCEPT

What about the actual self, to which one's self-concept refers? Just as there is a useful distinction made in the field of person perception between the actual characteristics of a person and the perceptions of that person by others, one can make a distinction between the perception of the self and the actual self. But exactly how to make this distinction in the area of the self has been a source of considerable confusion (e.g., see Alston, 1977). Above all, in spite of the distinction, there seems to have been an overemphasis on the self-concept, at the expense of what it is a concept of. A recent study (Ferguson et al., 1983) of self-schemata is illustrative. Knowing whether a person admires a trait (one's admiration for a trait being an aspect of the actual self) predicted how quickly that person could process information about the trait *just as well* as knowing whether the trait was perceived to be unusually self-relevant (that is, an aspect of the self-concept).

Another confusion arising from the emphasis on self-concept has been the tendency to see self-schemata or a "self-theory" as an actual agent of action—as a doer who initiates and controls. For example, Epstein (1973) implies that the self-theory acts, and makes an analogy between the "self-theory" and scientific theory—that one's self-theory influences the individual much as scientific theories influence scientists. But while theories certainly do "influence" scientists' behavior, theories don't *act.* The scientists themselves act. Similarly, Markus' (1980) argument that schemata may be "patterns for action" still leaves the question of patterns for *whose* actions?

Of course, it is possible that there is no agent of action at all, and stimuli become responses by being filtered through a set of higher-order internal processes. But why not then call these the self? They cannot be properly called self-schemata, or the self-concept, because such higher-order schemata do not seem to be something one perceives about one's self. Nor are they perceived as uniquely self-relevant. In other words, while they are not self-schemata, they are still a crucial part of the self. Further, they may even be said to cause behavior, in at least the sense that Sarbin (1952) has suggested—that behavior is determined by one's cognitive structure at a given point in time. In short, to refrain from calling that totality of structures the self appears only to invite confusion.

SELF ITSELF
OR "ACTUAL SELF"

Whether we are right or not that the self itself, the object of the self-concept, has been unduly neglected—it is very clear there has been little agreement as to what such an "actual self" might consist of. For example, the symbolic interactionist position is that the object of my self-perceptions is simply how others see my place in society. As Gergen (1977) put it, when it comes to self-knowledge, "there is no *thing* to know" (p. 19). While people seem to feel that there is something to know (e.g., James, 1890/1948), and there is evidence that people's self-concepts are not simply a function of how they think others see them (Shrauger & Schoeneman, 1979), this position remains influential.

At the other extreme from seeing the self as "nothing to know," personality psychologists such as Rogers (1947, 1959) and Freud make the self or ego the cornerstone of their theories. It is an active agent, integrator, and experiencer. Hall and Lindzey call this the "self-as-process," which includes "thinking, remembering, and perceiving" (1970, p. 516).

However, the actual self seems to be even more than these processes. Self-esteem, for example, is esteem for far more than just one's subjective processes, or even for all one's subjective experience (see Snygg & Combs' "phenomenal field", 1949). Individuals also esteem their characteristics, abilities, social positions, even their bodies and possessions. Indeed, when people are asked "Who am I?" they list all of these things about themselves (Kuhn & McPartland, 1954).

Lewin (1936) took a more general position about the self: He called it the person. He first defined the "life space" as the "totality of facts which determine the behavior . . . of an individual at a certain moment" (p. 216). He then defined the "person" as a region of the life space whose outer edge is the "sensori-motor stratum." Whatever the person does is a joint function of the person and the environment (represented together by the life space). Lewin expressed this elegantly with the formula B equals f (P, E). (This formula has in recent years been resuscitated, in response to W. Mischel's influential argument published in 1968, that behavior is almost entirely a function of the situation, i.e., environmental demands.)

Lewin's formula implies that the role of the person in influencing behavior is whatever is left over after the influence of the immediate environment is removed. (We realize that there may also be interactions of the person and the environment.) Thus the person would include effects of past environments (memories, habits, schemata, etc.), plus anything—if there is anything—not in the environment at all (e.g., inherited tendencies, releaser mechanisms, Piagetian potential cognitive structures, Jungian archetypes, Platonic ideals, or whatever).

COMPONENTS OF THE ACTUAL
SELF: "I" AND "ME"

So we might define the self as the total person, as does T. Mischel (1977), for example. Yet we may still be bothered by the feeling there is some deep central core of the personality which is one's "real" self. True, when asked to describe one's self, or when examining what influences self-esteem, it is clear that much more comes to mind than this inner core. Yet the subjective feeling that such a core exists is very strong.

James (1890/1948) dealt with the issue nicely. He described the self as including both the "I"—the actor/experiencer—and three "me"s—thought processes, social relations, and body and possessions. A similar distinction has been followed by most subsequent writers on the self, with some refinements: Today all the "me's" aspects—body, possessions, roles, and so forth—are typically treated as *cognitions* of body, possessions, roles, and so forth. Moreover, this collection of cognitions is typically assumed to be a system which is highly integrated and probably hierarchical.

The other half of James' distinction, the "I," is largely ignored. A minority (e.g., Rogers, Freud) have focused on what they call the "self" or "ego." But as James himself recognized, this "I" is usually so far from observable behavior—being the doer, and not any particular action done—that all discussions of it tend to wobble back into the realm of the subjective and unscientific. In particular, the I-as-free-causal-agent may be explained away as simply an illusion of responsibility for the spontaneous but not entirely conscious processes of transforming input to output via cognitive schemata.

The I as experiencer, however, is not so easily dismissed. Admittedly, it has not been easy to experience, much less observe the consequences of, such an experiencer. James tried but felt he could not; as did Mill, who wrote:

> There is something I call myself... or... my mind... distinct from these sensations, thoughts, and so forth ... something which I conceive not to be the thought, but the being that has the thought, and which I can conceive of as existing forever in a state of quiescence without any thoughts at all ... [yet] what this being is, though it is myself, I have no knowledge. (1904, p. 40)

Yet a sense of this self seems to accompany every experience, which is precisely why James (1890/1948) included the "I" in his description of the self. He wrote:

> Whatever I may be thinking of, I am always at the same time more or less aware of myself, of my personal existence. At the same time it is I who am aware; so that the total self of me, being as it were duplex, partly known and partly knower, partly object and partly subject ... must have two aspects ... we may call one the me ... and the other the I. (p. 176)

Myths have been perpetuated for millennia. Even a belief so universally held as the existence of a self as experiencer could simply be a socially supported false inference from experience.

On the other hand, the only argument for dismissing the existence of the "I" is parsimony: It has not been necessary to posit an "I" to explain most phenomena, so it has been simpler to do without it. But the parsimony argument is rather weak when weighed against an apparently universal and still unexplained sense of "something being there," the actuality of which is doubted only by a few philosophers and psychologists when in their most abstract mood. Thus, since psychology cannot yet explain everything, especially the subjective sense of self, some consideration of this rather difficult and abstract aspect of the self could yet be necessary.

Perhaps the strongest argument for the "I" is the repeated claim by some that they have fully experienced it. These included Socrates and Plato (the "Vision of the Form of the Good"), Augustine, Teresa of Avila, and even psychology's own

Gustav Fechner and Carl Jung. These and others, in a wide variety of cultural settings, have reported an experience in which, when the mind was sufficiently "settled," they experienced the "self"–free of thoughts, quiescent, yet aware. An example of this may be found in Gowan's discussion (1980) of the various experiences he groups under "syntaxic modes."*

In sum, the Western scientific approach to the self has distinguished the self-concept from what it is a concept of, and identifies that actual self as consisting of both a "me" aspect, which is a system of mental processes, knowledge, and cognitions of one's body, possessions, status, and so forth; plus a possible "I" aspect which imparts the sense of an underlying experiencer.

EASTERN VIEW OF THE SELF

Actual Self

If Western psychology, in its avid study of the self-concept, has only reluctantly described the actual self or person—and when defining it at all, only roughly dividing it into an "I" and a "me," and researching only the latter—Eastern psychology has done the complete reverse. The actual self is focal, being the determiner of the self-concept. And the most important aspect of the actual self is the perceiver or "I," which can be directly experienced. (Terms for the experience include *nirvana, samadhi,* and *kaivalya.*) In fact, the full development of this experience is considered the fundamental human motivation, whether a conscious one or not.

Vedic psychology treats this crucially self-defining experience with considerable precision. It is the experience of "pure consciousness," and in its simplest form it is said to be a subjective experience of alert yet quiescent awareness—without thoughts, feelings, or perception, but simply awareness by itself (Maharishi, 1972). In addition, objectively it is distinguished by certain thus far unique physiological correlates. Because this experience is so important in Vedic psychology's definition of the self, at this point we will delve more deeply into the evidence for its existence.

The idea and the reported experience of pure consciousness have been with us, even in the West, since the beginning of recorded history. In both East and West the experience was sometimes reported to occur spontaneously, but more often it was said to require some technique, plus some guidance from someone already having the experience. Either way, because of the relative rarity of the experience, it eluded scientific study until recently.

Then in the sixties and seventies the Transcendental Meditation ("TM") technique** and other forms of meditation began to be widely taught in the West.

*Even Freud was deeply impressed by the possibility of such an experience, as indicated by his discussion of it ("the oceanic experience") in the first pages of one of his last major works, *Civilization and Its Discontents* (1930/1961). Clearly he felt that if it existed, it would greatly change psychology, and certainly his own pessimistic conclusions about the possibility for individual happiness and social peace. But he admitted he'd never had the experience himself, and concluded it must be an extreme form of wish fulfillment.

**A mental procedure, said to be derived from Vedic sources. It is used twenty minutes twice a day and employs a "meaningless sound" as a "mantra," with a specific procedure for using the mantra. The technique is learned in about ten hours, spread over six days. (See Bloomfield et al., 1975).

The TM technique in particular was said to be a major breakthrough for Vedic psychology, providing the pure consciousness experience far more efficiently than even other Eastern techniques (because of the insight that a completely quiescent state might best be achieved with the least effortful technique, rather than by concentration techniques, which had become dominant in recent times; Domash, 1977).

Since 1970, the TM program has generated over 300 studies (of which we are aware). Although there is, of course, debate over the adequacy of and the conclusions drawn from some of these studies, several careful investigations have focused on the pure consciousness experience specifically (rather than TM effects generally) and have found physiological and behavioral changes which correspond strikingly to those reported by supposed experiencers of pure consciousness in other times and locales (e.g., Patanjali, Plato, Philo, Plotinus, St. Augustine, St. Teresa).

In one of the most interesting series of studies, Farrow (1977; Farrow & Hebert, 1982) had TM participants press a button activating a polygraph event marker during their meditations, immediately after they thought they had had the experience. The periods just preceding the button presses were reliably associated with sudden periods of breath suspension and could not be explained as intentional, since subjects did not know the hypotheses being tested or (thanks to some clever physiological apparatus) that breathing was even being measured. Moreover, there was no compensatory breathing afterwards, suggesting (along with other physiological results) that the breath suspension did not result in a loss of needed oxygen to the system, but that the subjects were simply using less oxygen during these periods.

In a comparison with control subjects, Farrow and Hebert found 28 experienced TM participants had an average, per meditation, of 5.9 breath suspension periods averaging 10.8 seconds each. The 23 controls had a mean (per eyes-closed relaxation period of the same length) of 0.6 breath suspension periods averaging 4.3 seconds. (The difference between groups was, of course, highly statistically significant.) Another group of 11 experienced meditators showed similar numbers and lengths of breath suspension periods, while a group of newer meditators showed significantly fewer and shorter periods—though still consistently greater than the eyes-closed rest control group. Finally, an intensive study of a single, experienced meditator showed that periods in which there were frequent experiences of pure consciousness (as shown by button presses and breath suspension periods) were also characterized by significant reductions in heart rate and increases in skin resistance and EEG coherence (see below), among other measures.

As for the subjective experience, one self-report stated, "There is a very dramatic change . . . like skiing down a ski jump; at a certain point you leave the ski jump and suddenly you are in the air. In transcending, you dive down and down, and 'click,' you find yourself in that other state, just 'there' " (Farrow & Hebert, 1982, p. 144).

Farrow summarizes his impression of subjects' reports of the development of the experiences as follows:

[There is a gradual change] characterized by an increasingly quiet and orderly state of mind, by an expansion of awareness, and by a reduction of mental boundaries until, all at once, a state of "unboundedness" is reached. . . . [It] is essentially the same for different people and is not affected by the circumstances preceding it, by the mood

of the experiencer, or by the passage of time during the period of [experiencing pure] consciousness. The duration and clarity of the experience may vary, but apparently not the basic characteristics of the experience. (1977, p. 109)

Another line of research has focused on EEG changes coinciding with reported pure consciousness experiences. Following a technique developed by Levine (1976), both Farrow and Hebert (1982) and Levine et al. (1977) observed dramatic increases in phase coherence of EEG alpha and theta among frontal and central scalp readings when subjects reported the experience. Subsequent studies by Orme-Johnson and Haynes (1981) and Dillbeck and Bronson (1981) confirmed a high correlation of EEG coherence measured in this way during meditation with subjective reports of the experience obtained immediately after meditation. The EEG coherence measured in these studies is described as "a measure of long range spatial coherence of the nervous system" (Farrow & Hebert, 1982, p. 149).

Finally, in some recent studies of college students, reports of this experience and/or its EEG coherence pattern appear to be correlated with several measures of functioning taken outside of meditation, including grade point average; creativity, intelligence, and moral judgment test scores; neuromuscular coordination; and cognitive flexibility (Dillbeck, Orme-Johnson, & Wallace, 1981; Orme-Johnson, 1981; Orme-Johnson & Haynes, 1981). This is consistent with claims by Eastern and Western experiencers through the ages that the experience of this ultimate self is beneficial to the overall quality of functioning.

This EEG coherence seems to be unique to the pure consciousness experience. The two have been associated with sufficient reliability for researchers to use the occurrence of this pattern as an indication of the pure consciousness experience, in the same way that REM plus the Stage 1 EEG pattern of sleep is considered to be a reliable indicator of dreaming. Further, this pattern has been observed to some extent in essentially all TM participants who have been tested. Thus in this book, when we have wanted to discuss pure consciousness, we have assumed that even though a study may not use physiological measures, if it employs TM participants it is a study of those who generally have the pure consciousness experience.

However, we do not mean to suggest that TM meditation is the only method producing pure consciousness in modern times. That simply is not known. But the few studies that permit comparisons among different methods of meditation, biofeedback, or relaxation suggest that different procedures produce different results (e.g., Abrams, 1977; Morse et al., 1977; Stroebel & Glueck, 1978). Even what would appear to be very slight differences in procedures seem to have substantial effects on results (Morse et al., 1979a, 1979b). Further, most of these techniques do not claim to produce the pure consciousness experience and involve repeating thoughts or concentrating on perceptions in such a way as to make the experience highly unlikely.

Self-Concept

As those in the West do, Eastern psychologies describe ordinary (non-"enlightened") persons as identifying the self with the "me" aspect: mental processes and cognitions of body, social roles, possessions, etc. However, unlike Western psychology, the Eastern approaches emphasize that the identification of self with only these "me" aspects is an error, due to lack of direct experiences of the "I." But once an individual has the experience, self-perception changes.

A parable from the *Upanishads (Chandogya Upanishad VIII:7-12*, part of the Vedic literature) illustrates the point. It mirrors the Western analysis of the "me" self as far as that analysis has gone, and then goes further. In the parable a student is given progressively more abstract explanations of the self: It is how one looks. No, it is the body, No, it is sensation. No, it is best experienced in the dream state. No, in one's sleep. Finally, after many years of exploring the concept, the student is shown that the self is the perceiver, separate from the senses or processes of perception and acting as a witness to all inner and outer events.

In keeping with this parable, Vedic psychology (Maharishi, 1969, 1972) contends that for most people the self is indeed identified with subjective processes and objects of experience. Those who really think about it, as James did, might deduce the existence of an "I" experiencer as a logical necessity, because someone must actually do the experiencing. Nevertheless, the most that can be known about the self without the pure consciousness experience is that "Deep within . . . we experience the 'myness' of feeling. We say 'I feel like this,' 'I feel.' 'I feel *my* feelings' " (Maharishi, 1972, p. 19-4).

All this is said to change, however, when one has experienced one's self as fully conscious and aware, but not aware of any particular thing. One has finally experienced the reality, not just the logical necessity, of the "I." At this point, the previous identification of the self with cognitions, perceptions, and behaviors begins to erode, so that all these phenomena are seen as merely the "interplay of the forces of nature":*

> The entire phenomenal world is nothing but the interplay of [the forces of nature] .... [These forces of nature] find an expression, for instance, in the meatabolic processes of the body, and on their basis feelings of hunger and thirst arise. The need for food and water is in the physiological sphere, but the ego feels 'I am hungry,' 'I am thirsty,' The [forces of nature] are responsible in a similar way for all experience. They are the basis of all events and activities, but the ego takes these upon itself and feels, 'I am acting.' As long as the Self has not been experienced as separate from activity, . . . it assumes the authorship of action, which actually belongs to the [forces of nature]. (Maharishi, 1969, p. 221).

When the self "knows itself," through the pure consciousness experience, it perceives other objects of experience as simply not its nature. This new self-concept is said to be the result of direct experience of the self, the subjective side of the physiological changes just discussed, such as EEG coherence and breath suspension. These are said to represent a change in the "style of the overall functioning of the nervous system," Vedic psychology's definition of the basis of states of consciousness. That is, the new self-concept is not a new way of understanding the same old self. The self-concept changes because the pure consciousness experience significantly changes what the person actually is. At first this change is restricted to

---

*This phrase raises the issue of free will. One common preconception about Eastern psychology is that it argues for a fatalistic determinism. (Actually, Western scientific determinism ought to produce the same fatalism.) However, this quote describes a stage in self-development, albeit an extremely crucial one. Later stages do imply a type of free will, when one *is* the "forces of nature." Maharishi suggests that any excess of fatalism in Eastern cultures is due to people adopting the *attitude* of "detachment," in an attempt to imitate descriptions of what others have actually experienced. The actual experience of pure consciousness is reported to produce not passivity, but increased energy and enthusiasm for activity, along with the deeper experience that the self is also more than this activity.

meditation and perhaps the time immediately afterward. This restriction eventually fades, permitting the development of still different self-perceptions, based on additional changes in the "actual self's" physiology.

Possible Evolution of the
Self and Self-Concept

In all, Vedic psychology describes four different and (in principle) physiologically identifiable states of consciousness in addition to the states of sleep, dreaming, and ordinary wakefulness. Each of these is said to give rise to a radically different self-concept. While research on most of these is difficult and only preliminary, we present them for the sake of completeness.

The first additional state (or the "fourth" after the usual three) is the experience of pure consciousness, just described. During it there is no thought of the self or anything else, but at other points in or out of meditation, the experience is remembered and changes the self-concept. The fifth is said to occur when the experience of the "I" predominates even outside of meditation, along with the sleep, dream, or awake states. The identification of the self with pure consciousness—rather than with one's activity, perceptions, body, and so forth—is permanent.

With still further experience of pure consciousness, all perceptions of the "me"— in fact, all perceptions of any type—are experienced more and more abstractly, until they seem to be subtle "fluctuations in consciousness" (the sixth state). Since the self already experiences itself to be nothing but this field of consciousness, all objects of experience are eventually perceived as aspects of the self, and "individual" self becomes "universal" self. This is called the seventh state, or "unity consciousness," described as the ultimate form of self-knowledge and self-development. The self-concept at this point is all-inclusive; or in Lewin's terms, the region of the person and the lifespace have become identical.

Again, these changes in self-concept are said to mirror those in the physiology of the actual person or self. While there is a little research (Banquet & Sailhan, 1977; Orme-Johnson & Haynes, 1981) on the states beyond the fourth, it is quite preliminary. We have discussed these states only to give a picture of the possibilities for self-development suggested by Vedic psychology, possibilities considerably beyond Western images of "formal operations" (Piaget, 1952/1963), "ego integrity" (Erikson, 1950), or an "integral ego" (Loevinger & Wessler, 1970).

A MORE COMPREHENSIVE
UNDERSTANDING OF THE
SELF

Finally we are ready to state how the self is defined in this book. This conceptualization combines the developments discussed in this chapter in Western experimental psychology and in Eastern Vedic psychology. It sees the person as including at least (a) an integrated cognitive system, including mental processes and cognitions of physical and social resources (the "me"); and (b) an experiencer or "I" which can be inferred, but also, when directly experienced, can be identified with "pure consciousness," or awareness itself.

Normally the self-concept is made up of the "me" aspects, plus, perhaps, an indirect sense of an experiencer or "I." But repeated and direct experience of the

"I" (as awareness by itself) leads the person to identify the self as the "I" and not as the "me". With still more experience of the "I," the self-concept might develop through stages until both the "I" and "me" are experienced as aspects of a single, unified field which includes all perceptions of everything.

When we speak of self-expansion in this book, normally this means expansion of the self by adding to or enriching "me" aspects. However, both Vedic psychology and the research on the pure consciousness experience suggest that the expansion of the "I's" identification to include this experience is very important both theoretically and practically. Thus it will receive our attention again, especially when we discuss the maintenance of relationships in Part III.

3

"Expansion" and "Including Others in the Self"

INTRODUCTION

Having explored what we mean by the self, we now discuss two points—first, the general motivation to "expand" the self, and then, in what sense "including others in the self" is one expression of this motivation.

MOTIVATION TO EXPAND THE SELF

Traditional Psychological View of Motivation

If there is a traditional opinion about "the energy and direction of behavior," it is probably that organisms seek pleasure and avoid pain; and, further, that pain is caused by tension due to a disturbance of the physiological equilibrium, and pleasure, by the reduction of this tension. Behaviorists (notably, Hull, 1943) typically called these hedonistic, homeostasis-oriented tendencies "drives." Before Hull, the clinicians were calling the same things "instincts" (notably, Freud, 1905/1953), and later, "needs" (notably, Murray, 1938).

This homeostasis approach seemed well suited to laboratory studies of how animals reduce hunger or avoid electric shock; or in the clinic, where therapists might employ such constructs as "repressed libido." Psychologists who have focused on the self have also found it useful, to explain the way an individual strives to *maintain* a current self-view (e.g., Gollwitzer et al., 1982; Greenwald, 1980; Swann & Hill, 1982)—although such self-theorists usually make no claims about underlying physiological mechanisms for maintaining homeostasis.

Problem: The Tendency to Seek New Experiences

Early on, however, a serious problem in the simple drive-reduction, homeostasis position became evident. Both those in the experimental (e.g., Woodworth, 1918) and psychoanalytic traditions (e.g., Freud, 1920/1959) were forced to confront the observation that organisms sometimes seek out new experience. They may even act to increase arousal rather than simply restore equilibrium. (For reviews of the data on these behaviors, see Berlyne, 1973; Deci, 1975; Dember & Earl, 1957; White, 1959; and Zuckerman, 1979.) Thus, while some tendencies may be explained by the drive for homeostasis, many others—such as curiosity, play, exploration, and the tendency to increase complexity (including what Zuckerman calls "sensation seeking")—were left to be dealt with.

Drive Naming

One approach to explaining this motivation for something besides equilibrium was to posit a new kind of drive: for example, a drive to explore (Montgomery, 1954) or to manipulate (Harlow, 1953). (Freud's 1920/1959, solution was similar, if more grand. He proposed an entirely independent motivational system—the "life instinct"—but it has been largely ignored both in and out of psychoanalytic circles.) More recently, some psychologists have posited drives to reduce uncertainty (Kagan, 1972) or dissonance (Festinger, 1957).

However, this kind of solution just gives a name to a set of motivations. It does not explain why or how they are motivating. Moreover, as White (1959) pointed out, such "drives" are categorically unlike the physiologically based homeostatic mechanisms to which the term "drive" originally referred. Exploration, mastery, and so forth are not associated with any known "tissue needs"—except perhaps of the nervous system. Furthermore, White noted, most of these drive-naming approaches still actually describe a tendency to *reduce* complexity, novelty, or whatever in the long run, through exploration and the like. They often do not consider the situation in which people appear deliberately to *increase* complexity and novelty, as if for its own sake.

Optimal-Level-of-Complexity and Arousal

Additionally, a very clever solution to complexity seeking is the suggestion that people seek an optimal level of complexity or novelty (e.g., McClelland et al., 1953; Dember & Earl, 1957). That is, the equilibrium level in the homeostatic system is not a zero level of complexity, but a mid-level, from which if one differs in either direction, one is motivated to return to this optimal mid-level. This is a very neat way of saving the intuitive appeal of homeostasis while dealing with the sensation-seeking tendencies.

There is, however, a problem with this optimal-level-of-complexity approach also. As Deci (1975) remarks, people sometimes solve puzzles completely, or explore all of a novel environment, rather than stopping at some optimal mid-level. Moreover, these approaches generally sacrifice the appeal to physiology of the traditional homeostatic theories.

In the face of these problems, Berlyne (1973) emphasized that novelty and complexity create arousal and that people have two motivations: to decrease arousal, and also to increase it in moderate increments. The two interact, so that stimuli creating a large increase in arousal activate only the desire to decrease arousal, and a small increase mainly appeals to the desire for moderate increments.

This approach does do a pretty good job of explaining the data. It also has the virtue of relating these motivations to physiology. But it still does not give any deeper understanding of why these two processes are motivating, or of any connection between them.

Effectance and Intrinsic Motivation

White (1959) took a somewhat different tack. He argued that there is a central-nervous-system need for the organism to master the environment. He described it as a motivation to feel competent through effectance: self-determined manipulation of the environment. This "effectance motivation" is then said to operate whenever the organism is freed from immediate demands to correct homeostatic imbalances—a position consistent in a general way with Maslow's (1967) hierarchy of needs.

Deci (1975) has developed a theory of "intrinsic motivation." He begins with White's ideas, adds a more cognitive interpretation, and elaborates the picture to include three motivational components: meeting tissue needs, reducing complexity, and seeking opportunities to reduce complexity. The first works by traditional drive-reduction mechanisms; the other two work in tandem to activate and control exploratory behavior and the like, and are based on the desire for effectance.

White's position has the virtue of relating the tendency to increase complexity and novelty to a physiological need, and Deci's approach connects it with the modern cognitive orientation in psychology. Also, both have the virtue of relating stimulation-increasing tendencies to a subjective experience (the feeling of competence), which mediates the motivational process.

On the other hand, White's connection to physiology is mainly speculative, and Deci's treatment of cognitive processes does not really permit any direct links with mainstream cognitive psychology research. Above all, we still do not have a deeper explanation from these theorists of *why* people want to feel competent.

Also—and this is important to our own approach—there is little evidence for White's, Maslow's, and Deci's position that "effectance," "self-actualizing," or "intrinsic" motivations occur only when "lower" homeostatic needs are met. On the contrary, even animals will sometimes endure pain to have the chance to explore a novel environment (Dashiell, 1925; Nissen, 1930). People can regularly be observed, from mountain tops to ocean depths, risking life and limb for the excitement of new experience. Moreover, they will sometimes purposely fail to meet tissue needs or endure privations, just to feel they have mastered their "lower" needs, or because they believe such asceticism might lead to some higher type of effectance.

The goal of life is usually considered to be survival. "Exploratory" behavior is then explained as having been "selected for" because it supports survival in new environments. But Darwinian natural selection is a theory of "evolution," not survival. A more "evolutionary" position seems to be that, in higher life forms, a different set of survival behaviors have been selected than those that promote the survival of plant life and the simpler animals. This particular set of survival behaviors has been selected because it supports the organism in attaining an active form of mastery and adaptation. Maybe humans, in particular, do not strive for mastery in order to survive, but strive to survive in order to explore and master.

On the whole, we agree with the important work done by White, Deci, Maslow, Berlyne, and the many others who have pointed out the importance of this tendency to increase stimulation, novelty, complexity, and the like. We also think that Berlyne's and Deci's specification of tendencies both to increase and decrease complexity is particularly helpful. We would simply note, however, that these various approaches still do not provide a unifying conceptual scheme to explain all motivation—and probably will not, as long as survival and homeostasis motives are seen as separate and equal to exploration and growth motives.

Self-Expansion as a Two-Phase, Cyclical Motivation

We propose that the central human motivation is to expand the self, and that this process is cyclical, involving two phases—expansion, then integration of each new expansion. The expanding phase accounts for the motivation to increase complexity, novelty, stimulation, and so forth. The integrating phase accounts for the tendency to reduce complexity. That is, we are defining integration as a motivated process, a striving to incorporate newly acquired perceptions into existing cognitive structures. But even though during integration the organism withdraws from external complexity, the overall process leads on to more and more expansion, knowledge, and competence. Integration—and also all activities which promote survival, including physiological homeostatic mechanisms—is in the service of this expansion.

Within a particular knowledge domain and at a given moment in time, a person may be situated at either of two main phases of this motivational cycle: (a) integrated, therefore seeking change and *expanding* (in this phase activity and contrast are sought in the environment); or (b) being expanded, and therefore withdrawing from change and *integrating* (in this phase restfulness and simplicity are preferred in the environment). When the complexity then has been integrated, motivation is again governed by the former phase.

Of course, a person can be simultaneously expanding in one knowledge domain and integrating in another. Indeed, this is probable, given the many demands and opportunities usually available. Thus the two phases may average out each other's visible, behavioral effect.

A person also may be expanding in two domains at once, but of course the total expansion from all sources cannot exceed the individual's capacity for expansion and integration. (We will return to this issue of individual differences in a moment.) In particular, while the integration phase may appear to be skipped, it cannot be. If a person is simultaneously having a baby, starting a new career, and buying a new house—an outsider may wonder when the integration phase is going to take over! It will have to be going on, though, and may be limiting how much expansion can be achieved from these changes—if all this activity exceeds the person's expansion and integration capacity. In that case, the individual may seek to avoid one or more of these "opportunities," or if they can't be avoided, they may be transformed from pleasures to stressors.

Looking at motivation as a desire for expansion plus integration clarifies a number of issues. For example, it suggests that Berlyne found only moderate increases in arousal to be rewarding because larger-than-moderate increases are too much to integrate, and the need to expand includes a need to *integrate* complexity and novelty*. If changes come too fast, we would argue they can not be integrated and become sources of pain rather than pleasure. Indeed, Cofer and Appley (1964) define psychological stress as anything experienced as a threat to the integrity—the integrated organization—of the self.

This model is also consistent with the phenomena emphasized by Solomon's (1980) opponent-process theory of motivation: At first a newly experienced situation (expansion) gives pleasure, but is not missed much if lost (as it is not yet integrated). Once it is well known (integrated into the self), its presence gives little pleasure (as it provides no new expansion), but its loss (necessitating disintegration—to be discussed shortly) is strongly resisted.

Ours is not, of course, the first model to emphasize an expanding and integrating process. Such processes are found in Piaget's work, and in Jung's idea of individuation and integration. The model also brings to mind Kuhn's (1962) description of the growth of science as an alternation between introductions and subsequent integrations of new paradigms. Perhaps science is just individual cognitive development writ large. (In fact, such wavelike patterns of activity and recovery are found everywhere in nature, from the wave function of particles and the firing of neurons to musical compositions and meteorology.)

According to Vedic psychology, the stages of development of self-knowledge described in the last chapter also proceed through phases of expansion and integration. First, pure consciousness is said to be experienced by itself during meditation (expansion). Then, with repeated alternation of other activity with the pure consciousness experience, both are eventually maintained simultaneously (integration). Next, the processing of perception begins to change, to focus upon more and more abstract invariants (expansion), until the most abstract quality, common to all objects, is experienced as identical with the internal reality of pure consciousness (integration).

The Self in Self-Expansion

The self plays a central role in all of this—as it tends to do in any psychological approach to motivation. First, it is the self or person (as defined in the last chapter) that is motivated. Second, one effect of motivated behavior is a modified self. (Depending on one's motivational theory, it may be a new, expanded, more effective self, or a renewed, returned-to-homeostasis self.) Third, the process of moving from old self to new self is mediated by our perceptions of the changing states of the self.

Both expansion- and integration-type processes have been emphasized in the research and thinking on the self.

With regard to expansion, Epstein (1973) lists the tendency to seek change and growth as one of seven key aspects of the self appearing in the literature, and posits it as a part of what he calls the "self-theory." Greenwald's (1980) paper on the "totalitarian ego" describes the ego as only an integrator. His analogy, however, seems to point as much or more to an expansive side to the ego, given the tendency for totalitarians to seek increasing territories of influence!

With regard to previous recognition of a motivation for integration, we have already noted the interest by recent social psychologists in the stability of the

*Moreover, the data of Berlyne and of others were based on averages which would have unintentionally combined observations of the two different hypothesized phases.

self-concept despite conflicting information, and Cofer and Appley (1964) made a similar point in their theory of psychological stress as a threat to the maintenance of the integrity of the self. Also, Greenwald's description of the "totalitarian ego" puts integration (creating a consistent world) ahead of any other goals for the individual.

Others have considered both the expansion and integration phases, and suggested the same relationship that we have—that integration of the self is in the service of expansion. For example, Jung (1940) wrote of "striving for wholeness" of the self through integration of greater and greater complexity, and Smith (1978) made the same point in his APA presidential address.

In the last chapter we defined what we meant in this book by the self. Two aspects of that conceptualization are especially important for the present discussion of expanding and integrating, and for the later application of all this to attraction and close relationships. These are (a) the "me" self as a cognitive structure, and (b) the self as including both the "I" and the "me."

Self as a Cognitive Structure—How It Determines What Will Be an Expanding Experience

In the last chapter we considered the "me" aspect of the self as a cognitive structure, and the idea is well exemplified by the person-as-scientist metaphor and Epstein's (1973) self-as-theory position. Given this view of the self, White's (1959) effectance behavior—self-determined manipulation of the environment—is really motivated not by a desire simply to feel one is being effective, but by a desire for real potential effectance in the future.

This real potential effectance requires knowledge. Self-determined manipulation of the environment serves the purpose of gaining knowledge about the environment (or gaining other resources which permit the application of knowledge). When we manipulate the environment, we learn about it, and thus improve the fit between the environment and our cognitive structure. We can predict and explain accurately and comprehensively. We have enhanced our ability to exert control over a greater territory of influence. Again, the goal of effectance behavior is not a "sense of competence"; the goal is knowledge. From knowledge comes power, or potential effectance, and also a well-justified feeling of competence or effectance. The basic desire, however, is not merely to *feel* that one has been competent, but to *be* competent.* This will have implications for understanding attraction.

Defining the self as, in part, a cognitive structure seeking to improve itself also helps us understand what, exactly, can and cannot expand the self.

Put simply, if whatever increases knowledge and therefore potential efficacy expands the self, then almost anything new, short of brain damage or complete misinformation—*if* it can be integrated—expands the self. Sources of knowledge, of course, include education, travels, skills training, and so forth—but also *all* new experience.

In addition, acquiring material and social resources—such as wealth, health, or status—can expand the self by helping one gain knowledge or helping one turn knowledge into actual effectance.

*People may prefer to *look* competent rather than gain knowledge—because appearing competent gives one status, a resource which increases the opportunity to put one's knowledge to work. But privately, it seems, people would rather have knowledge than simply act and feel as if they had it.

An experience will not expand the self if it cannot be integrated, if it disturbs current structures so much that no new structure can be made to include it. An experience can also cause "de-expansion" and/or "disintegration," if it reduces knowledge or resources, or reduces the cognitive organization of that knowledge.

Of course, what will actually be expanding (or de-expanding) may be different from what one expects and it is the expectation that creates the motivation for a particular action. Thus, even though all experiences differ in some ways from one another, and therefore could all potentially provide expansion if one noticed subtle enough differences, an individual may not perceive these differences as sources of new knowledge. Experiences that differ *too much* from the usual may also be perceived as nonexpanding (or if forced onto one, de-expanding or disintegrating), if the individual thinks the probability of integrating them into the self is slight (but we will come to the topic of individual differences in a moment).

The "I" and "Me" Aspects of the Self—How They Clarify the Goal of Self-Expansion

Logically, the process of expanding and integrating can have two outcomes: It can go on forever, or reach some conclusion. The conclusion, the process carried to its logical limit, would be the possession of all knowledge—complete potential efficacy, completely integrated. Or, if the process continues forever, it could be, as Rogers (1969) says, that the process itself is the goal. He describes a fully functioning person as "ever changing, ever developing, always discovering himself and the newness in himself in each succeeding moment of time" (p. 295). In the terminology we have been using, Rogers' position would be that one can (or must) be satisfied with making rapid progress in expanding. (Or as Huesmann, 1980, notes, steep reward gradients are in themselves satisfying, or secondarily reinforcing.)

So which is true—the point of the game is to play? Or to win?

We would suggest both. Continual expansion is the condition of the "me," while direct experience of the "I" provides an end state.

When it comes to processing items of information—expanding the "me" aspect of the self—there seem to be infinite amounts to know and integrate, or at least enough to fill a very long, active life. Thus the "me" continually seeks to expand and integrate its cognitive structure in pursuit of a seemingly unachievable ideal— to be structurally identical to the external world, constantly changing in exactly the same ways.

Yet some humanistic theories, many forms of Platonic idealism, and all Eastern psychologies describe an end state of self-development that involves the direct experience of the basis of knowing—the knower itself, or the "I" aspect of the self. This is described as an ultimate wisdom, enlightenment, self-actualization, knowledge of the Form of the Good (Plato), or the like. In Vedic psychology, we said it is called the experience of pure consciousness.

Those who claim to have achieved this end state describe it as involving some basic knowledge of the Forms themselves, or of the workings of the universe (Gowan, 1980), or of the "the home of all the laws of nature" (Maharishi, 1977). Thus all additional knowledge obtained by the "me" is experienced as familiar or "preintegrated" in some sense, because it is already within the self by virtue of the "I" aspect. The "me" continues to expand, yet the actual person, thanks to the "I" aspect, is simultaneously experiencing an end state to the process of expansion—a comprehension of infinity, an "unbounded awareness." This tinges the "me's" continual expansion into new domains with a certain sense not only of familiarity, but of fulfillment in spite of a process which can never be fulfilled.

If such a state of inner "knowingness" and fulfillment exists (and in the previous chapter we discussed some research on the question), we will see later that it would have special implications for maintaining relationships. For example, a sense of familiarity should facilitate the integration of novel experiences such as family transitions. In addition, relationships are so often uniquely (and impossibly) burdened with the task of providing their members with complete fulfillment through lifelong expansion, that some inner source of fulfillment might ease this burden considerably.

Individual Differences in Expression of Self-Expansion Motivation

In general, the more persons are already expanded, the more things they will perceive as offering expansion. True, things close at hand may be seen as offering little new expansion, but this is more than made up for by the vast realm of new knowledge and resources that being expanded permits one to acquire (learning to read, then with that skill learning to read math equations, foreign languages, etc.; learning to reason about physical transformations, and then about more and more abstract processes; gaining wealth and thereby traveling, buying new possessions, etc.; gaining a greater sensitivity to aesthetics through photography, for example, and thereby enjoying all the arts).

Besides creating a rich cognitive and resource system, expanding seems to add an even more general quality to the expanded person. He or she seems to learn to learn, or learn to attend to what matters. Plus, of course, self-confidence and persistence are acquired—the opposites of learned helplessness (Seligman, 1975). More expanded individuals can expand more from new experiences because they worry less about de-expansion (e.g., an experienced entrepreneur worries less about a new investment than the novice investor). The cognitive complexity literature (e.g., Harvey et al., 1961) also sees this ability to seek out and process diverse information as a product of experience (especially early experience in a warm but firm home environment).

This idea of "capacity to expand" is perhaps similar to intelligence, but we think it is even more affected by experience; by almost all experience, if it is at all expanding. Lukenbach (1978) has reviewed a variety of data indicating that rewards, success, and satisfaction—but also any type of learning—create widespread neurophysiological changes that facilitate further learning.

On the other hand, if certain classes of experiences have repeatedly been de-expanding, these will be avoided. And if, generally, many life experiences have been de-expanding, there will be a tendency not to try to acquire new experiences, knowledge, or resources out of fear of de-expansion. All of which implies a "positive spiraling" for the expanded, but a "vicious circle" for the less expanded—unless they find or are provided a means of expanding at which they will not fail, thus breaking the cycle.

We have already pointed out that yet another source of individual differences at any given time will be which phase of the expansion-integration cycle someone is in. These phases can last for minutes or years. After a difficult intellectual task, a "mindless" novel may be preferred by even the most literary. After six or so years of growing with one or more teenagers, parents may rejoice in the stillness of their "empty nest."

Finally, there are probably some inherited individual differences, particularly in the capacity to integrate experiences. However, the history of the issue within the study of intelligence and of mental illness tells us that measuring the amount of variance contributed by heredity would be difficult, to say the least. Whatever the heredity, since there is clear evidence that this capacity increases through expansion experiences—including the experience of pure consciousness—we prefer to leave that container of annelids alone.

We return to the topic of expansion facilitating further expansion when we discuss how individuals solve the problems that arise in the maintenance of relationship, in Part III.

"INCORPORATING ASPECTS OF AN OTHER INTO THE SELF"

To conclude our analysis of the phrase, "Individuals seek to expand themselves by incorporating aspects of an other into the self," we have only to understand in what sense a close relationship with an other expands the self.

Related General Conceptions in the Literature

The general idea that the purpose of relationships is to expand the self is not new, although it is rarely expressed in exactly these terms. Consider Bataille's (1962) dramatic explanation of love: "[Man] is born alone . . . He dies alone. Between one being and another there is a gulf, a discontinuity" (p. 12). "What we desire," he continues, "is to bring into a world founded on discontinuity all the continuity such a world can sustain" (p. 19).

There is also Hatfield and Walster's (1978) definition of "passionate love" as "a state of intense longing for union" (p. 9).

Likewise, Jung (1925/1959, 1965) calls the motivation behind love the seeking of wholeness of the self. Solovyev (1947) describes it as the desire to include another into our own egoism. Kelling (1979) sees it as the desire to make the ultimate, all inclusive accommodation (in the Piagetian sense) to everything. Hoffman and Hoffman (1973) actually use the phrase "expansion of the self" to describe one of several crucial reasons people choose to have children. And Maslow takes it for granted that "beloved people can be incorporated into the self" (1967, p. 103).

The related idea of "possessing" the other, or the attributes of the other, is widespread in the writing of clinical psychologists (e.g., Berl, 1924; Freud, 1951; Grant, 1976). Indeed, Reik (1949) comments that when we love, we desire "to own the other person" (p. 73). To Reik, love is like ambition—it is a product of individual ego development, especially the desire for self-improvement and self-fulfillment. It is "the unconscious but powerful striving to complete our ego ideal" (p. 97).

Nor is the idea of love as self-expansion foreign to general social psychology. McCall (1974) describes "attachment" as "incorporation of . . . [the other's] actions and reactions . . . into the contents of one's various conceptions of self" (p. 219). The schematizing of another social psychologist, George Levinger (1974), can also be adapted to illustrate this discussion. Figure 3-1a shows a relationship of a moderate degree (what Levinger calls "mutuality"); Fig. 3-1b represents a higher level of relatedness, called "major intersection." (Figures 3-1a and 3-1b are adapted from Levinger.) We would simply accent, as we have in Fig. 3-1c, that the relationship has created a region in each individual which is more dense than before, enriched by the aspect of the other included in his or her circle—expanded, if you will.

How Relationships Expand the Self

We have already said that the self is expanded by whatever expands its potential efficacy—that is, by knowledge and the resources to apply knowledge. Forming a relationship with another person obviously offers knowledge and resources in abundance. The individual person or self (P, from now on) not only possesses resources associated with his or her own person, but now also feels in possession of the cognitive structures and social and material resources of the other person (O, from now on). O's ideas, world view, abilities, achievements, statuses, and so forth are nearly as available for potential effectance as if they were P's own. The effect of a close relationship (and in fact, perhaps its definition) is that the resources of each are available for the other's use, and are even included within the self-concept of each.

Thus, for example, Tesser (1980) has shown what he calls "reflection": that people can experience pleasure over the accomplishments of their intimates. Stu-

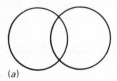

(a)

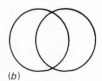

(b)

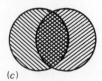

(c)

Fig. 3-1 Schematic illustration of degree of relatedness (inclusion of other in self) of two individuals: (a) moderate degree of relatedness; (b) higher level of relatedness; (c) same level of relatedness as (b) but emphasizing that the relationship enhances the contents of each self. (This kind of illustration of interpersonal relatedness is adapted from Levinger, 1974.)

dents of prosocial behavior often mention the notion of empathy, that individuals personally experience at least the suffering of another. It seems likely that other emotions, like joy and pride and confidence, are also empathized with.

Psychoanalytically oriented psychologists (e.g., Kelman, 1958) explain that the child "identifies" with the parent, and thereby takes into the self the feeling of having the power which resides in that parent. Rothbaum et al. (1982) call this "vicarious control". Bank and Kahn (1982) also emphasize the role of identification in the lifespan relations among siblings.

Reik (1944), however, claims the process behind loving is not so much one of identification as it is a selective process of incorporating those aspects of O which particularly fulfill P's ego ideal.

Effect of Including Aspects of the Other in the Self

The first effect is direct self-expansion through incorporating new skills, attitudes, resources, behaviors, and so forth.

The second effect is less direct. To include aspects of the other can enhance survival—which, as we said, is in the service of expansion. Aspects of O may enhance P's ability simply to maintain the self in a changing, potentially stressful environment. This effect is provided by the same things which provide expansion: knowledge, and also various material and social resources (such as those described by Foa, 1971). For example, the additional information and larger frame of reference gained through relationships seems to reduce anxiety (Schachter, 1959) and may very well be the reason that social support networks sometimes buffer individuals against stressors (e.g., Caplan, 1974; Dean & Lin, 1977) or increase their abilitiy to cope with stressors (Kessler & Essex, 1982). Another example is the way O's resources serve as part of P's cognitive network, which stabilizes self-views and role relations (Swann & Hill, 1982). While we have suggested that survival is in the service of expansion, and not the opposite, survival is still essential for self-expansion!

A third effect of incorporating aspects of O into the self is that these aspects may support self-expansion outside the relationship. Swensen (1972) feels his research suggests that the mutual promotion of each others' growth is the chief distinguishing characteristic of relationships of self-actualizing individuals. And Foote (1956/1963) has pointed out that the function of marriage to "further each other's career" in the broadest sense is the only basis for lasting relationships in our culture.

A fourth effect is that as P includes more and more aspects of O into P's self, P comes in a sense to include O—not just aspects of O—into P's self. That is, P feels as much or nearly as much satisfaction when O is satisfied, or pain when O is hurt, as P would if these had happened to P. P plans for O's happiness and welfare as if it were P's. P "identifies" with O, or is even in some sense "united" with O (an image frequently used to describe marriage in particular).

Yet a fifth effect is that P must form a relationship with O in order to include aspects of O. O is, to some extent, a "package deal." O will have many ideas, skills, possessions, behaviors, and so forth (or the cognitions thereof, if you prefer), very different from P's own, that P has not anticipated. P must either expand to include them or otherwise learn to deal with them (a learning which also expands).

Clearly P will find this fifth effect a mixed blessing. On the one hand, differences cause expansion because they provide contrast, challenge assumptions, and generally shake up one's world view. The more differences between P and O in knowledge, skills, and so forth—the more P's self gains by forming a relationship with O. But also, the more different, the more P will have to restructure P's self. Thus differences, both the known and the gradually discovered ones, are only attractive up to a limit. All these differences must be perceived as capable of being integrated; they must be seen as fitting somewhere within one's own values and understandings.

Jungian psychologists (e.g., Guggenbuhl-Craig, 1977/1981) typically see this fifth effect—integrating contrast—as the fundamental benefit of marriage. Marriage helps a person integrate all the opposite values of life one might otherwise manage to avoid and remain ignorant of (male-female, task-affect, physical-spiritual, artistic-scientific).

Further, P and O will find themselves expanding through something neither one possessed as an aspect of themselves, hidden or not, when they were initially attracted: the relationship itself. The knowledge acquired through the development of an ongoing relationship expands the self, regardless of whether P and O want and anticipate such expansion.

Expansion and Integration

As we have just said, the amount P can expand by incorporating O into the self is tempered by the requirement to integrate that expansion; and P may find a relationship to be impossible if too many salient aspects of O require simultaneous integration. However, once a relationship is formed and the expansion provided by O has been integrated, a different dynamic ensues: P wants further expansion still.

Thus, P may seek new aspects of O to incorporate, and perhaps "liven up" the relationship to bring them to the surface. On the other hand P may begin to seek new opportunities for expansion elsewhere—in other relationships or in other forms of expansion, such as career advancement. P and O may see this restlessness as natural and either sadly resign themselves to it and find ways to share their new involvements; or P may be disappointed that this boredom has arisen, while O may feel hurt. (Of course, in any relationship, both partners may go through the processes ascribed to P throughout this book, and both are also O's to the other.)

While the fading of romantic love may be the classic example of the effect of the expansion-integration cycle on relationships, Bischof (1975) describes a similar progression in the parent-child relationship, from the child's unification with the mother to separation at adolescence. Of course the child's expansion does not cease when he or she outgrows the close bond with the mother. Rather, expansion continues through schooling, marriage, the child's own children, friendships, career development, adult closeness with parents, and many other expansion opportunities.

This tendency for relationships to have difficulties after the "obvious" expansion opportunties seem to be exhausted is considered more in Chapter 8.

II

Implications for Attraction

4

Predicting Attraction

INTRODUCTION

This and the following two chapters give a brief overview of the social psychology of initial attraction. In this chapter we examine current definitions of attraction and the research on each of five variables that have been particularly successful in predicting attraction.

DEFINITIONS OF ATTRACTION

Attraction is often defined by researchers as a *positive attitude* towards a particular person (e.g., Huston, 1974). Relating attraction to attitudes is helpful because attitudes have long been a central topic of social psychology, and have therefore been extensively researched and conceptualized.

A traditional definition of attitude is that it is an "enduring system of positive or negative evaluations, emotional feelings, and pro or con action tendencies with respect to social objects" (Krech et al., 1962, p. 139).

These three components are also said to apply to attraction (Tedeschi, 1974). Thus, if P is attracted to O, P will *think* O is a good person, P will *feel* a liking for O, and P will *be predisposed* to want to do things with O.

Of course, we can only observe what a person actually does. Thus, some researchers have felt safer with definitions of attraction focusing on the "action tendencies" and employ measures involving objective observation of behavior—perhaps the distance from O that P chooses to stand (Byrne, Ervin & Lamberth, 1970), whether P will ask O out for a date (e.g., Folkes, 1982), whether P chooses to sit in a chair next to O (Stephenson et al., 1983), whether P will choose to go to a waiting room with O in it (Schachter, 1959), how long P gazes in O's eyes (Rubin, 1973), and so forth.

However, the above behaviors may also be due to factors other than what we feel we mean by attraction. For example, P might feel compelled by some social custom to stand near a relative whom P does not really like. Conversely, P may *feel* an attraction to someone, but be too shy or otherwise unwilling or unable to act on it.

Because direct observations of behavior do not always correspond with what we feel we mean by attraction, many researchers have focused mainly on the cognitive and emotional components. Thus to measure if P is attracted to O, one tries to determine whether P believes good things about O or feels favorably about O. Usually this means asking P about O, and usually in ways that disguise the purpose of such questions. For example, P might be asked to "describe" or give his or her "first impression" of O, and then the favorableness of the ratings on such scales as "mature/immature" or "genuine/phony" is summed (e.g., Archer & Burleson, 1980).

Occasionally it is possible to assess the cognitive and emotional components of attraction fairly objectively. For example, the degree of emotional response to another person can be measured physiologically (e.g., Clore & Gormly, 1974). (However, it is not always possible to tell from physiological indicators, such as changes in skin resistance, the positivity or negativity of the response, only the intensity!)

At the other extreme from such concrete measures as physiological response, attraction has been measured by analyzing the content of projective tests completed by P in the presence of O (e.g., Dutton & Aron, 1974).

However, the most common approach to measuring attraction is simply to *ask* P how attracted P is to O. Systematizing this approach, Byrne (1971) developed what he calls the "Interpersonal Judgment Scale" (IJS). Basically, P rates O on two 7-point scales: how much P "would probably like this person" and how much P "would enjoy working with this person in an experiment." Byrne's IJS has become a kind of standard in the field and has been widely adopted by other researchers.

It is, of course, appropriate that researchers should focus on definitions readily suitable for translation into measurement, and when a definition coincides with a construct which is already familiar and well worked out in other research—such as the attitude construct—so much the better. However, measurement-oriented definitions should also coincide as much as possible with what we feel we mean by a term.

In the case of attraction, certainly predispositions, cognitions, and especially emotions are involved, but do these categories exhaust what we mean by attraction? It seems that attractions can engage us deeply. For example, identity and sense of self-worth—beyond what is typically associated with attitude—seem to be implicated. Perhaps there is more still: physiology (e.g., Levenson & Gottman, 1983), archetypes (e.g., Jung, 1925/1959), and perhaps even transcendent experiences (e.g., Coleman and Coleman, 1975).

For now, we can accept the practical research value of the positive-attitude definition, while recognizing its frequent failure to touch deeper meanings. Certainly, whatever attraction "really" means, we would expect a positive attitude to be at least a quite common expression of that reality. Later, at the end of the next chapter, when we have considered theory, we will see if we can put together a deeper, more satisfying conceptualization.

RESEARCH

Each of the following sections provides a brief overview of research on one of the five most successful approaches to predicting who will be attracted to whom: similarity, propinquity, being liked, matching of admirable characteristics, and social and cultural influences.

Similarity

There is an old saying that "birds of a feather flock together." The idea that we like people who are like us goes back at least to Aristotle and has been the source of a rich research tradition.

In the 1920s and 1930s, researchers began by looking at background similarities between husbands and wives. Several large survey studies (reviewed in Jacobsohn & Matheny, 1962) did indeed find substantial likenesses in social class, education, race, religion, region of the country raised in, and so forth. However, later critics (e.g., Nimkoff, 1947) pointed out that these similarities probably arise because social circumstances make similar people more likely to meet and be acceptable marriage partners. Winch (1958) called this limited set of potential mates the "field of eligibles."

The next stage of the research focused on similarity of "temperament," "character," or what are now called "personality traits." Again, large survey studies found that husbands and wives (reviewed in Richardson, 1939) and also friends (e.g., Reader & English, 1947) had quite similar temperaments. (However, later research by Miller et al., 1966, suggested personality similarity, at least among friends, may be more perceived than actual.)

The general problem, however, with the personality-similarity findings was determining cause and effect. That is, does P want to be in a relationship with O because P and O are similar, or do P and O, as a result of being together in a relationship over time, become similar? It is a common observation that with enough time the members of any close pairing—spouses, students and teachers, parents and children, roommates—come to act alike, talk alike, and even look alike. Some experimental studies that have attempted to examine alternative explanations for similarity (e.g., Byrne et al., 1967) do suggest that general personality similarity can lead to attraction, but results of these and the correlational studies typically do not show large or consistent similarity effects when using standard personality tests.

It is possible, of course, that personality traits have not been well measured; or that they determine little, if any, of behavior; or that the wrong ones have been studied. One new line of research in this area is, so far, finding fairly strong effects for similarity of cognitive structures (e.g., Duck, 1973; Banikiotes & Neimeyer, 1981).

The most successful line of similarity research over the past 20 years has focused on similarity of attitudes. Donn Byrne established the major research paradigm in this area. In a typical study, attitude questionnaires were distributed to a large classroom of students. There might be 12 items, each asking for degree of agreement or disagreement on statements about "such varied topics as racial integration, political parties, and classical music" (Byrne & Clore, 1966), and other social issues, such as "smoking, reading books and magazines, strict rules for children, studying, religion, brothers and sisters, school integration and comic books" (Byrne, Griffitt, et al., 1970). After completing the questionnaire, the next day each student would be given what he or she was told was someone else's completed questionnaire. Actually all students receive questionnaires "fixed" to show either 100% agreement with the student's own responses, 0% agreement, or various degrees in between. After looking at the "other person's" questionnaire—and with no other knowledge of the person—the student would be asked to indicate on the IJS how likable he or she thinks that person is, and how much he or she would like to work together with that person.

By the beginning of the last decade, Byrne (1971) was able to cite enough independent studies of this kind to demonstrate a direct, linear relationship between amount of liking and amount of agreement. There are some exceptions, and there has been considerable debate over the meaning and precise details of the link between attitude similarity and attraction (e.g., Davis, 1981). As a general rule, though, the attitude similarity-attraction principle has held up quite well through the years.

Of course, these studies typically look at attitude similarity in a situation where it is the only information the participant has about the other person. However, some research suggests that even in much more realistic situations, attitude similarity is a fairly important predictor of attraction. Newcomb (1961) conducted a now famous study in which he administered questionnaires to a group of college transfer students (who did not know each other initially) at the beginning of a semester of living in the same boardinghouse. Newcomb found that those who had become friends by the end of the semester had similar initial attitudes to a greater degree than would have been expected by chance. Parallel results were found in a well-constructed conceptual replication conducted by Griffitt and Veitch (1974). Of course, there was considerable variability in the results, suggesting other factors played strong roles in the attractions, but attitude similarity was at least one important factor.

Propinquity

Propinquity, a kind of similarity of location, has also been found to result in attraction, apparently simply through frequent interaction. It is a typical observation, for example, that children who are seated alphabetically in their school classes make a disproportionate number of friends with children whose last names are alphabetically adjacent or nearly adjacent. Indeed, Segal (1974) reports a study of 60 police recruits, initially strangers, who attended a summer training program in which their roommate and class seatings were assigned alphabetically. At the end of the 6-week program, each was asked to indicate privately the name of his or her best friend. More than half of the choices were of a person with an alphabetically adjacent last name. Similarly, Festinger et al. (1950) found that people whose apartment doors were closer to stairways and elevators made more friends than those with more isolated doors.

Other researchers have noted that "mere exposure" to another person generally increases liking (Zajonc, 1968). For example, Brockner and Swap (1976) found that student subjects merely allowed to glimpse a fellow student through a window, for even four 2- to 3-second periods, were significantly more attracted to the fellow student than when only allowed two such glimpses—regardless of whether the subjects believed the fellow student to be similar or dissimilar.

Being Liked

It has been said that if someone likes us, we take it as a sign of intelligence, wisdom, and general good taste in the person! For whatever reason, it is certainly an old truth that we tend to like people who like us. Dale Carnegie's long-time best-selling book *How to Win Friends and Influence People* emphasizes that if you want people to like you, let them know you like them.

The effect seems to be very powerful. One of us (along with Don Dutton; Aron & Dutton, 1983) once administered lengthy, open-ended questionnaires to 50 college students who had said they had "fallen in love" with someone within the last few months. The single most frequent situation associated with sudden attraction for the respondents was the discovery of another's attraction for them. One description ran as follows:

> I met [her] in a department store in which she worked. I was looking for sandals, and she recognized me and came over from another section to talk to me. It took a few minutes to place her, and we didn't really say much ("Hi, it's been a long time," etc.), but it really freaked me that such a beautiful girl would remember me, and go out of her way to talk to me, and especially be so open and look so happy to see me. From that moment on, I thought a lot about her; fantasizing relationships, etc.

What is called the reciprocal-liking rule is so pervasive and obvious that research (reviewed in Mettee & Aronson, 1974) has focused almost entirely on the exceptions and limitations. The main limitation is P must believe that O is sincere in O's admiration for P.

Matching of Admirable Characteristics

First we will consider the question of what is considered admirable, and then the matching process. If you ask someone why he or she likes a particular person, the answer is likely to be that the person is good-looking, warm, intelligent, witty, or has some similarly admirable quality. The most straightforward explanation for attraction seems to be "attractive" characteristics in the person to whom one is attracted. In our study with Don Dutton (Aron & Dutton, 1983) of those who had recently fallen in love, 40 of the 50 participants mentioned appealing characteristics of the other. By far the most common traits mentioned were aspects of physical appearance.

Indeed, physical appearance generally does seem to be important—particularly when first meeting someone, when it is almost all one knows of the person (Murstein, 1977). Good looks seem to facilitate not only romance, but also friendship; and family, teacher-student, and business relationships as well (for a review see Berscheid & Walster, 1974; Hatfield, 1984). There is even some evidence juries will mete out more lenient punishment to good-looking offenders (Solomon & Schopler, 1978). While it is true that if we think well of people in other ways (for example, that they are intelligent), it enhances our estimation of their physical attractiveness (e.g., Gross & Crofton, 1977)—it is at least equally true that how well we think of people in other ways is strongly influenced by our estimation of their physical attractiveness (e.g., Dion et al., 1972)!

There are, of course, differing opinions about what is considered "good-looking" (e.g., Wiggins et al., 1968). Nevertheless there is also surprising consistency. For example, Byrne, Ervin, & Lamberth (1970) found high levels of agreement among students rank ordering photographs of strangers for attractiveness. Of course, there is more variation across cultures. Images of personal beauty also vary from time to time within a culture, such as males' crew cuts in the 1950s versus long hair in the 1970s. However, it does seem that in a given culture, at a given time, there is a relatively widespread consensus as to what patterns of physical characteristics are considered attractive.

Even across times and cultures, a few characteristics appear to be always desired: good health and youthfulness (Ellis, 1936; Ford & Beach, 1951; Frumkin, 1961; Malinowski, 1932; Westermarck, 1921), and perhaps also some nice kind of "spunkiness" (Beach & LeBoeuf, 1967)—though fragility, weakness, and passivity can also be considered attractive at times (Bataille, 1962). Also, the general characteristics that predispose one to positive aesthetic judgments generally (complexity, novelty, etc.–Berlyne, 1960), may play a role in judgments of personal beauty.

Finally, the fact that O *feels* attractive seems to influence how attractive O is to P. This seems to explain why those "in love," pregnant women, and children who have just been praised, all seem to shine. More systematically, Snyder et al. (1977) tape-recorded conversations, using an intercom, between male and female subject pairs, in which the male was shown a photo of either a very attractive or very unattractive female who he thought was his partner. (The photo he saw was actually determined randomly.) Another group of subjects then rated the attractiveness of the females, based on listening only to tapes of the female subject's half of the conversation, and without knowledge of either the purpose of the experiment, or of what kind of photo the male subject had seen. These raters thought that those females whom the males had considered attractive (and therefore the females who presumably felt more attractive) were significantly more attractive.

In addition to appearance (and feeling good about one's appearance), several other admirable characteristics have been found to play a role in attraction. These include, among others, intelligence (Solomon & Saxe, 1977), mental health (Murstein, 1971b), pleasant personality traits (Anderson, 1968; Posavac, 1971), and general competence (Aronson, Willerman, & Floyd, 1966).

Now that we have given an idea of what we mean by admirable characteristics, we can turn to the issue of precisely how they influence attraction. The clearest insight into this has come from research on what is called the "matching hypothesis" (Walster et al., 1966). It acknowledges that many P's might *prefer* to have a relationship with an extremely attractive person—a Burt Reynolds or a Brooke Shields—but unless P feels equally desirable in some way, P may not be willing to run the risk of rejection.

Indeed, the matching hypothesis must operate, since there is considerable agreement on who is attractive, and if everybody were attracted only to the most desirable other person, the situation sometimes seen in high schools would arise in which the football hero and the homecoming queen are happily in love, and everyone else in the school is miserable! In this vein, Zetterberg (1966) observed that even in an office setting there may be a "secret ranking" of attractiveness.

Obviously, P's still do form relationships with O's who are less than blatantly attractive. The match is said to occur because, were O more attractive than P, O might not like P—but if O were less attractive than P, P would try to do better! Thus, the matching hypothesis describes a kind of "marketplace of open competition." And there is considerable evidence that people end up making friends with, marrying, and dating others similar to their own level of attractiveness (for reviews, see Murstein, 1976; Walster et al., 1976). Besides these correlational data, there is also some direct evidence that matching determines initial attraction in a dating choice situation (e.g., Huston, 1973; Shanteau & Nagy, 1979) and predicts courtship progress (e.g., White, 1980).

Such a "matching" is not limited to physical beauty, but could be, for example, between good looks and career success (Murstein, 1976). Another interesting finding is that we may like someone who has many admirable characteristics better if he or she makes a mistake—becoming more human, as it were—whereas a less attractive person may be liked less for the same mistake (Aronson et al., 1970; Aronson et al., 1966; Deaux, 1972).

Social and Cultural Influences

In the case of attraction, as in other areas of human behavior, it is necessary to look at the social context to gain a full understanding of the phenomenon.

Kerckhoff (1974) has reviewed social/cultural effects on attraction and emphasized three main points. First, social structures and values largely determine whom one is likely to meet.

Second, social norms largely determine who among those one may meet is appropriate for a given relationship. For example, racial similarity is typically considered desirable for close relationships, but less important for more distant relationships (Triandis & Davis, 1965). Usually traditions consider same-sex pairings best for friendship or business partnerships, but prohibit them for romantic relationships. All cultures have some incest limitations, and in some cases they are very complex, e.g., "Though nowhere may a man marry his mother, his sister, or his daughter . . . he may marry his paternal aunt among the Marquesans and Yaruro, his maternal aunt among the Osset and Sema, his half sister by the same mother among the Lakher and Mentaweians [etc.]" (Murdock, 1949, p. 284).

Third, among people who are available and appropriate, social norms—and often subcultural norms—define what characteristics are considered attractive or important. We have already mentioned how criteria of physical attractiveness may be culture-specific. The relative importance of other kinds of qualities—and relationship styles—also seem quite culture-specific. For example, lower-class women were traditionally taught in our culture to value soberness and ability to provide for a family in selecting a husband, whereas upper-class women were more often led to emphasize breeding, style, and creativity. In some cultures the quiet, obedient child is most attractive to parents; in others, the active, exploring, independent child (Whiting & Child, 1953). Our culture seems to emphasize the potential for emotional closeness (love) as a criterion for marriage—but looks down on such attractions as a criterion for selecting a business partner. In many cultures, however, it is the reverse: Marriage is a serious business that is arranged for economic viability and long-run compatibility, while a "business partner"—such as a hunting or sewing companion—may be chosen for emotional appeal.

5

Understanding Attraction

INTRODUCTION

This chapter first examines the major theoretical explanations that have been offered for the five apparent attraction-predicting conditions considered in the previous chapter. It then explores how the idea of self-expansion bears on those theories, on understanding the five conditions that predict attractions, and, finally, on the definition of attraction.

GENERAL THEORETICAL PERSPECTIVES

Explanations for attraction typically arise from the same two broad theoretical traditions used to understand why people do things in general—the reward and Gestalt perspectives. Both have been applied with considerable success to attraction.

Reward Approaches

Reward-type approaches range from Skinnerian "schedules of reinforcement," to various exchange and social learning theories, to Freudian libido and classical philosophical hedonism. All these share one assumption: People seek pleasure and avoid pain. This very simple idea has been used in very sophisticated ways, particularly by behavioral psychologists and economists, to arrive at very precise understandings of human behavior.

In social psychology, one of the major variants of the reward approach has been "exchange theory" (Thibaut & Kelley, 1959), which takes a kind of economic perspective: A person will act so as to maximize perceived gains and minimize perceived costs. For example, in selecting a friend, P will choose among alternatives an O that leads to a relationship in which P expects to gain the most and lose the least.

While exchange theory may seem to describe a rather calculating approach to love, two points should be emphasized. First, the process of weighing rewards and costs among alternatives need not be conscious. Second, the kinds of "rewards" and "costs" involved in human relationships are very special. Although some researchers do focus only on material rewards, Foa and Foa (1974) list six categories of "resources" exchanged—money, goods, information, services, status, and love. When we have asked our students to describe what they have gained from close relationships, they do occasionally report such items as security, status, or wealth, but they also typically emphasize the "rewards" of growth, emotional support, sharing, being trusted and trusting, giving, learning about themselves, feeling good about themselves, and so forth.

In general, reward approaches simply point out that we will be attracted to persons who provide rewards or from whom we expect to receive them (Byrne, 1971), or even to persons accidentally associated with rewarding experiences (Aron, 1970; Lott & Lott, 1974).

Reward explanations can be readily applied to all of the previous chapter's five conditions that appear to predict attraction. Attitude similarity would lead to attraction because being agreed with is pleasant. It makes one feel good about oneself. Reciprocal liking (that is, being liked) works because people like to be liked; matching of admirable characteristics works because each seeks the maximum available in the open market of those characteristics that seem intrinsically pleasurable or practically useful; and the social context is important because people may be given social approval for doing what is expected or given social sanctions for failing to do so. Propinquity is somewhat less obvious from a reward point of view. However, Newcomb (1956) argues that since people are usually pleasant to strangers, as P comes to have more interaction with any O a net advantage of rewards over costs develops, which P associates with O. (For a fuller discussion of reward theory in relation to these prediction rules, see Berscheid & Walster, 1978).

The advantages of a reward approach are considerable. First, it is based on a very simple, intrinsically appealing idea that explains a wide range of phenomena. Equally important, its great success in other areas of psychology, especially learning and motivation, enables us to apply understandings that are already well worked out to this new area of research.

The reward approach as it has been applied to attraction does have at least two limitations. First, like any theory or conceptual framework, it cannot explain its own assumptions. *Why* do people seek pleasure and avoid pain? Second, and most important, reward theory is somewhat circular (e.g., see Murstein, 1971a). By itself, it does not predict what will be rewarding. If we know something is rewarding, we can predict an attraction. But how do we know something is rewarding other than by observing that people are attracted to it? This is not exactly a flaw in the reward approach—it is simply a limitation. As Byrne and Lamberth (1971) point out, the reward approach does permit us to generalize on similar phenomena, and the elaboration of the process of response to a reward has proven highly useful. In Chapter 7 we will consider the variant of reward theory—exchange theory—which especially applies to relationships.

Gestalt Approaches

Gestalt-type approaches include the classical Gestalt theories of Wertheimer, Kohler, and Koffka; Lewinian field theory; and the various social psychology

```
| |    | |    | |    | |    |          Fig. 5-1   Illustrations of Gestalt "law of
| |    | |    | |    | |    |                     proximity" (Koffka, 1935). The per-
                                                  ceiver spontaneously pairs lines a and
a b    c d    e f    g h    i                     b, c and d, e and f, and so forth.
```

cognitive-balance and attribution theories of Heider, Festinger, Kelley, and so forth.

A basic principle of the classical Gestalt approach is that the human mind spontaneously organizes its world in the simplest, most integrated way possible. "Gestalt" literally means "form" or "organization." Gestalt psychologists tradition-ally emphasize that such form or organization characterizes our perception of the world, and then go on to claim that these patterns of perceptual organization also apply generally to cognition and behavior. Thus it is worth briefly reviewing some Gestalt perceptual organization principles before proceeding to their applications to attraction.

One such principle of spontaneous perceptual patterning is illustrated in Fig. 5-1 (after Koffka, 1935, p. 164), where lines a and b, c and d, and so forth appear as pairs.

Although there is no logical reason why they should not be grouped bc, de, and so forth, the human mind opts for the "simpler," more organized picture. In this case the mind follows what the Gestalt psychologists called the "law of proximity."

In Fig. 5-2 the periods and slashes are spontaneously grouped together.

In Fig. 5-3 the areas above c and d are each seen as whole figures, while the space above f is seen as background. Figures 5-2 and 5-3 illustrate, respectively, Gestalt laws of "similarity" and "symmetry." Other rules are "good continuation," "common fate," "closure," "past experience" (i.e., commonness), and a catch-all "Law of Pragnanz"—that "psychological organization will be as good as prevailing conditions allow" (Koffka, 1935, p. 110).

Psychologists working in this tradition have emphasized different aspects of the approach. Those in the field of perception often stress simplicity. For example, "our nervous systems organize the perceived world in whatever way will keep changes and differences to a minimum" (Hochberg, 1964, p. 87). Clinical psychol-ogists discuss clear separation of figure from ground in personal experiences, or general wholeness and integration of the organism (e.g., Perls et al., 1951).

Social psychologists taking a Gestalt viewpoint emphasize the tendency of the individual to create a balanced, non-conflicting organization of mental elements— a cognitive balance (Heider, 1958), consonance (Festinger, 1957) or congruence (Osgood & Tannenbaum, 1955). These conceptions dominated social psychology in the 1960s. Social psychologists' more recent emphasis on attribution theory is also rooted mainly in a Gestalt tradition, both historically and in terms of its content. Although it is much less motivational than the balance theories, attribu-tion theorists typically assume that individuals' behavior is *consistent* with their attributions, and that the attributions will be consistent with their perceptions.

As for how Gestalt principles have been applied to the five conditions we have considered for predicting attraction, theories of cognitive consistency have been employed the most. For example, regarding the attraction of "similars," New-

..//..//..//..//..//..//..//..//..//..//   *Fig. 5-2*   Illustration of Gestalt "law of similarity"
                                                  (Koffka, 1935. The perceiver sponta-
                                                  neously pairs periods with periods and
                                                  slashes with slashes.

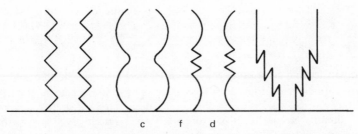

c   f   d

Fig. 5-3   Illustration of Gestalt "law of symmetry" (Koffka, 1935). The
perceiver spontaneously sees c and d as objects but f appears as a
space between objects.

comb's (1956) "A-B-X" model holds that if P ("A" in his model) likes hang gliding,
health spas, and yogurt (A's various "X's")—and so does O ("B")—the world is
simplest if P likes O. This is especially true if these things are important to P. On
the other hand, if P likes, for example, a particular political candidate whom O does
not like, they can still be friends, but with more difficulty. Other cognitive consistency approaches make similar predictions. Heider (1958) explains this connection
between the attitudes toward X and O as a cognitive "unit relation."

Cognitive consistency is also a straightforward explanation for another attraction
condition—reciprocal liking. If P likes P and O likes P, it is consistent for P to like
O. Notice that this approach makes P's self-esteem a prerequisite for liking others
(see Aronson, 1969), which is a favorite point of many clinicians.

Is is actually possible, though less familiar for social psychologists, to subsume all
five of the attraction-predicting conditions directly under Gestalt perceptual "laws"
(Table 5-1). Thus attitude similarity would be an example of "similarity,"
propinquity of "proximity" and "past experience," and reciprocal liking of "symmetry." The influence of social norms simply reflects the individual trying to put
his or her life in harmony with the social environment—perhaps expressing "com-

Table 5-1   Reward and Gestalt Explanations for Conditions Predicting Attraction

Condition predicting attraction	Explanation	
	Reward	Gestalt
Similarity	Consensual validation is rewarding	Similarity— unit relation, Cognitive balance
Propinquity	Over time, most others give more rewards than punishments	Proximity— unit relation
Being liked	Social approval is rewarding	Balance, Symmetry
Matching of admirable traits	Market forces	Symmetry, Similarity
Social norms	Societal approval is rewarding	Consistency with the social system

mon fate," "good continuation," "proximity"—or simply the "law of pragnanz." Matching of admirable characteristics is another case of "similarity;" and the source of a characteristic's admirableness can perhaps be found in its expression of one or more Gestalt organizational laws. For example, beauty is often described as a kind of elegance, of simplicity of form; and intelligence is typically measured by the ability to detect orderly patterns.

Overall, the Gestalt, like the reward approach, has the two virtues of being a simple, intuitively appealing approach that applies to numerous phenomena; and an approach whose implications have already been worked out in some detail in other fields (perception and cognitive consistency), so that what has been learned can be applied to the somewhat newer area of attraction. Of course, the consequences of the Gestalt approach for perception are probably less impressive than the effect of the reward approach on learning, but the Gestalt theories of cognitive consistency in social psychology have been very successful—and easily applied to attraction research.

The Gestalt approach also has its limitations. First, again like any theory, it cannot explain its own assumptions—in this case, it cannot say why balance and simplicity are perceived and preferred. Its more serious limitation, however, is that it does not obviously explain why people sometimes seek complexity and disequilibrium.

Relation of Reward and Gestalt Approaches

Reward and Gestalt approaches are rarely set in opposition to one another these days. Rather, social psychologists simply seem to use whichever best fits a particular phenomenon under study, or to consider each as explaining independent causal chains. Some theoretical purists subsume one within the other—a good organization is seen as rewarding, or a reward is seen as the final element needed to complete a Gestalt.* Regardless of how the two have coexisted within social psychology, they have largely dominated our understanding of initial attraction, and have been quite successful in the process.

ATTRACTION AS SELF-EXPANSION

Using the Idea of Self-Expansion to Synthesize and Go beyond Reward and Gestalt Approaches

We would suggest that a "reward" is whatever creates expansion of the self. And the Gestalt tendency to organize experience describes the integration phase of this expansion.

Viewing the two traditional approaches as phases of a unitary but two-phase motivation mitigates some of the limitations of each approach when considered separately. First, it places the assumptions of these approaches in the context of a higher-order theoretical model, giving an answer to *why* one seeks pleasure and avoids pain, and *why* organization is preferred. Second, it somewhat reduces the

*In fact, in the brief history of motivational research in Chapter 3, we emphasized that the traditional view has been that an organism feels rewarded only when it experiences a reduction in deviation from homeostatic balance—an idea not derived historically from Gestalt theories, but certainly Gestalt in spirit.

circularity of reward theory by pinning down what makes a reward rewarding: Something will be rewarding if it expands the potential effectance of the self. And third, it provides a consistent explanation for the Gestalt issue of why people sometimes seek to increase complexity or disturb balance or equilibrium: This increase or disturbance permits further expansion, which in the long run will lead to even more inclusive levels of integration of the self.

Attraction-Predicting Conditions as Preconditions

Another implication of self-expansion, however, is rather surprising and far-reaching in its significance for attraction research: It suggests that the five conditions that predict attraction are not direct causes of attraction at all, but function mainly as necessary *pre*conditions for attraction. ("Precondition" is meant in a logical and not necessarily temporal sense.) Under circumstances in which the necessary levels of at least one of these preconditions obtain, attraction will actually be increased by increasing the *opposite* of the other preconditions.

Even at first glance, the self-expansion motive seems to imply that attraction should result from the opposite of each of the five attraction-predicting conditions reveiwed in the last chapter. According to this approach, attraction should arise from P perceiving O as offering an opportunity for P to expand. But, for example, similarity between P and O would seem actually to minimize opportunities for P to expand. P should find a similar person *less* attractive. The same could be said for propinquity, reciprocal liking, matching on admirable traits, and normative social influences. Compared to their opposites, any of these conditions offer less opportunity for self-expansion, not more.

However, we would argue that the virtue of the five "preconditions"—and the reason they work so well in the research—is that they increase the feeling that it would be possible to actually form and maintain a relationship with the other. Similarity, propinquity and so forth facilitate interpersonal communication and interaction. For example, the findings of Davis (1981) and of Layton and Insko (1974) suggest that the real reason similarity is preferred is for its implications for future quality of interaction. And Levinger and Breedlove's (1966) results emphasize the function of similarity for facilitating the pair's goal attainment. Other researchers (e.g., Duck, 1973, 1977; Neimeyer & Neimeyer, 1981) have shown that the key aspect of similarity is "functional" similarity—that is, similarity of cognitive structure (in the sense of Kelly's REP), making communication easier. Indeed, Triandis (1977) concludes his very scholarly review of the similarity and attraction literature with the generalization that, "People are attracted to those with whom they can communicate effectively" (p. 178). In a similar vein, Triandis also says that similarity makes the other person predictable enough to create a relationship with.

In sum, similarity and the other "preconditions" promote attraction because they lead us to expect (and rightly so) that a relationship—and the attendant expansion—is possible. After all, if O offers tremendous opportunities for expansion, but is so different from P that P cannot form a relationship with O, the net effect for P is zero expansion. And no matter how similar, familiar, socially acceptable, and so forth any O is to P, every O has *something* unique or interesting to offer. Even the most similar O is not identical to P.

When P is not very confident about his or her relationship skills, the preconditions could be especially salient. If such a P meets someone who seems highly similar to P (or seems to like P, etc.), P's response is likely to be, "Oh, at last! *Here* is someone so much like me, maybe finally I can form a relationship."

We would argue, however, that given reasonable levels of expectation that a relationship is feasible (based on one or more of the preconditions), attraction is then increased mainly by increases in the *opposite* of one or more of the other five preconditions. That is, if P believes P *can* manage to form a relationship (on the basis of sufficient levels of one or more of the preconditions) with an O who is different, socially *pro*scribed, more attractive than P, or perhaps even unfriendly—P will prefer to do so. P will prefer to do so because such a relationship offers new perspectives on one's self, new challenges, new status, new reference groups, new experiences to try, new resources—in short, a greater potential for self-expansion.

This idea parallels Rotter's (1966) distinction between the reward value of a behavior and the perceived probability of getting that reward. (The former corresponds to the benefits to be gained from a relationship, through self-expansion; the latter to the probability of actually forming the relationship.) It also parallels the consideration in information theory (e.g., Buckley, 1967) that communication between two systems requires sufficient similarity of structure to interpret the message, but enough difference to have a message to send.

The "preconditions" cannot be ignored. Without them no relationship—and therefore no expansion at all—would be possible. As Darley and Berscheid (1967) found, merely anticipating interaction increases attraction. Likewise, even objects are more appealing if they vaguely resemble persons (Sears, 1983). That is, although we want interesting relationships with people, most of all, we simply want relationships.

In this vein, regarding similarity, Ellis (1935) commented: "It is a variation, but a slight variation that we seek" (p. 81). Or as Kelling (1979) put it: "Similarity is the background on which dissimilarity plays a highly figural role. . . . Similarity may allow people to get together, but it takes them no further."

We propose that this precondition-and-reversal idea applies to all five of the attraction-predicting conditions (Table 5-2). In the next sections we will focus on each one, examining the evidence for this proposition.

Similarity and Dissimilarity

Several studies focusing on perceived general personality characteristics support our suggestion that if P believes it will be easy to form a relationship with O, P may actually be more attracted to a dissimilar O. For example, Walster and Walster (1963) led participants in their experiment to believe that people with whom they would later interact would like them. Under these conditions, the participants actually indicated preferences for people who were believed to be dissimilar.

In a similar vein, Izard (1963) found that personality similarity was more important as a condition for friendship among college freshmen than among college seniors. Izard proposed that the reason for this result was the seniors' increased maturity—which presumably includes greater confidence in their ability to form and maintain relationships. Likewise, Goldstein and Rosenfeld (1969) found similarity to be less important for individuals who were assessed as low on "fear of

Table 5-2   Precondition and Attraction Variables

Precondition	Attraction
Contributing to expectation that a relationship with O is possible	Contributing to expectation that a relationship with O would expand self
Similarity	Dissimilarity
Propinquity, familiarity	Absence, distance, or mystery
Being liked	Initial dislike, which is overcome
Matching of admirable traits	Other has maximum admirable traits
Following social norms	Violation or independence of social norms

rejection" or who scored low on "need for approval" on a standard personality test.*

Nahemow and Lawton (1975) studied friendship patterns among 270 mainly elderly residents of a New York City housing project. They found that the more opportunity for forming a relationship via propinquity (high frequency of interaction because of close proximity in the housing project), the more likely it was that a person's best friends were of a *different* age and race.

A series of three others studies focused on attitude similarity. Each of the 40 male participants in Aronson and Worchel's (1966) experiment were led to believe that a fellow participant either liked or disliked him and either agreed or disagreed with him on several attitude statements. Subsequently, participants' ratings of their fellow participant indicated that attraction was mainly determined by these liking variables, and that similarity became essentially irrelevant. We infer that the liking manipulation produced so much confidence or lack of confidence in the probability of forming a relationship that additional confidence, from similarity, was redundant.

However, Byrne and Griffitt (1966) argued that the results of this study were due to the very small difference between the similarity and dissimilarity experimental conditions. They then repeated the study, intensifying the similarity-dissimilarity dimension: Even though they were able to decrease attraction to the dissimilar other, they were not able to increase attraction to the more similar other!

Finally, another study of this kind was conducted by Jones et al. (1972). These authors interpreted their complicated set of results as indicating that P prefers a dissimilar O who likes P over a similar O who likes P, given the participants are highly involved in the study and the measured response to O is an emotional one.

There has also been some work on the temporal patterns of influence of the various attraction predictors as close relationships develop, which is important for us to consider if these variables are indeed only preconditions. (True, we said P's

*Two studies (Murstein, 1971b; Snyder, 1979) have been conducted in which competent P's preferred "similars." But in these cases similarity was of competency-type traits (e.g. low level of neuroticism), so that the situation was more akin to one of admirable characteristics. These studies are consistent with the analysis we will offer shortly on admirable characteristics.

perception of a precondition being met need not always temporally precede the perception that O offers an opportunity for expansion. However, if P fails to perceive the presence of any of the preconditions, before sensing a strong level of a precondition's opposite, P might give up on attempting further interaction with O.)

After conducting studies with engaged couples over a period of several months, Kerckhoff and Davis (1982) described a "filtering model," in which similarity is used in the earlier stages to filter out those with whom one cannot easily relate. Then, in those relationships that survive the initial stage, further progress is a function of complementarity of needs.

On the basis of that study and his own extensive work with engaged couples, Murstein (1977) posits a three-stage "Stimulus-Value-Role" theory. Initially physical appearance matters most (the external stimulus). If O passes this test, value similarity becomes salient. The final stage refers to the "role fit" between the way each partner behaves in the relationship; a kind of complementarity idea. Thus both Kerckhoff and Davis's and Murstein's conclusions from their extensive data suggest that similarity is a precondition only (meant here in the temporal sense).

Propinquity and Distance

While propinquity often leads to attraction, there also is truth in the old sayings "familiarity breeds contempt" and "absence makes the heart grow fonder." Indeed, in the medieval romantic tradition, the love object was almost always hidden away in a tower, or otherwise made inaccessible. And today, as literature and the cinema tell us, people still seem to find themselves obsessed with the unknown, mysterious lover. In fact, it appears traditional that once the love object is "captured" and interaction becomes frequent, passion declines.

As for the data, the study of Nahemow and Lawton (1975) mentioned earlier also may be interpreted as indicating that when the probability of forming a relationship is perceived to be high, because of age and race similarity, then people who live further away may be preferred as friends. Of course, there is also the extensive data on the decline in marital satisfaction with time (e.g., Pineo, 1961).

Liking Those Who Like Us and Those Who Do Not

Mutual liking seems to be such an essential precondition that it is not easy to imagine situations in which P could feel O does not like P, and yet still feel confident, because of other preconditions being met, about the possibility of forming a relationship with O. The central role of reciprocal liking as a precondition variable is also suggested by its use as a precondition variable in the similarity-dissimilarity studies discussed above. Moreover, attempts to demonstrate a preference for a hard-to-get O have been rather unsuccessful. Only if O is hard for *others* to get, but easy for P, is P's attraction to O increased (Walster et al., 1973).

On the other hand, if O initially dislikes or resists P, and then comes to like P or accede to P's wishes, O is preferred over someone else who liked P all along. In one study (Aron, 1970), male participants first had to convince a female confederate that she should violate the experimenter's request that while the experimenter was out, she should not let anyone into the laboratory waiting room. Then in the "experiment" itself the subject had to try to overcome her physical resistance in a two-person test of strength (in which he did not know that his success was being manipulated through certain handicaps given him or her). Those participants randomly assigned to the condition in which they succeeded on both entry to the laboratory and the strength test—but only after strong initial resistance—were most attracted to the confederate. Those who succeeded against no resistance and those failing to succeed at all were less attracted to the same confederate.

This study, and others of what has come to be called "yielding" (e.g., Aronson & Linder, 1965; Cialdini & Mirels, 1976; Lombardo et al., 1972), suggests that although being liked remains an almost necessary precondition for attraction, if P feels that O did not always like P, then O appears even more interesting and the "conquest" of O is more satisfying. (However, Cialdini & Mirels, 1976, found that if P is low in perceived personal control, P will prefer an O that does not yield, presumably because this confirms P's expectations.)

A similar line of research (Brink, 1977; Lombardo et al., 1973) has found increased attraction to O under conditions in which P is simply given an opportunity to reply to a disagreeing statement made by O. As Brink explains these findings, the situation gives P the opportunity to experience "effectance."

Admirable Characteristics—Matching versus Going for the Best

The self-expansion approach suggests that, given the opportunity, every P should prefer to form a relationship with an O possessing maximally desirable characteristics. Thus P's self expands to include O's beauty, competence, status, wealth, and so forth. O's physical appearance is especially important for several reasons. It is the most available information, especially when first meeting O. Good looks can be, as Stendhal (1927) says, "an advertisement for passion." Moreover, at any phase of the acquaintance process, appearance is a valued potential addition to the self because, in our culture, attractive people are perceived to be more generally competent (Dion et al., 1972) and more socially competent (Goldman & Lewis, 1977). They also *are* more socially competent (Reis et al., 1982), and afford status to whoever is in a relationship with them (Sigall & Landy, 1973). In addition, the traits identified cross-culturally with personal beauty—good health, and youthfulness—have obvious value for potential effectance. And the only clearly identifiable characteristic of physical attractiveness in our culture for men—height (Berscheid & Walster, 1974; Graziano et al., 1978)—is associated with interpersonal as well as physical power.

However, as described in the previous chapter, in what appears to be a kind of "marketplace" of relationships, a P does seem to end up with an O of similar overall attractiveness. This matching may balance one admirable trait against another—a physically attractive P with a wealthy O, for example. But in general it is an easily observed phenomenon that people of similar overall attractiveness form relationships with each other. How then does expansion enter into the tight matching equation?

We would argue that the attraction-predicting condition of P preferring an O with a similar level of attractiveness—instead of a greater level—occurs for the same reason P prefers an O with similar attitudes: P perceives a greater probability of forming and maintaining a relationship. And the expected probability of forming a relationship seems to be a crucial variable in the matching hypothesis research.

In the first systematic study of the matching hypothesis, Walster et al. (1966) organized a computer dating dance at the University of Minnesota. Each of the 752 freshmen who signed up were surreptitiously rated by four "ticket sellers" for their physical attractiveness (self-ratings were also used). While at the dance with their "matched" date (the match was random), each completed a short questionnaire privately about how much he or she liked his or her date. In addition, participants were interviewed six months after the dance about whether they had attempted to date their partner again. The results were unambiguous. At the outset the students indicated on the computer dating questionnaire that they expected to be matched with a person of a similar level of attractiveness. However, those with the most attractive partners liked their partners best at the intermission, and were more likely to ask them out again later, regardless of their own level of attractiveness.

What is important about this study is that the participants' attraction to their partner was measured when propinquity, social etiquette, and inferred similarity (since they thought they had been matched by computer) all gave substantial support to an expectation that a relationship was feasible.

Consistent with our argument, subsequent studies (Berscheid et al., 1971; Cash & Darlega, 1978; Huston, 1973; Kiesler & Baral, 1970; Shanteau & Nagy, 1979; Stroebe et al., 1971) confirm the Walster et al. result, but also show that if P is not led to believe that O is a compatible match, or if P is not otherwise assured that O will like P, then the matching hypothesis is superior. For example, Shanteau and Nagy found P's preference among pairs of potential dates could be predicted by multiplying P's expected probability that O would go out with P by a rating of O's physical attractiveness.

Our point is that matching may be a precondition, but when a relationship appears to be possible because of other preconditions being met (or the issue is somehow made to seem irrelevant), P prefers the most attractive O.

Not only does the "matching" part of this precondition sometimes reverse, but so does the "admirable characteristics." In an extreme case of desire for expansion and confidence about being able to form and maintain a relationship, P may, as Jung (1951/1959; Hall & Nordby, 1973) describes, be attracted to P's "shadow"—an O of the same sex having traits that are only unconsciously attractive. These traits are usually aspects of P that P rejects as unacceptable and projects onto an O who shows any signs of them at all (the clergyperson's close friendship with a prisoner or underworld type; the monogamous wife's with a promiscuous single woman; the business person's with a poor artist). Of course such relationships only occur under otherwise strong preconditions, such as extreme propinquity (being stuck on an elevator together, being obliged to work together).

There is some evidence for such attractions under other strong preconditions. Murstein (1971b) found a negative (-.49) correlation in best friend's ratings of each other's physical attractiveness among college women residing together in a cooperative housing situation, where presumably propinquity and shared values would create strong preconditions for friendship. However, in a study in which such strong preconditions were not present (Cash & Darlega, 1978), including same-sex "close" friends (both male and female), physical attractiveness (as rated by judges) was positively correlated.

Social Norms and Violation of Social Norms

Several observers of human nature have noted that in the process of violating social norms about relationships, P may feel increased attraction to O. This is clearly the opposite of forming a relationship under the condition of social approval.

A major thrust of Bataille's (1962) work is that passion is increased by the violation of taboos. Life, according to him, is either in the rational world of work, or in the irrational world of violence, the supernatural, and passionate relationships. The scientific, rational world of work abhors disorderliness, so that taboos are placed on the irrational world. Bataille concludes that although society does provide certain specific channels for transgressing its own taboos, the experience of transgression almost defines for us what is passionate, and greatly increases the passion in these situations!

Douvan (1977) and Kelling (1979) put forward positions that are a little more down to earth. Human love, they argue, is greatest when it stands outside of the usual social structures, if not exactly transgressing them. Kelling emphasizes the psychological aspect: Love exists so long as the other person and the relationship are not psychologically pigeonholed (i.e., are not "accommodated," to use Piaget's term). Douvan's emphasis is more social: Love exists so long as the behavior in the relationship transcends the persona we express in our ordinary social relations.

Driscoll et al. (1972) found stronger romantic love among dating couples whose parents disapproved, and called it the "Romeo and Juliet effect".

In sum, it is easy to imagine that if any other preconditions are met—O is similar, close at hand, or fond of P—violating social norms could provide an unusual experience through which the self might occasionally expand towards greater autonomy, clearer personal values, new social roles, and the like.

DEFINITION OF ATTRACTION
RECONSIDERED

When we began our discussion of attraction, we settled for requiring that P have a "positive attitude" toward O, and we said that the attendant behavioral, cognitive, and emotional reactions were probably the easiest way to measure attraction. But we also suggested such a positive attitude is not necessarily identical with attraction, which may be considered richer and more complex. P may have a very positive attitude about O, i.e., P may act positively toward O, think highly of O, feel good about O, and yet not want to include O within P's self. We usually call such cases "respect" or "admiration," and do not usually associate them with the kind of attraction involved in close relationships. Thus, for example, Rubin (1973) includes "respect" items in his "liking" scale but not in his "loving" scale.

Another possibility is that P may be "attracted" to O, yet have a very negative attitude toward O. Such ambivalences, in fact, have even been considered to be a hallmark of stronger attractions (Berscheid & Walster, 1978; Hatfield & Walster, 1978). P may avoid O, think poorly of or dislike O—and yet still, somehow, want to incorporate something about O within P's self.

So what is attraction? We think the best definition is that P is attracted to O if P desires to enter a close relationship with O, which will usually but not always be refelected in attitudes or behaviors. This desire for a relationship arises when P perceives that O offers opportunities for self-expansion.

While this definition may be less easy to measure, we think it makes for better theory. Normally the perceived opportunity to expand will generate a positive attitude, and behaviors that bring P into O's company. Some expansion opportunities, however, arise precisely because O represents a deviation from normative values, and therefore P may not associate the desire to form a relationship with O with respect or other positive-attitude-type cognitions regarding O. Positive attitude toward O is a very frequent symptom of attraction, but not its substance. Expected self-expansion is its substance.

6

Strong Attractions

INTRODUCTION

In this chapter we first examine distinctions made between less intense attractions—usually called "liking"—and more intense attractions—usually called "loving." Then we turn to the various approaches offered for understanding the causes of strong initial attractions.

The studies and theories we will be citing tend to equate strong attractions with initial romantic attractions and, sometimes, weaker attractions with friendships. While we must accept this assumption in discussing the literature, we feel this limitation can and should be transcended. Strong feelings of love can develop in all intimate relationships, and can arise or be present at any time in a relationship. However, in this chapter, we are focusing on initial attraction only, and chiefly on romantic relationships.

TYPES OF ATTRACTION

Loving versus Liking

Until recently, most attraction research has focused on low-intensity attractions to strangers, which can be conveniently studied in the laboratory. Research of this type—what Clore (1977) has called the "Byrne paradigm" and the "Festinger tradition"—is mainly what we were considering in the previous two chapters. Nevertheless, even those researchers who in the past focused only on mild attractions have recently emphasized the need to study more intense attractions.

The first research comparing loving and liking was done in the early 1960s. Day (1961) reported that courtship couples showed a different pattern of similarities and complementarities of needs than did members of these same couples with their same- or opposite-sex friends. Banta and Hetherington (1963) studied 29 clusters of relationships—the engaged couple, and a male and female friendship for each partner—and found similar results.

Early clinical writers on attraction also made distinctions between loving and liking (or what they called friendship). For example, Grant (1957) suggested that, unlike friendship, love includes the desire to possess, occasional hatred or violence, and a preoccupation with aesthetic appeal. Suttie (1935) wrote that in friendship, interest is turned jointly onto the same things, whereas in love, interest is turned onto each other. Reik (1944) argues there are at least three additional differences: Friendship implies equality, love does not; friendship implies unconscious rivalry, love implies unconscious envy; and love is more passionate.

Among social psychologists, until the early 1970s there was no substantial interest in either intense attractions or the distinctions between these and less intense attractions.

The first influential work in this area was conducted by Zick Rubin (1970, 1973). He developed and validated questionnaire measures of loving and liking. Engaged couples with high scores on his "love scale" spent significantly more time "gazing into each other's eyes," as surreptitiously observed while they were "alone" in a waiting room prior to completing the questionnaires. Among other findings consistent with his distinction, ratings on the "like" scale for best same-sex friend and for fiance were similar, but fiances were "loved" more. Rubin's "liking scale" items are designed to measure how much P feels similar to O and how much P respects O. The "love scale" items, on the other hand, focus on P's feelings toward O of attachment, caring, and intimacy.*

Around the same time, Berscheid and Walster (1974) also made the important observation that, in addition to its greater intensity, "romantic love" differs qualitatively from more ordinary attractions. They cited the following three differences: (a) the importance of fantasy and the attendant idealization of the love object; (b) the prominence of ambivalent feelings; and (c) the different typical patterns of intensity over time (liking is a gradual increase over a long time, romantic love is a sudden initial increase, followed by—at best—a leveling off).

More recently, Hatfield and her colleagues (Hatfield, 1982; Hatfield et al., 1979; Traupmann & Hatfield, 1981) have emphasized the dimension of "intimacy" rather than the liking/loving distinction. They list seven characteristics that "distinguish intimate from nonintimate relations":

Intensity of liking/loving
Depth and breadth of information exchange
Value of resources exchanged
Variety of resources exchanged
Substitutability of resources
Commitment
The unit of analysis–from "you" and "me" to "we" (Hatfield, 1982, p. 271)

Very recently, Davis and Todd (1982) have approached the issue of nonintimate liking versus intimate loving by using a "descriptive psychology" paradigm (Ossorio, 1981). These researchers proposed "paradigm cases" of friendship and of romantic love which bring into focus the normally somewhat blurred relationship characteristics shown below (from Davis & Todd, 1982, p. 81).

*In an innovative recent study (Steck et al., 1982), subjects were asked to rate how much "love" or "attraction" was shown in Rubin love scales that had been filled in to emphasize different degrees of "needing" and "caring." Subjects' ratings suggested that caring is more central to love and needing is more central to attraction.

Friendship	Romantic love
Equal eligibilities	Asymmetric eligibilities
Enjoy	Enjoyment
Trust	Advocate/Champion
Mutual assistance	Give the utmost
Acceptance	Acceptance
Respect	Respect
Spontaneity	Spontaneity
Understanding	Understanding
Intimacy	Intimacy
	Fascination
	Exclusiveness

They emphasized that "the most obvious difference between a romantic love relationship and a friendship lies in a cluster of subrelationships which collectively might be identified as the Passion cluster—Fascination, Exclusiveness and Enjoyment" (p. 89).

To illustrate their ideas, Davis and Todd conducted a series of studies in which individuals described each of various love and friendship relationships by giving responses to a multi-item "Relationship Rating Form." In general, factor analysis of the responses were consistent with their concepual scheme, except for one unexpected result: Spouse and love relationships consistently scored lower than best friend (or other friends) on "stability."

Finally, Swensen (1961, 1973; Fiore & Swensen, 1977) found some justification for what we faulted at the start—treating the romantic relationship differently than other loving relationships. Swensen asked over 200 individuals to describe their "love relationships," including parent-child, sibling, spouse, and opposite-sex friendships or marriage. From these descriptions he derived 388 items, then administered them to 1200 more subjects, and factor-analyzed these results to produce a 120-item love scale divided into six factors or subscales: verbal expression of affection; self-disclosure of intimate facts about oneself; tolerance for the less desirable traits of the other; non-material evidence of interest, through moral support and encouragement; verbal expression of feelings of love for the other; and material evidence through financial support. All "love relationships" were found to exhibit one or more of these behaviors, but according to Fiore and Swensen, the opposite-sex-friendship/marriage relationship is the only one high on all six factors. (In his early research, shared activities, similarity of outlook, and physical expression of love were also found to be common experiences of love in opposite-sex relationships, but not necessarily for other relationships.)

Swensen's results both simplify and complicate the loving-liking distinction. While he only asked about "loving" relationships, some relationships clearly involved fewer—and different—behaviors than others. Swenson's data, and common impressions, suggest that one is supposed to "love" family members (whether liking them or not). Swensen found this type of love is expressed by giving material and nonmaterial (emotional and moral) support—plus, with siblings, by sharing activities. Another type of "love" is found between close, same-sex friends (although respondents might have called it "liking" if given the choice). Swensen found that same-sex friends do not express their love through material evidence or physical acts, but through all the other channels.

Only one loving relationship included every behavior associated with any of the other love relationships: opposite-sex friendship or marriage. Thus, at least in our culture, the form of love expressed most fully and broadly is between the sexes. However, when all these behaviors are present, more distinctions can still be made.

Types of Love

In addition to these global approaches to distinguishing loving from liking and the relationships where each are found, there have been attempts to distinguish among types of love.

Hatfield and her associates (Berscheid & Walster, 1978; Hatfield, 1982; Hatfield and Walster, 1978; Traupmann and Hatfield, 1981) have described in some detail a distinction between "companionate love"—"an affection we feel for those with whom our lives are deeply entwined" (Hatfield & Walster, 1978, p. 9)—and "passionate love"—"a state of intense absorption in another" (p. 9).

Lee (1976, 1977) has actually described six "styles" or "colors" of what people mean when they say "I love you":

Eros—fascination with beauty
Storge- friendship love
Ludus—game playing, flirtatious love
Mania—extreme romantic love
Pragma—practical, realistic-oriented love
Agape—giving, saintly love

While Lee's terms are largely taken from the rich tradition of more literary writings on love, his distinctions are based on an analysis of questionnaire responses. Lasswell and Lasswell (1976) have developed a measure of these styles, which has generated some interesting research (e.g., Johnston & Jaremko, 1979; Rosenman, 1978). On the other hand, Murstein (1980) cites an unpublished factor analysis of this measure by T. S. Hatkoff that suggests that one factor, intensity, may be the main dimension on which these various styles should be arranged.

Whether only much more intense, or qualitatively different, Lee's "mania" and Hatfield and Walster's "passionate love" both correspond fairly well to the notion of romantic love described by clinicians and popularizers (and by Berscheid & Walster, 1974). But while romantic love has been the subject of tremendous popular interest (evident in popular novels, movies, etc.), social scientists have typically considered it to be somewhat frivolous. Indeed, Linton wrote:

> All societies recognize that there are occasional violent emotional attachments between persons of the opposite sex, but our present American culture is practically the only one which has attempted to capitalize on these and make them the basis for marriage. The hero of the modern American movie is always a romantic lover, just as the hero of an old Arab epic is always an epileptic. (1936, p. 175)

Whatever serious work has been done on romantic love usually involves either its social history, its clinical indicators (e.g., Casler, 1973), or the extent to which its presence as a personality trait in marital partners affects subsequent success (e.g., Rubin, 1974).

Recently, however, Tennov (1979) presented an extensive collection of subjects' interview descriptions of an intense romantic love she labeled "limerence." Limerence involves constant, overwhelming, and even debilitating absorption in the unrequited desire for reciprocation of equally intense feelings from a love object. In addition to giving a strong sense of the phenomenon, Tennov also suggests that her interviews show that some people ("limerents") have this experience or are prone to it and others ("non-limerents") are not. (She does not give percentages.)

Steffen et al. (1982) developed a limerence questionnaire that correlated with self-reported degree of absorption in past relationships. Their factor analysis of subjects' responses found 14 dimensions of limerence. Especially important is that "some individuals emphasize the ecstatic nature of limerence while others obsess over fear of rejection" (p. 6).

Loving, Liking, and Self-Expansion

Much of what we have just considered about liking, loving, and kinds of love probably does boil down to differences in intensity and in early versus later phases of a relationship. For example, loving, especially mania or limerence love, does seem to differ from liking mainly in intensity. Passionate versus companionate love—as well as perhaps ludus and mania versus storge and pragma—are largely related to early versus later phases of a relationship.* But this analysis leaves out many details. Moreover, intensity and phase of relationships should be defined in a theoretical context to clarify how they interact and how they might be operationalized.

Using self-expansion as this context, we would analyze the development of a relationship along two dimensions: time, and the amount of other included into the self. As Fig. 6-1 shows, this analysis yields slopes of relationship development that are steep (at a given point in time) when the relationship offers rapid expansion, or shallow when the expansion it offers is slow. (These diagrams, for simplicity, do not include the phases of expansion and integration, which would make the curves step-like.)

Intensity, then, is simply the rate of expansion—on the figures, the steepness of the slope. If expansion from a relationship is very rapid (a) one would expect the characteristic experiences attributed to "mania," "romantic," "limerent," or "passionate" love. In this case, the rate of expansion from a relationship may approach the maximum total possible for that person from all sources. "Fascination," "exclusiveness," and "idealization" are both a cause and result of this steep slope. Similarly, because such expansion may occur at a rate beyond what can be easily integrated (the definition of stress), Berscheid and Walster's "ambivalence" and Davis and Todd's lack of "stability" are no surprise.

Liking, on the other hand, is associated with a gentler rate of expansion (c), well within the limits of what can be easily integrated and probably augmented with other sources of expansion.

If intensity of love varies in the different phases of a relationship, there are changes in the slope, whether the characteristics of the other have already been

---

*However, Traupmann and Hatfield (1981) describe a series of studies in which, to their surprise, subjective reports of the intensity of passionate and companionate love declined at about equal rates from early to later in relationships.

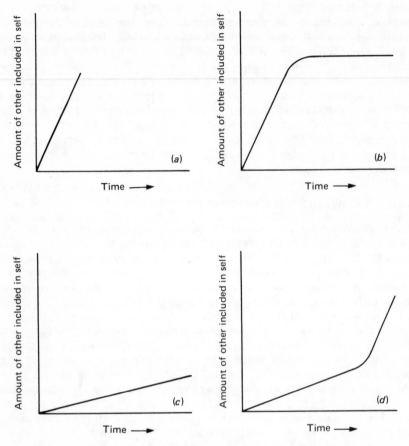

Figure 6-1 Theoretical patterns of changes over time in amount of other included
in self. Steeply rising slopes represent rapid expansion. Panels describe
(*a*) intense, "passionate" attraction; (*b*) initially passionate attraction
that has settled into less intense, stable love relationship; (*c*) slowly and
consistently developing relationship such as a friendship; (*d*) relationship
that was initially not intense, in which the individuals later "fall in
love."

largely included (*b*) or are suddenly found to be greater than supposed (*d*). In
the former case, the relationship may still be valued because it maintains a
great deal of expandedness (the height of the curve), even though the intense
feelings of pleasure and challenge associated with rapid expanding and integrating
may not be present. While that which Hatfield et al. call passionate love occurs
during any steep slope phase, companionate love occurs during any shallow phase in
which much of the other has already been integrated into the self. Table 6-1
explores the relation between expansion rate and amount of prior expansion.

Section one in the table seems to describe the cultural ideal of marriage, and
everyone's hope for romance. (We know O thoroughly yet keep learning more.
The relationship continues to provide strong rewards forever. This is in keeping
with the evidence for steep reward gradients being in themselves rewarding; see

Table 6-1   Relation between Integration and Expansion

	Rate of expansion from relationship	
Present level of integration	High	Low
High	1: seemingly impossible	2: companionate love
Low	3: passionate love	4: ordinary liking

Huesmann, 1980). However, a continued high rate along with an already high level of integration of other into the self seems not only impossible, but totally unsupported by the many studies suggesting a change from high to lower satisfaction after the early phases of a romantic relationship. Given the ideal of romantic love lasting "happily ever after," perhaps it is less surprising that Davis and Todd's subjects chose to describe their spouse relationships as more unstable (and thus perhaps meeting the ideal of being more exciting and passionate) than their friendships.

Section two, companionate love, means high amount integrated and low rate of further expansion. The other is very much a part of the self, but does not offer the excitement of further opportunities for rapid expansion. This could occur following a period of rapid expansion (as mentioned previously, and shown in Fig. 6-1b), as would happen in a marriage that began with passionate, romantic love and then settled into Reik's "warm afterglow" of companionate love. It could happen as a result of a long period of slower expansion (Fig. 6-1c), as in a lifelong friendship or kin relationship, or in a marriage that began with a less hurried initial attraction. (Either way, the curve has reached a considerable height and on the right side its present slope is not steep.)

Sections three and four are mainly about initial attractions (a steep slope, but not extended very far along the graph). Section three, rapid expansion, is the main subject of this chapter, while four, a slower rate of expansion, was that of Chapters 4 and 5.

Each individual has, of course, many sources of expansion—career, educational experiences, travel, hobbies, other relationships, and on and on. Different curves could be plotted for each. A summation of these at any point in time would yield a slope indicating the total rate of expansion occurring (its limit differs among individuals, as discussed in Chapter 3). Thus while the slope of expansion from a particular relationship (for instance, a friendship) may be shallow, this does not necessarily describe the individual's overall rate of self-expansion from incorporation of new experiences, skills, resources, and so forth—which may be very high on some other curve, for some other relationship (e.g., a new baby), or some totally different expansion experience (e.g., education or career).

COUSES OF STRONG ATTRACTIONS

Many cases of strong attractions, of course, are simply especially strong instances of the general attraction processes—that is, they are caused by especially strong occurrences of some of the five "preconditions," plus a large dose of one or more of the opposites of these.* Other strong attractions, however, seem to be the results

---

*However, the more different, distant, etc. O is, the stronger the preconditions must be in order to help P believe that a relationship is possible. Therefore, to produce a strong attraction, both precondition and expansion variables must be very strongly present.

of additional, special mechanisms. At least four are described in the literature: (1) P's idiosyncratic responsiveness to highly specific characteristics of O; (2) P's arousal or affect when meeting O, or the unusualness of the situation; (3) P associating O with relief from punishment (or presumably, though we are not aware of any such research, P associating O with strong pleasure); and (4) P's "readiness" for strong attractions.

Responsiveness to Specific Characteristics

Some P's appear to be idiosyncratically predisposed to respond to a particular aspect of an O—the shape of face, posture, tone of voice, or whatever (Binet, 1887; Grant, 1957, 1976). Grant (1957) argues that this phenomenon accounts particularly well for (a) love-at-first sight attractions, (b) the apparent irrationality of attraction, (c) the intensity of passion associated with some attractions, and (d) attraction being based on cues that are easily recognized at first meeting.

Several different explanations have been proposed to explain how an individual might become unusually responsive to a particular cue. Grant (1957), Stekel (1943), and Gebhard (1965) emphasize "one-shot conditioning" from some experience in early life.

Tridon (1920) and Bridges (1935) focus on O's resemblance to P's image of the opposite-sex parent as remembered from infancy. According to Tridon, this explains the desire for youthful mates and why P may feel less "in love" as O grows older, and hence resembles less P's image from infancy of the parent. These writers were, of course, elaborating on Freud's (1927) idea that a woman seeks her father in her husband, and a man seeks his mother in his wife. Jung (1925/1959) also thinks that the child's perception of the parent contributes greatly to the anima/animus archetype, discussed below.

In addition to clinical observations, there has been some weak support for the parent-image theory in questionnaire-type research (Hamilton, 1929; Schiller, 1932; Strauss, 1946). However, for many key traits, Strauss found the same degree of correlation between spouse and parent characteristics for both parents. Mangus (1936), in his study of 600 college women, found that the husband-ideal mate correlations were higher than the father-ideal mate correlations.

Furthermore, Aron et al. (1974) administered questionnaires to 98 members of engaged couples waiting in line for their marriage licenses in Toronto. They found that a respondent's relationship with the fiance was significantly more similar to the relationship the respondent had had with the mother than with the father—*for both sexes!* These data suggest it is the first love object—for both sexes usually the mother—that is most important.

Another explanation for highly specific preferences is that they are inherited—that is, they are "releaser stimuli," like those said to bond an infant to a mother (Bowlby, 1958).

However, the most prominent inherited-predisposition approach is C. G. Jung's (e.g., 1925/1959) archetype theory. Jung held that all men have an image of their ideal woman (anima) and all women an image of their ideal man or men (animus) in their unconscious. The anima archetype, for example, is a man's composite of all of his personal experience with women, the ideas of women held by the various cultures and subcultures to which he belongs, and an inherited image based on all women of all times. It is by virtue of this anima or animus archetype that P is attracted to an O of the opposite sex.

Above all, the anima or animus archetype represents an unexpressed part of oneself (if a female, the unexpressed male qualities present in the genes but inhibited by sexual differentiation; if a male the unexpressed female qualities present in the genes but inhibited by sexual differentiation). Thus P seeks vicariously to express the unexpressed and to attain wholeness by forming a relationship with an O who represents that archetype. Jung feels that this drive for wholeness through the projection of the anima/animus archetype "upon the person of the beloved" is "one of the chief reasons for passionate attraction" (1925/1959, p. 540).

Likewise, the shadow archetype (Jung, 1951/1959; Hall & Nordby, 1973) is said to represent the unexpressed, rejected parts of one's self, which are sometimes sought in or projected onto a same-sex friend. Again because of the motivation for wholeness that Jung describes, one may then feel intensely attracted to the person in whom these shadow characteristics have been found or on whom they have been projected.

P's Arousal or Affect at the Time of Meeting O, or the Unusualness of the Situation

A series of studies conducted in the early 1970s (Aron, 1970; Brehm et al., 1978; Dutton & Aron, 1974) found that male subjects are more likely to be attracted to a female confederate if they meet her under conditions in which they have been exposed to anxiety-provoking or other arousal-creating conditions, such as while anticipating an electric shock or role playing a highly emotional situation.

The most influential explanation for these findings is based on an extension of Schachter and Singer's (1962) two-component theory of emotion. This theory suggests that a person experiences nonspecific physiological arousal and then uses perceptual cues to cognitively label it. In terms of love, Berscheid and Walster (1974) argue that "individuals will experience passionate love whenever two conditions coexist:

1. They are intensely aroused physiologically;
2. Situational cues indicate that 'passionate love' is the appropriate label for their intense feelings" (p. 360).

In a study widely cited to support this view (Dutton & Aron, 1974), an attractive female confederate stood in the middle of a frightening walk-over suspension bridge. The confederate was instructed to stop each male (of the appropriate age group) crossing over the bridge and request that he write a creative story about a Thematic Apperception Test picture. Afterwards, the confederate told the subject that he could phone her that night for an explanation of the study if he chose.

A substantially higher proportion of those who were stopped on the bridge also phoned her, compared to others who were stopped on a small, safe bridge, or to those who were stopped ten minutes after crossing the frightening bridge. Similar results were found in an analysis of romantic content of the TAT stories. And, as predicted by the researchers, the same results were not observed in a comparison of same-sex subjects stopped on or off the bridge, presumably because possible attraction to a same-sex O did not represent an appropriate explanation to which one could attribute such arousal.

In a laboratory replication (Dutton & Aron, 1974), individuals that expected strong electric shocks (versus those expecting very mild shocks) were more attracted to the confederate (whether or not she was also perceived as expecting high or low shock).

In subsequent research, Kenrick et al. (1979) attempted to replicate the laboratory part of the above study. They did not find the same result, perhaps because they gave the subjects a chance to interpret the arousal as fear on an anxiety questionnaire administered before the attraction measure.

Riordan and Tedeschi (1983) found that an attractive female confederate was more liked by a male subject expecting shock only when the confederate was present before and after, but not during the threat. They also found that this result was not affected by sex of confederate. However the attraction measures in the Riordan and Tedeschi study were entirely of liking (versus "loving" or strong attraction). Aron (1970) and Dutton and Aron (1974), on the other hand, evaluated such things as "desire to kiss" and romantic imagery in TAT stories. In these studies, when attraction was measured on both these strong-attraction items and also on the liking items (e.g. "How much would you like to work with this person?"), effects were found only on the measures of intense attraction (Aron, 1970)!

Finally, two other recent studies obtained results consistent with the two-component theory. Dutton (1979) had subjects view videotapes of persons involved in conflict. The "battle of wills" depicted on the screen produced high physiological arousal (measured by electrodermal response) in the observing subjects when the subjects believed the conflict to be real. If they believed the persons on the screen to be only role playing a conflict situation, physiological arousal was significantly reduced. An attractive opposite-sex person shown on the screen, involved in the conflict, was perceived as significantly more attractive when the subjects were in the physiologically-aroused condition.

White et al. (1981) report an interesting variation, in which running in place for 120 seconds or listening to a very funny or upsetting tape was used to manipulate arousal. Their results were straightforwardly consistent with the two-component theory: Aroused males were significantly more attracted to an attractive female confederate than were unaroused controls. Moreover, the study gave further support to the two-component theory in that (a) the arousal yielded attraction only to attractive confederates (who thus presumably provided an appropriate explanation for feeling arousal), and not to unattractive confederates; and (b) the effect was the same regardless of whether arousal was due to a neutral (running in place), positive (very funny Steve Martin tape), or negative (very upsetting description of mutilation) stimulus. White and his associates found the same basic pattern of results for both strong "romantic attraction" (e.g., desire to kiss) and "general attraction" (e.g., how much would you like to work with her) items. However, an inspection of their tables shows substantially stronger results for the "romantic attraction" items.

As was previously noted, the most widely cited interpretation of the results of these various studies is based on the two-component, misattribution-of-arousal approach. However, two other closely related explanations have been suggested.

Clark (1982; Clark et al., 1983) proposes that arousing situations call forth memories of past arousing experiences. Thus, the attraction in these various studies did not result from a need to label an undifferentiated arousal, but simply through associations. Clark's approach does, indeed, seem more parsimonious. However, (a) there has as yet been no direct experimental test of this position versus the two-component, misattribution-of-arousal paradigm; and (b) the theory would seem to predict that the positive or negative affective tone of the arousal should affect attractions, contrary to White et al.'s findings. Nevertheless, it is a promising suggestion that may well account for some, if not all, cases of what had been seen as misattribution.

One of us (Aron, 1970) has in the past suggested that strong emotion at the time of meeting O is only one of several *boundary breaking* experiences that, when associated with an O, can attract one strongly to that O. In addition to intense emotions, the feeling of power, isolation, and mystery are examples of such experiences. Boundary breaking or unusualness—and the associated excitement—has also been linked with attraction by other researchers. The idea of novelty, for example, is at the core of Berlyne's aesthetic theory. Also, at least one experimental study illustrating supposed arousal effects has been mimicked by manipulations of unusualness (McDonald et al., 1983). Berscheid (1983) says that it is precisely the breaking of a "highly organized behavior sequence" that produces arousal and develops emotions, including love.

Relief from Punishment

The series of studies focusing on the two-component theory have also been cited (and in some cases conducted) in support of an alternative view: P is attracted to O in these studies because, just when P is feeling anxious, O's presence provides distraction and/or comfort. That is, O is valued because P associates O with reduction of punishing stimuli: "While it may be true that high levels of aversive arousal are often associated with high degrees of passionate love, it is our major hypothesis that it is more often the reduction of that arousal, rather than its labeling, that intensifies the relationship" (Kenrick & Cialdini, 1977, p. 385).

This phenomenon could explain some of the results of the Dutton and Aron (1974) study, and could fit with findings on attraction under conditions of shared stress and bonding under aversive conditions among animals (reviewed in Kenrick & Cialdini, 1977). Moreover, this approach seems to fit the Riordan and Tedeschi (1983) data better than the two-component theory, since in that study attraction was greatest when the confederate was present only during the period preceding and following the threat; thus any direct association with the threat was minimized (and association with relief from threat maximized). Moreover, the possibility for misattribution should have been greatest in the condition in which the confederate was present during the actual shock threat.

However, while this view no doubt explains some cases of attraction, it is not very convincing about strong attractions. As noted earlier, in all the studies where reduction of punishment is the best explanation for attraction, only generalized non-intense attraction was measured. Moreover, as Kenrick and Cialdini and Riordan and Tedeschi admit, the relief-from-negative-affect explanation does not explain away all cases of two-component findings. In terms of the studies we have just reviewed, it would not easily explain the findings of Aron (1970), Dutton (1979), or White et al. (1981)—since in all of these the source of arousal was either not aversive or the object of attraction could not easily be construed as reducing arousal.

Readiness

Closely related to the relief-from-punishment view is an idea suggested by Reik (1944): Strong attractions are more likely to occur for P during certain periods of time. That is, Reik hypothesized a "readiness" for strong attractions. Readiness is said to coincide with such things as recently being rejected and being in an appropriate life situation to enter a close relationship.

Focusing on the rejection theme, Walster (1965) found that female college student subjects were more attracted to a potential male partner when the subject's self-esteem had just been lowered (through an experimental manipulation).

Although Reik, Walster, and one of us (Aron, 1970) have emphasized romantic relationships in discussing readiness, a parent's sometimes sudden interest in a child, or an adolescent's suddenly taking up with a new best friend after being rejected by the previous one, also seems to fit this picture.

Causes of Strong Attractions and Self-Expansion

The various special mechanisms for strong attraction we have considered can be explained in terms of threshold phenomena within the expansion-integration process, and by the process of the association of O with an expansion experience.

Threshold Phenomena

If a system tends to enlarge in steps of expanding and then integrating, there will be times when the system will be primed for a major advance in expansion or integration, and only one crucial additional experience will be required. It is this kind of situation, we think, that may account for the first cause of strong attractions just described—the sudden, powerful effect of specific cues. It is also what Jung seems to mean by the function of the archetypes to *complete* the self.

The last two causes for strong attractions proposed in the literature, readiness and relief from punishment, can also be seen as thresholds of expansion. Both readiness and relief from punishment imply a state of preparedness for significant change.

Association of O with Expansion Experiences

We have argued that generally P is attracted to O because P perceives O as a potential means of expansion. Normally that association is a kind of instrumental conditioning, in which O has been instrumental for P's expansion by providing new resources that expand P's self. It is also possible, however, that P could perceive O as a course of expansion through a kind of classical conditioning in which O is directly or indirectly associated with some strong attraction experience, either because something about O or the circumstances of meeting O reminds P of that experience, or because that strong expansion experience and P's meeting of O occurred or is occurring at the same time. Either way O becomes a conditioned stimulus for that feeling of sudden, strong expansion.

Actually, Lott and Lott (1974) have proposed just such a position, regarding more mundane rewards and more ordinary attractions. That is, P will be attracted to an O associated with P's receiving rewards such as security or wealth. We agree; but we would specify the important rewards to be expansion of the self, and note that if the association is with rapid expansion, then more-than-ordinary attractions might occur.

This kind of process, in fact, seems to be exactly the kind Grant (1957) offered to explain the source and importance of specific cues in the attraction process—that they are the result of learned (or innate) associations.

Similarly, the strong attractions occurring in the many arousal studies—whether because of relief from punishment or P's affect, arousal, or other boundary-breaking experiences—could be considered examples of O being associated with P's expansion. That is, if P meets O *while* experiencing expansion, owing to circumstances that might have nothing to do with O, P might still connect O with the expansion, and hence see O as very attractive. This idea is not very dissimilar from Clark's (1982) notion of a kind of affective-arousal-state-specific memory.

Obviously, the kinds of experiences subjects have been given in the series of studies associating autonomic arousal with attraction fit this bill very well. Walking across a suspension bridge over a 400-foot ravine or expecting an electric shock are certainly dramatic experiences. Or at least they create the kind of strong arousal associated with certain kinds of very expanding experiences—great challenges, moments of great happiness, tragedy, insight, and so forth. If the experience is not so overwhelming that integration is completely impossible, we would expect anyone met during such times to be associated with dramatic expansion of the self, and hence be objects of attraction. It is not necessarily the arousal—but rather, perhaps, the expansion or the association of expansion with arousal—that gets misattributed to O.

Of course, some experiences (such as threat of shock or listening to an upsetting tape) may be perceived as de-expanding the self, by threatening it, rather than expanding the self. However, subjects in the various studies cited were exposed to these conditions and then presented with an attractive potential object of attraction, and they appear to have taken the unusualness aspect of the negative arousal source and attributed it to excitement about a perceived opportunity for expanding through a relationship. Indeed, an interesting asymmetry was observed in recent study by Clark et al. (1984) where they found that arousal produced by a presumably affectively-neutral situation (exercise) intensified P's interpretations of O's positive emotion as being highly aroused. But the corresponding effect for interpreting O's negative emotion was not obtained.

In sum, whatever the specific mechanisms are that cause strong attractions, they are probably, in some way, caused by P's perception of a dramatic new possibility for self-expansion through O.

III

Maintaining Relationships

7

Theoretical Perspectives

INTRODUCTION

In the remaining chapters of this book we consider the maintenance of relationships—why they are and are not maintained, and what the ideal ongoing relationship might be.

Because both individuals and society want marriages in particular to last, available research on relationship maintenance and satisfaction deals most with the marriage relationship—and Part III does the same. Part III is also more practically oriented, for when we get to the obstacles to maintaining relationships we not only describe the problems but the typically proposed solutions. We also consider how thinking in terms of self-expansion sheds a new light on both the problems and the solutions.

First, however, this chapter examines the maintenance of relationships rather than their nonmaintenance. We consider major current theoretical perspectives on relationships, looking for their explanations of why and how relationships are maintained. Then we explore the implications of the self-expansion idea for integrating these theoretical perspectives and for offering additional insights into several issues on which these perspectives have been compared. Finally, before going on to two chapters that, in part, predict that self-expansion helps maintain relationships, we discuss the concern occasionally voiced that because of expansion the self may somehow lose its autonomy or ego boundaries.

PREVALENCE OF MAINTAINED RELATIONSHIPS

As we said, the data on marriage is most plentiful. Roughly 40% of marriages will probably end in divorce (Markman, 1982), but a marriage still usually represents a maintained relationship in that it was intended to be and generally is maintained well beyond the initial attraction and acquaintanceship stage. According to Campbell's (1981) extensive quality-of-life surveys, undertaken in the U.S. between 1957 and 1978, 95% of people over 40 had married. Of those who had also divorced, 3 of 4 women had remarried; 5 of 6 men had remarried.

As for other relationships, over 90% of couples capable of having children had had at least 1. About 90% of those interviewed lived within 2 hours of another household of relatives and more than 4 of 5 of these saw such relatives at least once a month. A friend to "call on for advice and help" was claimed by 19 of 20; a confidante with whom they felt they could discuss any personal problem, by 5 of 6.

Besides survey researchers like Campbell who are directly observing the ubiquity of ongoing relationships, those in the therapeutic and counseling professions are also impressed and even surprised by the determination of people to stay in relationships, even when those relationships have become for some the source of terrible suffering (Guggenbuhl-Craig, 1977/1981).

MAJOR IN-DEPTH STUDY

Only one major study has examined the dynamics of long-term relationships and the reasons they were maintained. Cuber and Harroff (1965) conducted lengthy interviews with 211 upper-class men and women married 10 years or more who had never seriously considered divorce or separation, although the majority had been increasingly dissatisfied with their marriage over time.

From their data, Cuber and Harroff described five categories of marriages: total (deeply satisfying; couples almost always prefer each other's company over anyone else's), vital (similar to total marriages, but to a lesser degree), devitalized (spouses spend little time together, are dissatisfied compared to first years of marriage), passive-congenial (marriage was never highly satisfying, but adequate), and conflict-habituated (tense, constantly in conflict, but under control or stabilized). These five were further reduced to two categories, intrinsic (vital and total) and utilitarian (the other three). The immediate reason the intrinsic marriages had lasted was obvious: Both partners still enjoyed the relationships greatly.

The reasons spouses in the other three categories gave for staying together were usually costs, constraints, and poor alternatives—the high social or emotional costs of divorce, the difficulty of finding another mate that was the boss's daughter, and so forth. Thus the label "utilitarian" to describe "marriage . . . for purposes other than to express an intimate, highly important *personal* relationship between a man and a woman" (Cuber & Harroff, 1965, p. 109).

These marriages may have been practical, but many of the couples at some level apparently felt that the utilitarian advantages did not compensate for their loss or lack of intimacy in marriage. These marriages were maintained, Cuber and Harroff concluded, by means more devious than simply the acceptance of expedience. Spouses developed avoidance devices, rationalizations, and other relationships. Mostly, however, the utilitarian marriages seemed to simply maintain themselves:

> *For the passive-congenials it all comes quite undramatically and naturally; for the devitalized it seems about the only sensible way 'at this time of life'; and for the conflict-habituated it serves about as well as any conceivable arrangement to contain the contest. Once set up, the valences are mutually reinforcing and the tide is therefore very hard to reverse. Chiefly, they do not want to reverse it; they are content with the current order of things, whether or not in other compartments of their minds they might like it otherwise. (pp. 130-131)*

In other words, Cuber and Harroff concluded that those in utilitarian marriages (the majority of their sample) simply accepted nonintimacy as a workable arrangement in marriage. They remained in such marriages mainly for practical reasons, but also largely because of inertia.

All of which is not too surprising—the happily married stay together because they are happy; the less happy that do stay together have utilitarian reasons to want to continue, or rationalize their inertia; and the unhappy but less inert have left the picture through divorce. Is there anything deeper to be seen here?

THEORETICAL PERSPECTIVES

In the literature on ongoing relationships, four theoretical perspectives have been widely used: social exchange, role/symbolic interaction, psychodynamic, and general systems theories. For each we will briefly describe the basic model, then consider how it applies to (a) why people maintain relationships and (b) how ongoing relationships differ. Then we will consider (c) the model's strengths and unique features in relation to these issues and (d) its limitations.

SOCIAL EXCHANGE THEORY

The basic idea of social exchange theory (Blau, 1964; Homans, 1958; Thibaut & Kelley, 1959) is that behavior in social relationships is mediated by the members' perception of the rewards and costs as compared to their internal standards and their available alternatives. Thibaut and Kelley define "attraction" as occurring when the perceived "outcome" (the advantage of rewards over costs) of a relationship exceeds the "comparison level" (one's internal standard of an adequate outcome). Attractions, whether initial or ongoing, are also weighed by their members against available alternatives (the "comparison level of the alternative").

Many theorists influenced by the social exchange approach emphasize the importance of the participants' perceiving that the distribution of rewards is *equitable* in relation to each member's contribution to the relationship (e.g., Adams, 1965; Hatfield et al., in press; Walster et al., 1977). Moreover, equity theory asserts that people are dissatisfied with unfair relationships even if they are unfair in their own favor!

Why People Maintain Relationships

People will desire to maintain a relationship as long as the perceived outcome exceeds that of available alternatives. "Available" is important here: One may be attracted to many persons who offer outcomes exceeding one's internal standard, but they may not be truly available. The relationship is maintained—in Thibaut and Kelley's terms, "commitment" occurs—as long as the perceived outcome exceeds the "comparison level of the alternative."

Types of Maintained Relationships

There are two "comparison levels": one that is internal, or what a person would like, and one that compares what a person has with alternatives. According to exchange theory, for a relationship to be maintained, its perceived outcomes must exceed the comparison level of the alternative, but need not exceed the internal comparison level. This implies two types of relationships. Satisfying relationships are those in which one feels one has gotten the best among alternatives *and* has more than met one's expectations for a relationship. In the not-so-satisfying type, perceived outcomes are below one's internal comparison level but above the comparison level of alternatives. In this case one stays in the relationship even though unhappy with it, because the alternatives are even worse!

Strengths and Unique Features

The most important contributions of exchange theory are its calculus of costs, rewards, and alternatives, and the attendant sensitization to the importance of alternatives. In fact, while studying several hundred couples, Udry (1981) found that the perceived availability of alternatives, should the relationship end, predicted divorce during the next two years better than marital satisfaction.

The basic ideas of social exchange theory seem both well articulated and intuitively plausible. Its theoretical propositions are easily derived, empirically testable, and have frequently been tested. Indeed, the approach has generated a considerable body of research. It also invites extrapolations from well-established work in the general psychology of learning and motivation, in which reward-type theories have already demonstrated great success, and from economics, which exchange theory clearly emulates.

Exchange theory's equity-theory offspring has also generated considerable research and theory, with important implications for both attraction (the "matching hypothesis" studies) and relationship satisfaction (e.g., Walster et al., 1978). It has also sensitized researchers to the general importance of perceived fairness in relationships.

Limitations

One limitation of exchange theory is the same limitation pointed out in Chapter 5 for reward-type theories generally—the means or bases for predicting rewards and costs are not specified. They are simply whatever turn out to keep individuals in the relationship or cause them to leave it.*

The theory's other drawbacks fall into two main groups: those implied by the tradition of research, but which are not logical limits of the theory, and those limits in the system itself as it is usually articulated. We first consider the several issues raised by the research traditions.

The typical emphasis of exchange-oriented research is on rewards and costs that can be tested in the laboratory or with survey or archival data, and those that have been the historical focus of economic and learning theorists. These are usually

---

*Of course, exchange theorists *do* specify rewards when conducting a particular study, and very good and extensive research has been done to determine empirically what will be rewarding (e.g. Foa & Foa, 1974; Safilios-Rothschild, 1976). However, although one can tack a list of such rewards on to the theory, the very appealing logic behind the theory gives no clues for generating that list. One must use common sense to know what variables to try out. Even equity theorists, who helpfully specify fairness as a kind of reward (or lack of it as a cost), do not indicate what kinds of resources must be equitably exchanged, except again by tacking on a list of empirically derived rewards. The self-expansion approach does not entirely solve this problem, but it does give some direction when it posits expansion of potential efficacy as a criterion.

conceptualized as pleasures and pains, satisfactions and punishments, black ink and red ink, win-lose, and the like. But Hansen (1982) argues in his review of Kelley and Thibaut's (1978) latest book that this focus is unfortunate because it excludes those human motives which are "higher" than the "lowest" level, "pleasure-pain," or the next highest, "success." These higher motives are "duty" and, finally, "transcendence."

Hansen attributes this hierarchical categorization of motives to Allport's interpretation of Eastern psychology, but similar hierarchy of motives has also been made in the West. Plato subdivided his Republic into four strata according to a system of this kind. Much more recently a developmental approach to motivations, involving increasingly expanded connections with society and the world, has been suggested by Kohlberg's (1969) description of levels of moral development, by Loevinger and Wessler's (1970) stages of ego development, and by other stage theories of adult development (Erikson, 1950; Gowan, 1974).

To be fair, one can imagine no logical reason why exchange theory could not explain how these "higher" motivations of duty and transcendence become more rewarding than pleasure and profit. The problem is more one of the tradition of research and thinking associated with this perspective, not its intrinsic logic.

However, a history of a particular way of operationalizing concepts weighs strongly in science. Hansen (1982) points out that these approaches provide an image of human motivation "that is grossly distorted and of limited relevance to family theory" (p. 247), and that there is danger in the real but limited successes that a theory like this brings to practitioners and researchers.

A somewhat different concern is that exchange theory pictures people as static: they are either satisfied or they are not, their outcomes either do or do not exceed comparison levels. Changes in aspirations (i.e., in comparison levels) are mentioned, but not really considered systematically. In particular, the possibility that people are always seeking more and more, because of habituation or because of a fundamental motivation to grow, is not considered. Again, there is no logical reason why this could not be included within exchange theory—but it does run counter to the homeostasis/survival-oriented tradition in which exchange theory has been firmly rooted.

Yet another limitation of the tradition associated with exchange theory is that it minimizes the role of non-economic societal factors. Other theoretical perspectives emphasize that relationships involve role behaviors sanctioned by society, that the rewards, costs, and alternatives provided by relationships are largely socially determined—yet this theory describes those social influences very little.

A final limitation of the tradition as it has been applied in the family area is that although it officially (and often emphatically) describes rewards, costs, and alternatives as those *perceived* by the individuals involved—in practice the definition of the situation is made by the researchers' choice of objective measures. The applications of exchange theory are only occasionally sensitive to phenomenological reality, although in the last few years this has begun to change.

Now we turn from traditional but not inherent shortcomings, to some more direct challenges to exchange theory's understanding of maintained relationships. The main problem arises when the theory is applied to the special conditions of very close relationships. Social exchange theory posits that as people continue to interact with others, they continue to try to maximize rewards and minimize costs. However, it is precisely in our most intimate relationships that the usual self-interest motivations seem not to apply; we appear to become more "communal" rather than "exchange" oriented, as Clark and Mills (1979) put it.

It may be, of course, that there are simply more subtle, less obvious rewards and costs in close relationships. As Hatfield (1982) notes, in casual relationships the rewards are usually practical, so that their equitable exchange is easy to recognize—while "generally, what lovers care about is love" (p. 283).

Those in the social exchange tradition have attempted to deal with the "convoluted, murky" factors determining rewards within loving relationships by making several modifications (McDonald, 1981), which can be summarized as follows:

1. *Social norms* about certain roles instruct those in the roles to accept as equitable many situations that appear inequitable. The official norms for marriage are, "For better or worse, for richer for poorer, in sickness and in health, till death do us part." Norms for parent-child relationships are even more demanding of sacrifice. Thus, when inequities in these relationships are sensed, they may be accepted as "natural" (McDonald, 1981, p. 831). And Murstein, Cerreto, and MacDonald (1977) found that to feel otherwise is associated with less marital satisfaction. McDonald also suggests that cognitive consistency may apply here: "I'm still here so I must be getting something from this relationship."

2. People have *different cognitive orientations*. McDonald cites Burns' (1973) typology, borrowed from Meeker (1971) and McClintock (1972): Some people are oriented to maximizing outcomes for the self, some for joint self and other, and some for the other's negative outcomes or positive outcomes.

3. McDonald (1981), Hatfield (1982), Kelley (1983), and many others have noted the importance of *commitment*. According to McDonald, commitment minimizes the exploration of alternatives. Above all it "transfers the relationship from a 'specific goal-based exchange to a diffuse commitment-based exchange.' Commitment indicates to the exchange partner that the marketing of resources is no longer necessary and that the partner can be assured that the current exchange will continue regardless of market conditions" (1981, p. 834).

McDonald and others have noted that one commits both to an individual and to a lifestyle-relationship—marriage, parenthood, loyal friendship—in which alternatives are not to be considered.

4. Finally, social exchange theory is being modified to take into account the *"we" feeling* and the sense of being rewarded by outcomes that benefit the relationship or the other (as, for example, Tesser's 1980 "reflection" idea discussed earlier). Kelley and Thibaut (1978) lucidly elaborated one explanation of the "we" feeling, based on extending the exchange calculus to include perceived benefits that require the interaction of P and O. Other explanations are in terms of norms, a joint-other cognitive orientation, or a commitment (owing to norms or to the rewards of not being in an overtly reward-oriented relationship). When two people define themselves as a unit (Hatfield, 1982), social exchange within the couple is said to be governed by concern for the couple's best interest.

These four modifications to social exchange theory to account for lasting, superficially unrewarding relationships are often brilliantly clear when considered separately. But when taken together they seem to obscure the original theory a bit. If a house has had its roof, floor, and four walls replaced, is it the same abode? One especially wonders this, given that many of these modifications to shore up reward theory's explanations for loving, long-term relationships are borrowed from role and personality theories. However, the remodeling job certainly demonstrates a very commendable commitment by researchers in this area to adjust to the data!

ROLE THEORY/SYMBOLIC INTERACTIONISM

Each of the four theoretical perspectives we are considering has many variations and different approaches within it, and in each case we can only focus on one or two. In the case of role theory, we will emphasize the conceptualization offered by Sarbin and Allen (1968), and the suggestions for application of the general symbolic interactionist position to the family, which have been articulated by Burr et al. (1979).

Symbolic interactionism emphasizes the individual's perception of the situation in terms of the social symbols available, particularly roles and role expectations. A role is a set of behaviors defined by a social position. The major determinants of behavior are the roles a person believes he or she is expected to perform; the perceived social expectations of how the roles should be performed; the person's ability to fulfill those expectations in terms of the person's competence, personality, and goals; and conflicts of expectations within and among roles.

Why People Maintain Relationships

Role theorists seem to hold that once in a role, a person will stay in that role so long as role performance is not hindered by undue difficulties. Three main kinds of difficulties can arise:

1. Conflicts within the socially defined expectations—if the various expectations for a particular role are contradictory or if they conflict with expectations for other roles the person is expected to enact. For example, the role of mother-in-law may be perceived to involve conflicting demands to both criticize and support the daughter-in-law, or the role of loving husband and father may be perceived as conflicting with being a successful businessman.

2. Conflicts in role expectations (or "lack of role consensus") between those enacting reciprocal roles in a relationship. If the adolescent believes the father's behavior should be friendly and equal, but the father believes it should be formal and authoritarian—there is a problem!

3. Conflicts between the role expectations and their suitability for the individual expected to enact it. These are of three main kinds: (a) inadequate competence to meet the role expectations; (b) the personality does not fit with the role; and (c) role performance conflicts with personal goals.

Types of Maintained Relationships

Role theory seems to suggest that stable relationships differ in two main ways: how much "organismic involvement" is displayed (Sarbin & Allen, 1968; more or less the effort and bodily engagement in the role), and how the role is defined and valued by self and society. Cuber and Harroff's (1965) categorization of married couples can be understood in these terms. Obviously the total, vital, and conflict-habituated have more organismic involvement than the devitalized and passive-con-genial. And each of the five seem to represent different meanings of what the spouse role entails. (Conflict-habituated spouses probably also struggled with what has been described as inadequate role consensus; e.g., Bahr, Chappell, & Leigh, 1983.)

Strengths and Unique Features

The primary contribution of this approach is its insistence on viewing the situation from the actor's point of view and its consistent sensitivity to the impor-tance of the social influence on that view of the situation.

The result of these advantages is that role theory/symbolic interactionism implies strong forces for staying in a relationship that result from simply the time spent in it: We have learned to play the role well, have come to a shared definition of reciprocal roles in the relationship, and are organismically involved in it. Similarly, role theory/symbolic interactionism makes obvious the significance of the social barriers to leaving a relationship. And, in a fairly effective way, it allows for individual differences in personality and competencies.

Limitations

The main limitations (for the issues of this chapter) exist because the approach is not very motivational. Admittedly, some theorists have spoken of a greater motivation to stay in roles that are congruent with personal goals (Burr et al., 1979), but that is about all. Of course, symbolic interactionists would point out that motivations are strongly influenced by socially-determined perceptions of reality, so that people are motivated (in a sense) to meet role expectations simply because they perceive them.

The approach works amazingly well without a true motivational theory until one wants to ask, for instance, why people enter and stay in relationships. The role-theory explanation—that role conflicts are not sufficient to drive them out of it—is helpful, but is it sufficient? Would this alone really predict who will and who will not stay in a relationship?

Second, like exchange theory, role theory is basically homeostatic in its view of individual behavior, saying that we continue to enact a role unless there is some reason to leave it. Reasons to leave it, or to change it in any way, are scarce. Society might change the role's definition. If individuals were troubled with role conflicts, they might try to reduce the conflicts. Also, the idea that people might seek oppor-tunities to enact roles that increase organismic involvement, or increase the ability to fulfill personal goals, or whatever, is not intrinsically inconsistent with role theory (and is very much consistent with its spirit). However, the idea has rarely influenced research or applications, particularly in the area of close relationships.

Third, one could interpret role theory as focusing on the level of motivation that Hansen (1982) labeled "duty." This could be seen as an advance over the reward approach, which emphasizes pleasure/pain or success. A theory focusing on only one of these four, however, still fails to give the whole story. Also, pleasure/pain and success are largely ignored in role theories, unfortunately, and transcendence is con-sidered only rarely.*

*However, transcendence has been considered! Sarbin and Allen (1968) treat it as the limiting case of organismic involvement.

PSYCHODYNAMIC THEORIES

The psychodynamic view of personal relationships emphasizes the unconscious motivation to repeat and/or fulfill the early childhood relationship with the parent. The long history of this view has led to several quite independent lines of thinking, each with considerable richness of terminology and principles, even if we restrict our discussion to the topics of importance for this chapter.

As far as we know, psychodynamic theorists have not considered the motivation to maintain any but the romantic-love-marriage relationship. (Of course Freud at times considered sexual sublimation to be the basis of all emotional attachments, and just about everything else. But the equal importance of close relationships in cultures where sexuality is less restricted, along with other evidence and arguments, suggests that the sublimation approach had its problems; see Grant, 1976).

The "British School," or "ego-oriented psychoanalysis," or "object relations theory" yielded most of psychoanalysis' lasting ideas on attachment (Segraves, 1982). As we discussed earlier, the basis of romantic attraction is said to be the intense need to project one's ego ideal onto, and then merge with, someone having the qualities the ego-ideal demands but one's own life lacks (Reik, 1944). Another idea is that one unconsciously wishes to be accepted unconditionally, loved tenderly, and told one really has fulfilled all one's ideals (or would have except for bad luck)—all as one wishes one's parents would have done (Bergler, 1946). In yet another version, unconscious "archetypes" determine attraction (Jung, 1925/1959).

Why People Maintain Relationships

Transference or projection, although the basis of attraction, is not seen to be a stable basis for long-term relationships. As Reik says, after a few years of marriage, what is left, at best, is an "afterglow" (Reik, 1944, p. 150). As usual, something else is offered to replace romance: "a new kind of companionship . . . the peacefulness of tender attachment." While "passion is gone," the new stage is "no less valuable," but "clear and calm" (p. 150). However, this transformation is precarious, and its mechanics not explained.

Marital therapists with a psychoanalytic orientation (e.g., Fitzgerald, 1973; Nadelson, 1978; Sager, 1976; and Segraves, 1982) have considered marital stability a little more than the earlier theorists. Perhaps because of their therapeutic experience, however, most of this stablility is seen as a balance of neurotic needs—an "unconscious contract." The goal of therapy is to analyze out the transference neurosis, "so that behavior is motivated more in the service of the ego and less by impulse and intrapsychic conflict" (Nadelson, 1978, p. 146). Then, one presumes, the analyzed couples are still stable, but happier.

Jungian psychology has more to say on maintenance of the marriage relationship. Jung (1925/1959) himself said that during the first half of life, until one's children are grown, the individual is largely an unconscious "instrument for maintaining the species" (p. 534). Mate selection is also instinctual. ("The idea of 'instinct' is of course nothing more than a collective term for all kinds of organic and psychic factors whose nature is for the most part unknown," p. 534.) "The peculiar harmony that characterizes marriage during the first half of life—provided the adjustment is successful—is largely based on the projection of certain archetypical images" (p. 540). The man chooses a woman resembling his anima archetype, the "eternal image of woman (p. 534)"; the woman chooses a man resembling her animus. They project this ideal (an ideal having both personal and collective components, rather than the strictly personal projection in psychoanalytic theory) on to the other. Then they settle down into their biological roles. "The woman becomes the mother, the man the father, and thus are robbed of their freedom and made instruments of the life urge" (p. 534). Thus, for awhile, the maintenance of the relationship is no problem—one is imprisoned (especially in the Swiss society of Jung's time).

In the second half of life, according to Jung, children and work lose their hold and at least some people begin to examine consciously the meaning of their lives and relationships. Many difficulties ensue, and only a few will "pass from a collective to an individual relationship. This amounts to full conscious realization of the relationship that marriage brings" (p. 542).

Guggenbuhl-Craig (1977/1981) has gone into more detail about maintenance of the marriage relationship from a Jungian perspective. A couple must be motivated not by the goal of happiness, but rather see marriage as a path to "salvation" (p. 41), to full development of the personality, including its spiritual side. Or in Hansen's (1982) terms, marriages cannot be on the basis of pleasure/pain or profit, as it is today; nor is duty a sufficient motivation today. According to Guggenbuhl-Craig, transcendence is the only reason to put up with the impossible demands of marriage:

> *Two people of different sex, usually with extremely different images, fantasies, and myths, with differing strength and vitality, promise one another to be with each other night and day, so to speak, for a whole lifetime. Neither of them is supposed to spoil the other's experience, neither is supposed to control the other, both of them should develop all their potentials fully." (p. 10)*

According to Guggenbuhl-Craig (1977/1981), if psychologists cannot explain what keeps couples together, it is because they have not considered the human desire for transcendence.

> *One frequently sees aged married couples in which one partner is spiritually and physically robust while the other is physically ill and spiritually reduced. And still they love one another, and not out of compassion or protectiveness .... The love on which marriage rests transcends the 'personal relationship' and is more than merely rational. (p. 41-42)*

Guggenbuhl-Craig says that marriages take archetypical forms that express individual and collective paths for development. Examples are the Holy Family, warring Zeus and Hera, physical Ares and Aphrodite, and the queen and her prince-consort.

He notes that from his clinical experience, the amount of conflict in a relationship does not predict its likelihood of ending. People stay together to achieve growth through their difficult relationships, whether they know it or not. "The observer who sails under the flag of well-being [such as a reward theorist!] has difficulty understanding this" (p. 123).

In sum, according to the various psychodynamic approaches, romantic or marriage relationships (other close relationships are rarely discussed in this tradition) are maintained by deep, unconscious, personal, and/or collective motives to be complete and ideal, to return to a happier narcissistic state of infancy, or to achieve some degree of full spiritual development or "salvation" in the second half of life.

Types of Maintained Relationships

The main categorization of relationships would be neurotic, immature, or instinctual versus normal, adult, or conscious. In addition, the Jungian view suggests relationships follow different archetypical patterns, with different reasons for maintenance (to fight, to raise perfect children, to work together, to rule together).

Strengths and Unique Features

The main strength of this approach is its thorough treatment of unconscious motivations. Moreover, it is unique among the four theories we are considering in this chapter in its attempt to relate motivation to some deeper principle. This principle is homeostasis (for all but the Jungians, who are the minority). Psychodynamics could even provide a kind of calculus for computing forces for maintaining and not maintaining relationships in terms of cathexis, or perhaps the balancing of demands of the id, ego, and superego—although these would admittedly be difficult to quantify.

In addition, the developments suggested by Jungian perspective are unique among major theories for dealing with the full range of motivations described by Hansen, and with the role of growth and expansion in relationships.

Limitations

The main limitation is a failure to explain why people should maintain a relationship if they are not neurotic or immature. It is simply assumed that for them to do so is somehow normal. The Jungian version is more helpful in this respect—positing a desire (in only some, however, according to Jung; in all according to Guggenbuhl-Craig) to be whole or to achieve "salvation." It shares with mainstream psychodynamic theories, however, the tendency to deal very little with contemporaneous social influences.

Finally, psychodynamic theorists have said little about any but the marriage relationship.

GENERAL SYSTEMS THEORY

The many versions of family systems theory share at least two features: (a) they see relationships (and particularly the family) as an interacting collection of elements that is more than the sum of its parts; and (b) they believe that there are general principles of systems as true for personal relationships as they are for organisms and societies.

The approach has been most influential in family therapy where it facilitated the transition from individual therapy to "conjoint" therapy, dealing with the entire family at once. Those in this clinical tradition (e.g., Watzlawick, Weakland, Haley, Beavers, Jackson, Satir) have typically emphasized the parallels between families and organisms, or other open systems; the importance of communication among the parts (a type of negentropy or entropy-reversing, order-increasing process); and stability and adaptability ("morphostasis" and "morphogenesis").

During the seventies, the systems approach to relationships seemed to be the theory of the future, but as Holman and Burr (1980) have observed, it "has not matured as quickly as many had hoped" (p. 732). It has provided some interesting, new, cross-disciplinary concepts and descriptions. However, perhaps because its main proponents are clinicians for whom formal theory construction and testing is not a main interest, there is some uncertainty about where to go with these concepts in predicting human behavior. Perhaps to some clinicians the implications are obvious. For whatever reason, though, descriptions of systems theory tend to be provocative but brief.

Why People Maintain Relationships

Systems theorists have generally looked more at the patterns of interaction within relationships than at the motivation to maintain those relationships. Indeed, by frequently making parallels between families and organisms, systems theorists imply that if the system were to fall apart, the parts would die! The motivation to stay together seems to be a basic assumption of the theory, a motivation intrinsic in all systems.

Perhaps another reason that family systems theorists (usually therapists) ignore the motivation for relationship maintenance is that it is uniformly present in almost all couples and families who agree as a unit to come for treatment. Further, families, unlike friendships or even marriages, are biologically defined units that can vary in quality but can not easily be totally dissolved.

However, the marriage aspect of a family does frequently dissolve, and thus family system theorists have had to consider what makes a system resilient to destruction. The key term is "adaptability," i.e., how well the system can survive the forces of entropy. Broderick and Smith (1979) summarize an unpublished paper by Wilkinson that neatly lays out five variables contributing to the adaptability of a system such as family:

1. "variety in the system" (leading to "openness to outside input")
2. lack of "conflict and tension in the system" (thus less "differentiation" and "alienation of units from the decision-making function")
3. "stability of membership over time"
4. "number of multiple alternate channels of communication among units"
5. "efficiency of the subsystem responsible for memory (records, etc.)"

Other theorists (e.g., Beavers, 1976; Speer, 1970) have emphasized that a system will maintain itself only so long as it grows and elaborates itself.

Types of Maintained Relationships

Olson, Russell, and Sprenkle (1983) describe a circumplex model that places families on two orthogonal dimensions, with extremes of rigidity-chaos and disengaged-enmeshed. Successful families are placed in the midranges, but still fall into four types (a 2 × 2 organization of these dimensions): flexible and separate, flexible and connected, structured and separate, and structured and connected.

Beavers and Voeller (1983) argue for a continuum instead, on the single dimension of flexibility. From their observation, a family can never be too flexible— because these theorists equate flexibility with adaptability to change, or competence. In categorizing families according to their quality of functioning, the lowest level is characterized by amorphous internal structure, poor communication, and lack of boundaries with the environment. Normal families, the middle level, have clear and strong internal and external boundaries and rigid structure. Optimal families have clear but highly flexible structure and boundaries. Presumably the middle and optimal families are readily maintained and their spouse relationships might resemble, respectively, the utilitarian and intrinsic marriages described by Cuber and Harroff (1965).

To our knowledge, systems theory has not been applied to intimate human relationships other than those of the nuclear family.

Strengths and Unique Features

The main strength of the systems approach is its focus on the relationship as a whole and on the characteristics of the interaction in the relationship. In addition, the approach encourages new ways of thinking about relationships by comparing them to other kinds of living systems. Moreover, it focuses the researcher constantly on all systems levels, so neither the individual nor the social system is easily ignored. Finally, it has the virtue (from our perspective) of emphasizing growth, not just homeostasis, in relationships.

Limitations

The major limitation of the systems approach in the context of the issues considered in this chapter is that it deals very little with individual motivation. It also does not discuss other individual factors, such as individual differences in personality and competencies.

COMPARISON OF THE FOUR APPROACHES

Our discussion of the major theoretical perspectives brings out, as we see it, five topics related to maintaining relationships. In this section we will compare the ways in which the various perspectives treat each of these.

The Forces for Maintaining versus Not Maintaining a Relationship

This is treated most completely and elegantly by the social exchange theorists, who specify a quasi-mathematical formula of outcome (rewards versus costs) in terms of comparison level and comparison level of the alternative.

We said psychodynamic theories also could offer an analysis of such competing forces, in terms of either cathexis or id, ego, and superego. As far as we know, however, these dynamics have not been directly applied to the issues at hand, and this approach does not consider the contemporaneous social forces influencing a person to stay or not stay in a relationship.

Role and systems approaches suggest a few reasons for leaving relationships—role conflict, entropy—but mostly assume members stay simply because parts gain their meaning from social roles or their relationship system.

Alternatives

Only social exchange theory deals explicitly with alternatives.

Individual Motivation

Of the theories discussed, only social exchange and psychodynamic approaches emphasize individual motivation. They can be compared on three issues.

The Basis of Motivation

Only psychodynamic theory provides an explanation (instinctual drives, tension reduction, cathexis as wish fulfillment, the desire for wholeness or salvation) of what will be motivating. Social exchange theory does not attempt to specify on what basis to expect something will be experienced as rewarding or costly.

The Range of Motives

As noted earlier, Hansen (1982) argues that human motives cover a wider range than simple hedonism, and refers to Allport's list, from Eastern sources, of pleasure/pain, profit and success, duty, and transcendence. Reward theories focus mainly on the first, and to some extent the second, as do psychoanalytic theorists— although Jungian theories consider duty and emphasize transcendence. (Role theorists imply a focus on what Allport labeled "duty.")

Growth Motivations

All the approaches considered, to the extent they are motivational at all, are homeostatic. Especially when considering the maintenance of relationships, they assume that unless there are forces for leaving the relationship, people will maintain the status quo. Only systems theory hints that individuals are sometimes motivated to expand and grow (they are more explicit about this sometimes for social systems). Also, of course, there is the Jungian motivation to achieve an ever-elusive wholeness.

Social Influences from outside the Relationship

Once we move to the social level, role and systems approaches take the lead in thoroughness. Role theorists incorporate society at every aspect of the analysis, since the individual's construction of the situation is based on the social reality as it impinges upon him or her.

Systems theorists emphasize the interrelatedness of systems, and that families and other relationships are living systems, constantly interacting with their environment.

Psychoanalytic theory traditionally treats social influences only in the context of the internalization of social values in childhood. Otherwise, such influences are just one more aspect of "reality" for the ego to deal with. Similarly, exchange theorists see social influences as types of rewards and costs—except the social norm of reciprocity is central to equity theory.

Differences among Ongoing Relationships

The social exchange approach emphasizes that any relationship will be maintained only if it provides outcomes better than alternatives, but that these maintained relationships still might differ as to whether the outcomes provided are perceived to be better or worse than what one feels one ought to have in life.

Table 7-1   Thoroughness of Major Theories' Treatment of Relationship Issues

	Social exchange	Role	Psychodynamic	General systems
Forces to maintain	***		*	
Alternatives	***		*	
Motivation to maintain relationships:				
1. Basis			**	
2. Levels	pleasure/ pain and profit	duty	pleasure/ pain	
3. Growth				*
Societal influences for maintenance	*	***	*	***
Types maintained	attracted vs. not	involvement, how roles are defined	neurotic vs. adult; relationship archetypes	differences in boundaries, structure, communication

Role theory seems to imply that relationships differ according to the members' involvement in the relationship roles and according to how they define and/or value those roles.

Psychodynamic theorists focus mainly on whether relationships serve neurotic needs or are on a mature, adult level. Jungians add the idea that different maintained relationships might represent different cultural archetypes.

For systems theorists, degree of adaptability and of cohesion have been particularly important systems concepts for producing typologies.

Table 7-1 gives a visual picture of the varying strengths of the four approaches when compared on these five points. In the next section we consider the same five issues of relationship maintenance from the self-expansion perspective.*

SELF–EXPANSION AND THE MAINTENANCE OF RELATIONSHIPS

Considering the first two issues—forces that maintain a relationship and alternatives—we suggest that individuals will maintain a relationship as long as it is perceived to promote expansion. Alternatives that involve withdrawing from the relationship will be preferred if they are perceived to offer enough additional expansion to offset the perceived costs—that is, the de-expansion and disintegration that would result from not maintaining the current relationship (these costs, and the perception of them, could vary widely).

As for the motivation to maintain relationships, fundamentally it is the desire to expand the self. Relationships are usually maintained because P is continually including more and more aspects of O into the self—more and more subtle aspects,

---

*One essential issue is missing from this list: How—with what techniques or stratagems—do members maintain their relationship? It has not been a major topic for these approaches, but it is obviously important and will be discussed in Chapters 8 and 9.

plus whatever new aspects appear as O's life develops. However, there are other ways in which a relationship might promote self-expansion, and these are discussed in a moment, under relationship types.

Considering the range of motivation, or Hansen's levels, this desire to expand the self operates on each level and also explains how individuals move up this hierarchy of motives: Each subsequent level offers greater opportunities for expansion.

Of course, Vedic psychology (like all Eastern perspectives, and many Western ones as well) would hold that the motivation to expand the self only achieves its ultimate aim through transcendence, the experience of infinite expansion, which relationships can facilitate but not in themselves provide. (However, according to Hansen, and we would agree, Eastern psychology does not consider these levels to be exclusive. Every individual is motivated to some degree by each—only the proportions contributed change as one moves "higher.")

Societal influences foster relationship maintenance when individuals perceive society as enhancing the expansion of those who remain in relationships—as when an executive needs to be married in order to advance; or when one simply feels expanded by feeling more a part of one's community and the larger society. Social disapproval for not maintaining relationships in accord with social norms can also keep relationships together out of fear of de-expansion through guilt, disapproval, exclusion from certain expansion opportunities, or the like.

Types of Ongoing Relationships

Considering that people may stay in relationships either to gain expansion or to avoid de-expansion, and that expansion and de-expansion can arise from the relationship directly or from its larger social context—we can construct four "types" of relationships that might be maintained (although, in practice, any relationship will be a combination).

1. The members are actively expanding or integrating through the relationship; they still feel challenged, they haven't plumbed the depths of the other fully yet. Cuber and Harroff's (1965) intrinsic marriages might fit this category, as well as relatively new romantic and parent relationships, and many ongoing friendships.

2. To separate from the other will de-expand the self. Other social disapproval and constraints are not a problem, other alternatives are not lacking, but P has come to enjoy whatever expandedness was gained by including O within P's self and P can perceive the pain and loss that would arise from separation from O—the pain and loss of de-expansion and disintegration.

This situation probably particularly describes why certain long-term friendships are maintained, or some adult child-parent relationships. It is also reminiscent of Cuber and Harroff's devitalized marriage category, and the category of stable-but-unrewarding relationships described by exchange theory (Lewis & Spanier, 1979).

3. The relationship was established or is now maintained to support expansion and integration of the self outside of the relationship; for example, to further one's career, to have children, to do what society expects. As we saw in the Cuber and Harroff data, the majority of marriages begin or become utilitarian, and many North Americans, and even more members of other cultures, expect marriage to function mainly for this purpose. For most other relationships too—friends, kin, or whatever—the major culturally sanctioned reasons for the relationship are often utilitarian. Any additional expansion through the relationship itself is "all gravy."

4. To separate would bring de-expansion and disintegration in other areas of life—beyond simply the loss of a support base—through social sanctions, intense guilt from strong religious or personal feelings, or the loss of resources only available in the context of the relationship.

Table 7-2 shows this typology. Clearly the third and fourth reasons for staying in a relationship involve the social context of the relationship, not the relationship itself; and the second and fourth reasons are to avoid de-expansion rather than gain expansion. Thus only the first category describes a relationship that is not only maintained, but intrinsically satisfying. The many obstacles to a relationship of this type are the topic of the next two chapters.

One additional point: Unlike exchange theory, the self-expansion perspective does not predict that the lack of alternatives is in itself an adequate reason for P to maintain a relationship with O. First of all, P would rarely lack alternatives—if any form of expansion experience can be considered an alternative—since many kinds of alternative expansion opportunities can be maintained along with P's relationship with O. However, a crucial issue for P when weighing the attractiveness of an alternative is whether expanding through this alternative will damage or end the current relationship, and if so, how much P's self will de-expand or disintegrate as a result.

Alternatives have an extremely important effect on relationship maintenance, since people always seek the opportunity to expand maximally. They must also consider the costs of de-expansion or disintegration, however, as interestingly shown by Udry's (1981) finding that if a spouse feels he or she has alternatives, this predicts divorce better than that spouse's marital satisfaction. However, since we think alternatives exist for everyone, and it is the quality of the alternative in relation to its de-expansion costs that P must consider, we see this study slightly differently. Udry asked spoiles about their resources and alternatives *given* the hypothetical situation that their current relationship had ended, so that in this case de-expansion was a "given" rather than a cost to be calculated. Udry's study probably actually measured how dependent a spouse was on the relationship for expansion. When problems occurred or boredom set in, the costs of de-expansion by leaving the relationship were lowered. Less dependent spouses already had lower costs, however, so they were especially likely to divorce.

Relation of Self-Expansion to Other Theories

As noted previously, we consider the self-expansion approach to be not so much another competing theory, but rather a heuristic conceptual framework

Table 7-2 Four Reasons for Maintaining Relationships (in Terms of Self-Expansion)

	Opportunities to expand through . . .	Fear of de-expansion through loss of . . .
Interaction with O	1	2
Resources provided by O that expand P outside the relationship	3	4

that includes, organizes, and goes somewhat beyond the existing theories. Thus the reward-cost-alternatives calculus of exchange theory is included, but recast, so that rewards and alternatives are understood as opportunities for expansion and integration, and costs include the threat of constriction or disorder. Roles are included as expansion opportunities. Unconscious forces are acknowledged, but the significant psychodynamic forces are those urging expansion of the self (a view shared by some but not all in that tradition). In the systems theory view, we would say that relationships are maintained because they offer a potential for expansion by participation in a system that includes emergent properties otherwise not available to P.

Perhaps one could rework any of the four perspectives into a higher-order framework that included what was valuable in the others—plus the idea of self-expansion (which could be very interesting and valuable, though perhaps not very different from this book!). Not one of the four as they presently exist, though, easily deals with *all* the points considered in the previous section, while we think self-expansion does. In addition, the history and commitments of researchers and clinicians associated with each of these perspectives indicate that none will be sufficiently modified in the near future to include all the other perspectives.

A complete, intuitively satisfying theory of ongoing, loving relationships still ought to be possible, and perhaps an entirely new, unfettered approach is precisely what is required.

DOES EXPANSION OF THE SELF IMPLY LOSING THE SELF?

The next three chapters will refer more than once to the practical importance of self-expansion for maintaining relationships. Before proceeding, therefore, let us answer a concern heard from time to time: Can one's self, identity, or ego boundaries be lost by expanding the self?

This concern usually arises in two contexts: in discussions of extremely expanding experiences in general, and of very intimate relationships.

In normal development, the expansion (and integration) process is what *creates* ego boundaries. Through this process, as the maturing human tries to incorporate everything, the boundary between self and environment is discovered, shaped, and firmly established. (The infant learns, for example, that one's own toes can't be incorporated—they are already part of the self—but food can be incorporated; mother's breast can be, but only temporarily; mother can't be, but mother's behaviors can be, by imitation; her esteem can become self-esteem; and so forth.)

This process never ends, but it is most active in childhood and adolescence. During this period it is true that individuals seem more susceptible to being overwhelmed by expansion experiences, so that they may incorporate so much of one thing into the self (the skill of skateboarding, the attitudes of a favorite friend or teacher, or even the parents' identities) that the process of sorting out self from non-self and gaining autonomy may seem, or even be, threatened.

This loss of integrity is rare, however; and if it does occur, it is not the fault of the expansion process per se, but of pressures on susceptible individuals to expand too quickly, or in ways that prevent graceful integration. (And with adolescents, often the problem is not the youth's expansion process, but the inability or unwillingness of adults in the vicinity to expand to include those new aspects of the youth, especially when the youth's self reflects on the adult's.)

Normally the selves of youths expand into the richly complex, well-integrated selves of adults. In this culture especially, one aspect that everyone wants to incorporate is competence in maintaining one's independence (the development of which Erikson describes very well). As the youth struggles to learn and then solidify this skill, experiences that would seem to be expanding (close relationships with parents) may come to seem de-expanding, threatening the acquisition of this culturally treasured knowledge of how to think and act for one's self (whereas a "constant war" with one's parents might teach this skill very well!).

Of course, if any expansion experience is going to be a concern, the pure consciousness experience of complete expansion will require special explanation.

Subjectively described, this experience is seldom a "loss" of self, but rather a finding of the self, separate finally from roles, relationships, and all objects of experience (Carrington & Ephron, 1975). This fits with the discussion of the self in Chapter 2–that there is a "me" self including all possessions, experiences, cognitions, and so forth; and an "I," separate from all this and directly experienced through pure consciousness.

That this experience does reinforce the self's integrity and autonomy is suggested by studies associating practice in Transcendental Meditation with increases in ego-strength (Van den Berg & Mulder, 1976) and field independence and ego-distance (an internal sense of self rather than identification with externals, measured by ability to see the autokinetic effect; Pelletier, 1974), along with decreases in depression and neuroticism (Ferguson & Gowan, 1976; Hahn, 1975; Shapiro, 1975; Tjoa, 1975; Van den Berg & Mulder, 1976) and conformity (Shecter, 1978).

Much of the problem here probably lies with the use of similar words for normal and abnormal situations. Just as being "excited" describes a pleasant feeling as well as a condition requiring hospitalization, a feeling of "unboundedness" as we have described it in this book—accompanied by the physiological parameters of EEG coherence, breath suspension, and so forth—is not *in this case* a symptom (much less a cause) of the "loss of ego boundaries" associated with psychiatric conditions. In fact, in the only study bearing on the issue, Glueck and Stroebel (1977) found the experience to be "the most appropriate technique to use with psychiatric patients" (p. 320) to reduce their stress levels.

Now we turn to the concern that intimacy specifically may lead to loss of self, to Jung's "nondifferentiation" (1925/1959, p. 534), among siblings to Kohut's "merging" (Bank & Kahn, 1982), or in the larger family to Bowen's "undifferentiated ego mass" (1976).

In an article titled "The Dangers of Intimacy," (in press) Hatfield cites a number of valid reasons to fear intimacy (rejection, loss of control, etc.), basing them on the literature and her clinical experiences. Nevertheless, the "fear of losing one's individuality or of being engulfed" is, in her opinion, especially unrealistic for most people. A real loss of personal identity in a relationship is seen only when an individual completely lacks independence.

However, Hatfield admits the fear is very common, unrealistic or not, and represents a need to further develop one's competencies in relationships. She sees intimacy and independence not as opposites, but as the same skill—which we could call skillful self-expansion. She states that "people must be capable of independence in order to be intimate with others. People must be capable of intimacy, if they are to be independent." In our opinion this translates well to, "people must be integrated in order to expand, expanded if they are to have anything to integrate."

Similarly, while Levinson and Harris (1980) warn that "loss"-of-self experiences like meditation can be threats to the development of identity, they also conclude that this "loss" of self is as natural a tendency as self-differentiation (what Hatfield calls independence, or what we would call a product of integration). Also like Hatfield they see these "two poles" of identity and its loss as one—the artifacts of a "linear conceptulaization" (p. 280). Speaking of romantic love as one class of transcendental experiences, which includes meditation as well, Levinson and Harris say, "One's sense of identity gains in relation to The Experience of romantic love, and romantic love can only be experienced in terms of an individual's identity" (p. 281). Levinson and Harris cite numerous other clinicians holding the same view.

The peculiar dread in some clinical literature of "losing oneself" is understandable; and both mental disorders and expansion experiences have been described with similar words. Although we think that the motive to expand is a relentless one, thoroughly comprehensible to most people, one aspect of it can sound threatening to some: During the actual expanding phase, there has to be some period of nonintegration of the self—some loss of the old, orderly schemata. While for some this phase is a pleasure, for others it may be experienced as a slight cognitive untidiness, or an annoying sense of uncertainty, or even for some, while it lasts, a threat to the integrity of the self.

.

8

Getting Tired of the Other

INTRODUCTION

The many dedicated professionals concerned with helping people maintain satisfying relationships have, naturally, concentrated their efforts most on those who seek their help, and as we will see in the next chapter, these professionals can teach us a great deal about the obstacles to maintaining relationships. But a relationship can end without its members ever seeking help. Perhaps one or both of them are dissatisfied, but cannot see any specific problem worth presenting. The troubles of these nonclients might give a quite different picture of the obstacles to long-term relationships.

In this chapter we deal with what we guess may be the major underrated, undertreated obstacle to lasting love: P simply ceasing to expand or perceive any further potential for self-expansion through O. Since we have said expansion or the perception of potential self-expansion is the fundamental reason to maintain a relationship, this is a serious problem indeed.

Focusing mostly on marriage, where the problem seems most relevant and both research and theory have been most abundant, we first discuss the evidence for the problem, then the explanations proposed and the solutions offered for it up to now. Next, we suggest how the self-expansion approach contributes to an understanding of boredom and satisfaction in relationships, and derive three solutions to the problem of P getting tired of O. Finally, we delve into the central concept of Vedic psychology, pure consciousness, to see how it relates to this perplexing question of "how to keep love alive."

THE SCOPE OF THE PROBLEM

The strongest, best-validated fact about relationships (at least marriage relationships) is that satisfaction with them declines as time passes. This decline is very clear during the first decade, after which the pattern is somewhat debatable (Udry, 1974). In any case, after the first few years, companionship declines (Burgess & Wallin, 1953; Pineo, 1961; Rollins & Feldman, 1970), common interests and attitude agreement decline (Burgess & Wallin, 1953; Pineo, 1961), and expressions of love and affection decline (Burgess & Wallin, 1953; Swensen et al., 1981).

At the outset, the pattern is even fairly clear: The husband's satisfaction declines early after marriage, the wife's dips more drastically after the birth of the first child (Burr, 1970; Rollins & Feldman, 1970). Toward the end of this chapter we will look at the evidence for what happens after that.

Yet even while satisfaction declines, problems do also (Swensen et al., 1981); and some measures of marital happiness, sexual adjustment, and ratings of the mate's positive qualities do not decline (Burgess et al., 1963). One set of studies (described in Traupmann & Hatfield, 1981) suggests that both "passionate" and "companionate love" decline only slightly over the years, and at about the same rate; and personal adjustment appears to increase (Pineo, 1961; Uhr, 1957). Thus perhaps what these data show is not an increase in troubles, and not a decline in love either, but a decline in the general relevance of the whole relationship!

Data on friendships are much scarcer. Apparently friendships seldom last through the life cycle, the way marriages are expected to (Foote, 1956/1963; Dickens & Perlman, 1981). It is understood that friends may change interests or choose to move away without considering the relationship (Reisman, 1979).

Still, boredom is probably less of a factor in the ending of friendships. Friendships tend to take more time to develop than romantic relationships and the contact is often more sporadic. Thus usually when friends are together there is considerable potential for expansion both through "catching up" and "getting closer." Nor are friendships expected to be as intense and fascinating as romance or marrriage. However, even if the loss of novelty is less of a factor in the ending of friendships, friends who are known longer have been found to be seen less often (Jackson et al., 1977).

The parent-child relationship is seldom considered in terms of satisfaction, but it may contain an interesting antidote to boredom anyway—the child's constant change. Perhaps this is one reason why, around adolescence, children seem to get tired of their parents faster than parents get tired of their children! Parents may also tend to see children as an extension of their selves (Hoffman & Hoffman, 1973), and boredom with one's self seems to be less common than boredom with others! Alternatively, perhaps parents do get tired of children, but the feeling is suppressed, or irrelevant, because of the involuntary nature of the relationship.

THEORETICAL EXPLANATIONS

Habituation

The fundamental explanation for the phenomenon of getting tired of the other seems to be less a theory than an established fact: The nervous system habituates to all stimuli (Peeke & Herz, 1973). Habituation occurs at every level, from the single neuron to the whole organism. Our eyes accommodate to bright light; we get used to having a doctoral degree. Habituation reverses when one is no longer exposed to the repeating stimuli ("absence makes the heart grow fonder"). An ongoing relationship almost by definition is repetitious in some ways, and therefore eventually subject to habituation.

Learning Theories

Explaining habituation in learning terms, Miller and Siegel (1972) say love deintensifies as the reinforcement becomes predictable. Similarly, Huesmann (1980) points out that rewards from a relationship, like all rewards, are evaluated according to recent experience. "Since habituation is an inevitable fact of life" (p. 164), loving behaviors, or satisfaction with status gained from the relationship, or whatever are the relevant rewards, all cease to be satisfying with time. "The lover's failure to recognize the inevitability of habituation and to correct their comparison levels for it may, in fact, lead to dissolution of the relationship" (pp. 164-165). Further, what we really fall in love with may be, not a person, but "a steeply sloping reward function," which is known to have "secondary reinforcing properties" (p. 166), especially in a society emphasizing growth and achievement.

Again, Jacobson and Margolin (1979), behavior modification-oriented marital therapists, note that "the partner's reinforcing potential" diminishes over time "simply due to habituation." They observe that while couples usually come for help with more specific problems, if they also feel bored they are less able to cope with troubles. Plutchik's (1967) model also makes "lack of novelty" a prominent force for marital instability.

Cognitive Theories

Livingston (1980) has applied to romantic love the concepts of uncertainty from decision theory, and information from information processing theory. Uncertainty reduction, in mild amounts, is said to be an adaptive and sought-after behavior of the species. This process of uncertainty reduction is said to generate the feeling of love, in that it creates arousal and vigilance—a focus on O, the source of uncertainty-reducing information. "Since uncertainties must either be reduced or not, it is inevitable that these cumulative probabilities will eventually stabilize, making nearly inevitable the end of the romantic phase of the relationship" (pp. 145-146).

Kelling (1979) has also taken a cognitive view, as a sort of nouveau Piaget. He says one adapts to the other or incorporates the other in one's schemata (in this book's terms, expands to include the other in the self) by the usual Piagetian process of alternating between what Kelling calls "being on the rim" (beginning to try to accommodate to this mysterious other) and "being in the pit" (focusing on one's self, one's own developing schemata, and trying to assimilate the other.) Romantic love, though, lasts only as long as this process remains "preadaptational"—before one has had much success "pigeon holing" one's partner within some schema.

Once adapted to, O becomes just another person, not an object of intense romantic love. According to Kelling, intense romantic love symbolizes the hope that we are about to achieve not just the blissful unity with the womb suggested by some psychodynamists but a future utopian unity with the environment—an unlimited final adaptation to everything, the ultimate goal of the knowledge process. Humans want this experience, symbolize it (have some words for it), feel frustrated that it hasn't happened yet, and often mistake love for or try to make a love relationship into this total expansion we seek. Then, because it is only another symbol of it, we become frustrated again.

Thus, Kelling says, the lover inevitably falls out of romantic love, which "is that infinitesimal moment between fantasy and reality" when the lover feels his or her dreams of infinite union have finally come true, but before the lover has "had to face the fact that the loved one is not all the fantasy desired, because anything experienced in time and space must be limited" (1979, p. 76).

Psychodynamic Theories

These have suggested a similar disillusionment after the breakdown of the transference—that is, when the projection onto O of an ego-ideal (Reik, 1944), an all-loving parent (Bergler, 1946), or an archetype (Jung, 1925/1959) ceases to work and reality impinges.

Social Exchange, Symbolic Interaction, and Systems Theories

Surprisingly, the major approaches to families and relationships do not appear to predict or discuss this loss of interest. They imply a homeostatic approach: If an internally comfortable homeostasis or adequate role enactment is achieved, no social forces impinge, and no alternatives present themselves, people should live happily ever after.

Conclusion

Unlike problems of communication or money or in-laws, getting tired of the other is *intrinsic* to ongoing relationships. In our terms, the motivation for self-expansion is inescapable. Habituation, reduction of uncertainty, or whatever one calls it (we call it completion of the integration phase of the expansion-integration cycle) inevitably leads to a need for novel stimuli (the expansion phase). There may be individual differences in this need for novelty and growth (see Zuckerman, 1979; or our own discussion of possible sources of differences in Chapter 3), but the tendency to habituate and seek new experience is ubiquitous.

To conclude our discussion of the problem of people getting tired of each other, we've enjoyed the comments of Venditti (1980), a clinician, on the marriage relationship:

> Boredom is perhaps the most common denominator of all marital problems. It is not always recognized as such, because by the time problems have developed, their cause—boredom—has long since been forgotten. . . . Children who are bored usually become irritable, dull, unproductive, uninteresting, dissatisfied, argumentative, inconsiderate, gullible, prone to delinquency, disrespectful, and generally obnoxious. When adults are bored, they are prone to all of these traits also, but on an even larger scale. (p. 65)

CURRENT PROPOSED SOLUTIONS

Several theorists and clinicians describe a change that must take place if a romantic/marriage relationship is to be maintained. Basically, passionate love must somehow, at some point, develop into something more "mature" and "clear and calm" (Reik, 1944); "companionate" (Hatfield, 1982); "fully conscious" (Jung, 1925/1959); "generative" (rather than fixated on the intimacy stage; Erikson, 1950); and "salvation"-oriented (Guggenbuhl-Craig, 1977/1981).

According to the data, the couples who make this change become Cuber and Harroff's (1965) intrinsic (total or vital) couples, or become at least the passive-congenials.

However, how couples manage to achieve a long-term satisfying relationship, neither researchers, theorists, or clinicians seem to know.*

Although the means to solve the problem of boredom are not clear, the task has become better defined in recent years: Couples simply have to develop "an ever-changing array of exchanges of behavioral and rational rewards that are mutually satisfying" (Huesmann, 1980, p. 166). They must expand their repertoire of reinforcing behavior capabilities (Jacobson & Margolin, 1979). To maintain true romantic love, they can try, in the language of uncertainty theory, "near random behavior," which is all that "can continue to induce in one's lover the feelings of passion that characterize romantic involvement and even this is a highly delicate process. Unpredictability becomes predictable in its own way . . ." (Livingston, 1980, p. 147). So, again, the favored solution is for a couple to "come to terms with the satisfaction that may be realistically possible in adult life within the specific existential situation of their marriage" (Goodwin & Mudd, 1976, p. 75). Good luck.

Perhaps one of the most astute analyses comes from an earlier, remarkably prescient article by Foote (1956/1963), in which he suggested that in our culture, at least in some strata of it, a marriage might best be kept interesting if it helped both partners develop their careers (in the broadest sense). He also predicted the coming emphasis on self-development.

Arrest in the development of either partner makes [marriage] vulnerable to breakdown. Strengthening it by this definition consists of multiplying the number of overlapping sequences of matching phases of development in which they are involved either as collaborators or as performer and significant audience. (p. 18)

In 1956 Foote noted that wives have understood this supportive role for years, but husbands had better learn it soon.

The usual husband whose wife is discontented . . . may expostulate that if he only knew what she wanted, he might be able to supply it. That is, he makes the simple and misleading motivational assumption of many psychologists, that discontent arises from unsatisfied wants and only requires gratification to disappear (a view that can create havoc in parent-child relations as well). (pp. 20-21)

Of course we could not agree more that this motivational assumption is misleading!

As for more specific solutions for "keeping love alive," they are not to be squeezed from any of these theorists. Many (e.g. Kelling, Jung, Guggenbuhl-Craig) describe the process of turning initial attraction into an interesting, ongoing relationship as simply too mysterious and unique to each couple to explain: After the loved one no longer symbolizes "infinite potential," the loved one is allowed to become him or herself. According to Kelling (p. 79) "everything further is

*One study (Emery & Dindia, 1982) asked couples how they maintained and rejuvenated their relationship, but found that most replied either with how they solved problems—for example, "communicating," "threatening"—or maintained stability—for example, keeping to relationship "ground rules," keeping a pleasant home, observing ceremonies, spending time together, staying attractive. The strategies they mentioned that, by creating novelty, might have been truly rejuvenating, tended to be negative—for example, "preliminary relational termination," "sacrificial extravagance," discussing problems, and exhibiting violence. Also, these were consciously applied only in times of crisis. The couples apparently did not consider the idea that the crises themselves might have arisen out of boredom.

specific and peculiar to the relationship." (Given the equal lack of ideas for keeping the love lively in other family relationship or in friendships, the maintenance processes in those relationships seem to be equally difficult to articulate.)

Clearly married couples especially, expected and expecting to be in love and fulfilled in their marriages until death, need some help. While it has not come from psychology, religious institutions (perhaps feeling some responsibility for the predicament) have tried to offer that help.

Their solutions tend to fall into two categories. One is to develop more shared, outside interests, including having children or working together, but also recreational interests, hobbies, friends, and the numerous church groups available to married couples. The second is to deepen the relationship—"enhance" it, "enrich" it. For the latter purpose churches and temples frequently offer "marriage encounter" programs—well-named, it seems, to re-arouse a sense of excitement or even a kind of mild, interesting threat to the status quo. Numerous secular programs have followed suit (e.g., Guerney, 1977).

In the end, most clergy would probably agree with Guggenbuhl-Craig (1977/ 1981) that marriage is more than a place to enjoy a "steeply sloping reward function." That is, there are "lessons to be learned" in marriage—some "salvation" to be gained—with which comes a deeper type of happiness. Thus, the time has come to consider this slippery emotion.

MARITAL HAPPINESS AND BOREDOM IN LIGHT OF SELF-EXPANSION

Some Data on Marital Happiness

Everyone can cite exceptions to the gloomy picture we have painted for voluntary, long-term relationships. ("Right up to the day they died, Grandma and Gramps were in love"—hopefully with each other.) The data show exceptions too, and they are obviously very important for understanding this persistent and perplexing problem of boredom among those who love.

First, Cuber and Harroff (1965) did find that interesting minority of intrinsic marriages. In these, even after ten years or more together, spouses reported such vitality, sharing, and joy, such deep involvement and contentment, such "fierce monogamy," and such a desire to be together always—that the relationship got "better all the time."

Surprisingly, another place to look for long-term satisfaction is in the generally disheartening longitudinal and cross-sectional marriage data we mentioned earlier, which found that dissatisfaction with marriage increases as time passes. While some studies (e.g., Pineo, 1961) and the interpretation of the data generally (e.g., Hudson & Murphy, 1980) suggest a simple decline over the life cycle, others have found marital quality to be curvilinearly related to years married or stage of life cycle (e.g., Rollins & Feldman, 1970), with the marriage improving after the children have left home. The validity of one model or the other was a hot issue during the 1970s (Spanier and Lewis, 1980). At present, the application of better statistical methods seem to confirm a slight curvilinear trend (Anderson et al., 1983)—for couples still married at all. (An obvious problem with these studies is that divorced spouses are not included.) However, this upturn does not reach the high level that newlyweds report. (But what do those youngsters really know about love anyway?)

Campbell's (1981) monumental quality-of-life surveys are even more optimistic about long-term relationships, in the long run. He found that while satisfaction with marriage does take a dip during the years young children are in the home (especially for women), it rises after the "nest empties," as other studies have found (e.g., Van Reken, 1977, in which engaged couples and those married over 25 years were most satisfied, least troubled, and most expressive of mutual affection). In fact, in 1978 Campbell found no differences between the numbers of young and old married populations describing their marriages as "very happy." About seven out of ten said that they were "very happy" with their marriages, about six out of ten, "completely satisfied." With all this general happiness in view, Campbell doesn't see a downturn in the happiness of married people, but a temporary dip in what is otherwise an upward trend!

Swensen and his associates (1981) hypothesized that couples probably contribute more or less to this average upswing according to how they experience these later years, and that their different experiences might depend on their ego development, as measured by Loevinger and Wessler's (1970) scale. Comparing 36 couples at the retirement stage of the life cycle who had scored above Loevinger and Wessler's conformist level to 36 similar couples who had scored at conformist level or below, Swensen found that the postconformist couples scored significantly higher on Swensen's own six-factor love scale. Also, the difference in scores between the "empty nest" and retirement couples showed lower love scale scores for conformist couples in the later, retirement stage, while postconformist retired couples showed a significant gain on the love scale. In fact, postconformist retired couples scored at a level close to that of the newly married! Interestingly, the number of problems in the marriages declined for all couples with time, and was unrelated to ego development.

In short, it seems that some apparently rather special individuals develop very satisfying long-term relationships, even though most theories say very little about how they may be managing this feat.

Solutions Implied by the Idea of Self-Expansion

In Chapter 7 we found that the idea of self-expansion suggested four reasons why P might maintain a relationship: continued expansion by incorporating aspects of O into the self; continued expansion outside the relationship through resources or opportunities provided by the relationship; fear of de-expansion or disintegration through loss of the aspects of O that P has incorporated; fear of de-expansion or disintegration in settings outside the relationship through the loss of resources provided by O or the social repercussions of violating norms of fidelity, loyalty, and so forth.

All these forces can maintain a relationship, but only the first maintains what is typically called a close, loving, intimate, "intrinsic" relationship—the ideal of marriage and close friendship. Furthermore, the other forces for maintenance are getting weaker—at least in our culture, for the present—as individuals increasingly strive to keep themselves autonomous financially and in every other way; as social norms about commitment grow less stringent; and as opportunities to meet new O's multiply. It seems that now more than ever a relationship may be maintained solely by virtue of the first force. P has to see the relationship itself as a means of self-expansion, difficult as it may be to maintain this process against the tide of habituation.

Still, it is a fact that some people do manage to be happy in long-term, close relationships. From the self-expansion perspective, we see three possible processes that might explain their success. The first is by doing that which we said in the last chapter seems impossible. The other two are going to sound only a little harder.

1. P might attempt to continue to see deeper, novel aspects of O, or O might continually change to keep P interested—all in order to make O an inexhaustible source of expansion. This seems to be the principle behind most of the solutions proposed in the literature, which we have already discussed.

2. In sharing experiences with O, P might perceive that by virtue of being with O some additional self-expansion is gained from experiences. We might call this an indirect, synergistic, or catalytic effect of O on P's expansion.

3. Discovering that all experiences eventually cease to be expanding (because of habituation), P might simply cease to expect O, or anything else external, to satisfy this recurring internal craving.

Although we will discuss these three solutions to boredom separately, successful couples probably employ all three, plus at least some of the more utilitarian reasons for staying together.

Making the Relationship a Continuous Source of Expansion

While discussing their data, Swensen et al. (1981) suggested that happy older couples, which were usually postconformist in their ego development, applied a solution that could be categorized as making the relationship a continuous source of expansion. Rather, life applied it for them. With the children gone and retirement upon them, these couples perceived so much change in each other and their relationship that each became a fresh source of expansion for the other.

Swensen et al. feel that while couples are busy raising their family and pursuing their careers, they probably grow apart, and they certainly change. All this time, conformists have maintained their marriages through "stereotypic sex-role expectations." When the roles change, as the children leave home and retirement comes, conformists haven't the flexibility to integrate the many changes in each other. Postconformists, on the other hand, can integrate and probably even relish the expansion these changes bring in each other. This explains their upswing in satisfaction.

Besides the major life cycle transitions, people change all the time, and our ability to appreciate subtler aspects of them can also change. Between life cycle changes and P and O's individual development, theoretically, at least, P ought to find enough opportunities to expand from a deep relationship with O to last a lifetime. How exciting a life each leads, how tuned in each is to subtleties in people, how much these subtleties provide real expansion for the other—these would all be mitigating factors.

Quite frequently couples manage to keep things interesting by alternating between the utilitarian use of the relationship as a "support base," and the discovery of new aspects of each other. They each expand separately through outside experiences, return to the relationship changed by those expansion experiences, and expand to include each other's new aspects, sometimes in a quite passionate period of reacquaintance. This may be a conscious approach (Foote, 1956/1963) of pursuing separate but mutually enjoyed careers; or it may be an unconscious pattern they have fallen into, often the precarious pattern of fighting, separating, and making up (Emery & Dindia, 1982).

Perceiving Greater Self-Expansion through Experiences Shared with the Other

With O present, P may feel that experiences are more expanding, that novelty is added, perhaps by seeing things through another pair of eyes. O also may push P to expand and integrate as much as possible, or may even do part of the process for P (perhaps by being more daring in an adventure, more astute at business, more intuitive with people, more sensitive to aesthetic qualities, or whatever).

Cuber and Harroff's (1965) interviews with their "intrinsic couples" suggested just such synergy. Spouses in the "total" category (in particular) emphasized finding all experiences more enjoyable when shared, and preferred being together over almost any possible way of spending time alone.

Couples' spending time together may be an effect of their being happy with each other, or noticing greater expansion when together. However, spending time together may also *cause* marital happiness, by offering the *chance* to discover the additional expansion that sharing an experience can provide. Huston (1982) found that newlyweds, in spite of their intention to be close, quickly settled into those patterns of spending leisure time usually associated with marital *un*happiness. Their patterns probably reflected a carry-over from single life, not a lack of pleasure in being together. Thus, paradoxically, one solution to getting tired of the other might be to do more things together, not fewer.

Ceasing to Rely on External Sources of Expansion Experiences for Satisfaction

Since psychologists have discovered that organisms habituate to everything, including each other, P might reach the same conclusion through self-observation. This discovery is bound to lead to fewer demands on O to provide P with self-expansion experiences, but it will also be associated with other changes in their relationship.

One possibility is that P's actual motivation to expand might diminish. As a result, P's interest in life would probably diminish, P and O's relationship would stagnate, and in extreme cases P might become quite depressed, as described in the learned-helplessness findings (Seligman, 1975). P says, in effect, "Yes, I'm satisfied with this relationship, because no relationship would make me happy, because *nothing* would make me happy."

Another possibility is that P's lessened dependence on external sources of expansion experiences (such as relationships) would be associated with the development of some inner happiness or contentment that simply has little to do with outer circumstances or events (although well-being probably cannot ever be completely independent of them). How often does this inner well-being arise? Possibly far more often than one would think.

In Campbell's (1981) extensive surveys of the sources of the feeling of well-being in the U.S., he found two big surprises. First, most people report that they are quite happy most of the time, and more so with age. And second, all the various "objective indicators . . . succeed in accounting for less than a fifth of the variation we see" (p. 230) in reported well-being. Similarly, Gallup (1977) and Easterlin (1973) have found no consistent connection between economic improvement and increased happiness.

There have been some other surprises in the study of happiness and well-being in recent years. Kammann (1982), looking at objective life circumstances and also life events, has failed to find any consistent factor that accounts for more than 10% of inter-individual variance in reported happiness.

Philip Brickman and his colleagues (1978) looked into the reported happiness of subjects who had recently been crippled and confined to a wheelchair for life or who had won major lotteries. These studies found that one month to one year after these two types of quite extreme events, lottery winners were no happier than controls, and not much happier than accident victims! These life events accounted for only 10% of the variance in happiness scores, and there was no difference among the groups in expected future happiness. (Although people around them rated lottery winners as much happier and victims as much unhappier than they actually were.)

Other research suggests that the blind, retarded, and malformed are as happy as other people (Cameron, 1972; Cameron et al., 1973).

Kammann has found that even though "happenings" and "happiness" are apparently independent of each other, people still are convinced that external factors such as wealth and health are the main determinants of happiness: Subjects think that people with these assets are happy even when the actual correlations turn out to be zero (Kammann and Campbell, 1982). Thus expectations oppose rather than support what one might call a "field-independent happiness."

Kammann is convinced that if the social sciences "cannot adequately account for happiness on the basis of what is happening 'outside' a person, it seems logical to look 'inside' for mental processes that could give circumstances their favorable and unfavorable meanings" (1982, p. 7). Such a mediating mental process might be a "happiness set," an idea Kammann has borrowed from Dember and Penwell (1980). This factor is a tendency to have more positive free associations, and Kammann found that it added about 15% to the variance accounted for in happiness scores. Campbell (1981, p. 50) draws similar conclusions: "It may well be that some people have a general orientation toward life, more or less accepting or demanding, that is reflected in their readiness to express satisfaction both with specific domains of life and with life in general. . . . A basically optimistic person may be able to contain the effects [of a negative event] and maintain the positive quality of other life domains."

Some people are happier than others, and since life circumstances account for so little of this variance, it is worthwhile to investigate how the happy (or those with Kammann's "happiness set") do vary from the unhappy. Campbell found that items in the "domain of self" have the greatest effect on well-being. Satisfaction with self was most important, and "the intriguing characteristic" was the way self-satisfaction was "almost completely unrelated to the individual's income, education, age, or marital status" (p. 229). What did affect it, Campbell found, was "the individual's sense of controlling his or her own life" (p. 229), what others have called internal locus of control. "If we isolate the part of the population which expresses both a strong sense of personal control and high level of satisfaction with self (about 15% of the total), we find that we have identified a group of people with extraordinarily positive feelings of well-being" (p. 217–218).

In short, the data on happiness suggest that it is not an uncommon feeling; and it is mainly determined by inner rather than outer conditions, even those external factors such as health, wealth, and education, which are usually associated with expansion and opportunities to expand.

How can relationships arrive at this happiness set? One way might be for P to notice the importance of inner mood, of life's small pleasures, or of attitudes and life philosophy.* As a result, P might decide to improve daily feelings by being more positive. Another way might appear if P, after sacrificing much to attain certain major forms of self-expansion (or to avoid certain forms of de-expansion), decides that the results are not worth the imbalance they've created and their effect on "life's little pleasures." For example, P might conclude, "I'd rather be my own boss, work out-of-doors, and spend more time with family"—or whatever—"even if it means I make less money," or, "I'd rather have a pleasant, harmonious home life, even if it isn't very exciting, rather than be bitter or sad or have affairs or whatever."

To review, we have described two situations that could be associated with this third, probably fairly rare solution to getting bored with O (i.e., P no longer expecting O, or anything, to provide lasting self-expansion). One might be a giving up on self-expansion when it proved insatiable; but the people in this cul-de-sac are not usually going to be very happy. There is also the situation just described, in which people apparently cease to rely on others for self-expansion because they have become "older and wiser" about what really expands. They appear to have firm internal loci of control too, so they probably see their happiness as something they can do something about—but not by external expansion experiences so much as by changing their attitudes.

However, there is yet another situation. Ceasing to rely on external sources of self-expansion experiences might be associated with finding a satisfying *internal* source. According to subjective reports of those experiencing it, pure consciousness seems to be such an internal source.

However, it is our impression that the experience probably also benefits relationships by facilitating the first two solutions to getting tired of the other. Thus at this point we would like to delve into the data on this experience more intensively, and afterwards return to the possibility of the experience enhancing all three solutions.

---

*Following the principles of adaptation level theory, Brickman et al. (1978) suggest that in the short run a shift in adaptation level accompanies any major life change, making mundane pleasurable events less pleasurable in contrast to a happy major event and more pleasurable compared to a tragedy. Plus, in the long run, habituation makes even the major event itself less important. In other words, people are not made happy (or unhappy) by major events. Rather, they are happy if they take pleasure from "the little things in life." A major positive event can actually decrease this pleasure. We suspect, however, that an awareness of the effect of their own perception of events could conceivably change this impact.

PURE CONSCIOUSNESS EXPERIENCE
AS A FACILITATOR OF SOLUTIONS
TO GETTING TIRED OF THE OTHER

Evidence

Suarez (1976) found that 146 couples practicing the TM technique for two years or more had significantly higher scores on measures of marital adjustment than 58 couples who had been practicing the technique for less than two years, the former group presumably having more experience in pure consciousness.

In another study of marital satisfaction (Aron & Aron, 1982), a nonmeditating matched control group was employed and precautions were taken to ensure that participants did not know the hypothesis being studied. Couples practicing the TM technique scored significantly higher on the Locke Wallace (one of the measures used by Suarez), and the effect was even stronger for those most regular in the practice (and thus, again, possibly experiencing pure consciousness more).*

The pure consciousness experience is also associated with increases in a number of attributes that are associated with marital satisfaction or adjustment. Some examples are listed in Table 8-1.

Of course, one can only draw very tentative conclusions from this kind of analysis. Moreover, the studies relating the variables to marital satisfaction are primarily correlational. The studies in the pure consciousness column are experimental or quasi-experimental, but in most cases the link they show is with the TM program, not with the pure consciousness experience directly. Finally, in most cases, the measures used for the variable by the studies in the two columns are not the same.

Nevertheless, it is plausible that these characteristics would be associated both with marital satisfaction and TM practice. If the happily married are generally more expanded and expanding individuals, by our definition, then they ought to possess characteristics (in most cases without meditating) that are similar to those possessed by people who expand themselves through meditation. These characteristics no doubt help married people deal with the problem most intrinsic to long-term relationships, this problem of getting bored with the other. Finally, if the TM program enhances these traits (presumably through providing the pure consciousness experience), it is reasonable to presume that the development of these characteristics might be mediating the possible effect of the program on marital satisfaction suggested by the correlational findings of Suarez and ourselves. However, the hypothesis that the pure consciousness experience causes these traits to develop in meditators, and thus can facilitate solving this problem of boredom—or other relationship problems—deserves further consideration.

Explanations

We have argued that any expansion is satisfying and any expansion increases the capacity to expand—all of which should facilitate the methods members of relation-

---

*An additional study (Kukulan et al., in press) may be related to the satisfaction of children with their parent-child relationship. It found that children in meditating families scored lower on anxiety and higher on internal locus of control than matched controls from nonmeditating families.

Table 8-1   Studies of Positive Variables Associated with Marital Satisfaction and Pure Consciousness Experience

	Association	
Variable	With marital satisfaction	With pure consciousness
Ego development	Swensen et al., 1981	Alexander, 1981
Self-esteem	Cohn, 1976	Nystul and Garde, 1977
Intelligence	Terman and Oden, 1959	Shecter, 1978
Creativity	Litwak et al., 1960	Travis, 1979
Cognitive complexity	Crouse et al., 1968	Dillbeck, 1982
Lack of neurotic traits	Burgess and Wallin, 1953	Ferguson and Gowan, 1976
Good health in later years	Renne, 1970	Wallace et al., 1982

ships use to maintain their interest in and commitment to one another. However, we also side with Vedic psychology in suggesting that the self-expansion produced by the pure consciousness experience is qualitatively different, as well as quantitatively greater, than the expansion provided by any other experience.

Similarly, Maslow (1971) observed even among the "self-actualized" a clear qualitative as well as quantitative difference between "transcenders" and the "merely healthy." Although Maslow listed quite an assortment of experiences under transcendence, they all seem related to or approximate indices of the basic pure consciousness experience, which he also described.

What gives this experience its special ability to change how individuals perceive and enjoy their experiences?

During the early years of TM research (1968-1973), the observed physiological changes during meditation and improvements on many health and performance measures outside of meditation were explained as the result of the unusually deep rest meditation seemed to produce (Bloomfield et al., 1975).

Then, beginning around 1973, Banquet (1973) and Levine (1976) noticed the unusual pattern of very high EEG coherence during TM practice, especially among those reporting clear experiences of pure consciousness. Later studies replicated these findings (Dillbeck & Bronson, 1981; Farrow, 1977; Farrow & Hebert, 1982; Levine et al., 1977; Orme-Johnson & Haynes, 1981), and also found strong correlations between degree of EEG coherence during and after meditation with performance measures outside of meditation, such as those listed in Table 8-1.

In this latest research, the strongest relation with EEG coherence (and also with subjective reports of the pure consciousness experience) was with creativity—a remarkable .61 in the Torrance Test (Orme-Johnson & Haynes, 1981). Creativity is probably one of the better measures of global functioning (frequently defined as arising from integrated communication among information stores in the brain, as in Mednick, 1962).

Coherence has also been associated with better problem solving (Orme-Johnson et al., 1981). Interestingly, meditators do not show simply a better performance on tasks requiring right brain functioning, as early "altered state" theorists hypothesized (and later found: Pagano & Frumkin, 1977). Rather, if both hemispheres are monitored and tasks specific to each are given, meditators show an increased lateralization of either hemisphere, according to the type of problem solving required (Bennett & Trinder, 1976).

In the concept of coherence, researchers felt they finally had an empirically based explanation that also captured the flavor of both the subjective and the Vedic descriptions of pure consciousness. Coherence means "dynamic integration," and it seemed reasonable that while the brain is integrated in its activity, rather than diversely active with localized neural processes, one might subjectively experience a sense of "wholeness" and "unboundedness," devoid of particular thoughts, yet aware. It also seemed reasonable that afterwards, as a result of this period of uninterrupted integration, one might function better.

Of course EEG measures provide only a very rough picture of what might be going on in the brain. Banquet and Sailhan (1977) suggest that the usually open circuit between environment and brain is closed by meditation, yet vigilance is maintained, so that there is "a kind of diffuse recruiting response." A loop might then result, between the cortex and the hippocampus and certain thalamic nuclei, allowing for the retrieval and reprocessing of stored information.

> *[This loop] eliminates the information if it is unuseful and reprocesses it for recoding and elaboration if it is redundant or noisy. Thus, this process participates in the organization and structuring of the mind content, that is to say, the brain itself. In the long run the repetitive occurrence of this specific functional mode induces an integration between the closed circuit and open circuit modalities. This new integration could be on the basis of a better functional individualization of specific and nonspecific areas of the cortex and/or of superficial and deep cortical layers." (p. 172)*

Another, similar theory (Glueck & Stroebel, 1975) begins with a "driving mechanism" created by meditation, which quiets limbic activity and the subcortical areas generally, allowing those mechanisms that control the transmission of signals between the hemispheres to respond to signals from the limbic system which are usually not detected. The result, again, is a freer exchange of information between the hemispheres. Glueck, a psychiatrist, sees this "freer interchange" as an explanation for his finding that teaching psychiatric patients to meditate speeds their progress in therapy, compared to nonmeditating patients. He thinks they have greater access to repressed material because in meditation the affect (coming from the limbic system) normally associated with a threatening idea is quieted, allowing the idea to be examined more rationally. (Perhaps similarly, a meditating P becomes aware of repressed feelings about O, and thus has the chance to resolve them internally or take some action such as discussing them with O before they adversely affect communication with O.)

Whatever the mechanism, Orme-Johnson (1977), the leading researcher in the field, concludes that "there is experimental evidence that this high degree of linear coupling of the EEG is related to the transfer of information between cerebral systems," creating "a state of unobstructed information exchange or 'flow of intelligence' " (p. 707).

Thus at least for now EEG coherence seems to be a plausible explanation for any observed improvements in the quality of functioning associated with the pure consciousness experience. It also may turn out to be the best single descriptor of what many have sensed to be some global quality of competence (e.g., those in the field of intelligence testing, Cronbach, 1960; or optimal human functioning, Maslow, 1970; Rogers, 1961). The term also has the advantage of connoting very nicely the expansion and integration experience: Dynamic [expanding] organization [integration]. Above all, the physiological, behavioral, and self-reported data portray a unique experience, which has to have some unique effects on relationship maintenance and satisfaction.

Effect of the Pure Consciousness
Experience on the Solutions to Boredom

Making the Relationship a Continually Fresh Source of Expansion

Each partner must change rapidly and/or become increasingly appreciative of subtle changes in the other. Regular exposure to the pure consciousness experience may do both, as suggested by the studies cited in the previous section, plus by findings associating TM practice with positive changes on such variables as perceptual discrimination and cognitive processing (Bennett & Trinder, 1976; Dillbeck, 1982; Miskiman, 1977; Pagano & Frumkin, 1977; Pelletier, 1974; Pirot, 1977), tolerance (Shecter, 1978), "capacity for intimate contact" (Seeman et al., 1972; Nidich et al., 1973; Hjelle, 1974), and "trust in others" (Van den Berg & Mulder, 1976). However, the association of creativity and cognitive complexity with both the pure consciousness experience and marital happiness might especially explain the role of pure consciousness in facilitating this particular solution: Creativity makes people both interesting and interested; cognitive complexity is said to make a person "sensitive to environmental change" (Crouse et al., 1968, p. 643).

Perceiving Greater Self-Expansion through Experiences
Shared with the Other

This also would seem to be helped by greater attunement to the subtle aspects of an experience, such as the effect of the other on one's own experience.

We have also mentioned that merely spending an adequate amount of time together might be enough to enhance this solution. To do so, however, requires the ability to recognize the larger pattern one's life is taking, and to make changes when necessary. This in turn requires a number of the attributes we found common both to those experiencing pure consciousness and the happily married—intelligence, cognitive complexity, ego development, creativity, and so forth—plus the internal locus of control associated with life satisfaction generally (Campbell, 1981) and with regular TM practice (Hjelle, 1974).

Relying Less on External Means of Self-Expansion

This would seem to be an inevitable result of the pure consciousness experience. Like all expansion experiences, it brings a feeling of satisfaction and happiness. In fact, the subjective experience of pure consciousness is frequently described in terms such as "pure happiness" or "heavenly, sublime sweetness" by modern meditators (Orme-Johnson, 1977). Their historical counterparts chose equally impressive terms, examples being Teresa of Avila's (1583/1960) "raptures" and the pure consciousness described in the Vedas as *satchitananda*, or "eternal bliss consciousness." Although EEG coherence in adults is rare in non-meditators, something much like it has been observed in infants after feeding (Maulsby, 1971) and in cats while purring or while successfully appraching a goal (Adey et al., 1961).

One of the few researchers in the area of happiness, Maynard Shelly (1973a, 1973b), took an interest in the experience's effect on happiness because of his theory that those who are hyperaroused are satisfied only by very intense experiences and consequently enjoy daily life less. He reasoned that since, in contrast, those practicing TM generally show unusual autonomic stability (Goleman & Schwartz, 1976; Orme-Johnson, 1973) they ought to enjoy more daily activities, and to a greater degree than even the average person. Thus since Shelly had defined happiness as simply a sum of daily satisfactions, he reasoned meditators should report greater overall happiness. Comparing 160 meditators to 145 controls of similar age and background, he concluded, among other things, that meditators appeared to be happier, to enjoy more experiences, to develop deeper personal relationships, and to depend less on their external surroundings for happiness. Van den Berg and Mulder (1976) also found that meditators report more "life satisfaction."

Yet clearly the pure consciousness experience is qualitatively as well as quantitatively different from other sources of expansion and happiness, even extraordinary sources. The reason is that this experience is fundamentally not an experience *of* anything—it is simply awareness by itself. For example, one person gave this description: "The predominant experience in meditation was a deep, expansive silence;" another, "I was infinite, unbounded, existing everywhere the same" (Orme-Johnson & Haynes, 1981, p. 214).*

Of course, pure consciousness can only be an "infinite, unbounded" self-expansion experience in the sense of the "I" aspect described in Chapter 2, for though the "me" aspect may strive to include everything and be expanded completely, it does not seem physically possible. The expansion resulting from the direct experience of the "I" aspect is complete, according to Vedic psychology, since this "I" aspect includes, in a sense, all experience, by including the common denominator of all experience—the experiencer.

However, the reported "unbounded" quality, whatever it means exactly, appears to make the experience very resistant to habituation. Most subjective reports repeatedly emphasize that meditations become, if anything, more enjoyable with each experience—of what is literally nothing! For example, "meditations become more and more effortless, blissful, and comfortable," and "this experience of wholeness has grown in greater clarity and fluidity during the [past] three months" (Orme-Johnson & Haynes, 1981, p. 213). Similarly, many experiencers in various cultures have described an unceasing desire to repeat that state (Bucke, 1901/1969; Teresa of Avila 1583/1960).

There are also some research data suggesting that the experience does not

_____

*It can probably be called an "experience" only in the sense that it can be remembered and described after it has happened, since no thoughts or perceptions can occur during the experience (at least in what is considered the simplest form of this state. After considerable familiarity there are sometimes descriptions of "impulses of natural law cognized within the unmanifest structure of pure consciousness," but in an infinite variety; Dillbeck, personal communication, November 1983). This absence of sensation makes it very much like sleep, except that individuals are aware and alert, according to both EEG measures and self-report (Farrow & Hebert, 1982).

habituate.* Glueck and Stroebel (1975) randomly assigned psychiatric patients to relaxation training and biofeedback, and also to the pure consciousness experience by means of TM. The subjects reported that experiences using the first two techniques were boring, anxiety-producing, or otherwise unpleasant (in spite of equal amounts of intensive instruction), and the methods eventually were dropped from the study. On the other hand the TM practice was "the most appropriate technique" because it was most able "to hold their interest over a considerable period of time" (p. 320). Other comparison studies have found similar results (Abrams, 1977; Lewis, 1976; Morse et al., 1977; Riddle, 1979; Tolliver, 1977). The most obvious explanation seems to be that techniques are boring if they do not allow the user to "transcend" the prescribed activity, which eventually habituates.**

Finally, the experience is unique among expansion experiences in that, according to Vedic psychology (Aranya, 1963; Maharishi, 1972; *Rig Veda* 4.412) it can eventually be present at all times, integrated with every other experience. At first the experience is isolated to meditation, then eventually becomes simultaneous with other experiences, and finally becomes the common "substance" of all experience.

In short, we have described how the experience might solve P's problem of boredom or dissatisfaction with life. The remaining question, however, is the effect of all this inner expansion and satisfaction on P and O's relationship.

One might think P would lose all interest in O, or in anything else external to P's experiences of pure consciousness. Paradoxically, however, this interest apparently does not decline. One reason is that even "infinite" inner happiness can obviously be augmented by sources of outer self-expansion—new experiences, skills, successes—perhaps in the same way that in mathematics some infinities can be called larger than others.

Vedic psychology claims that the inner contentment makes outer events less crucial. With P feeling daily this sense of expansion and inner contentment, P not only puts less of a demand on O (or on anyone or anything else) to supply such feelings, but this greater self-sufficiency can actually free P to enjoy O more. For example, Maslow (1967) found that self-actualized people, despite their "peak experiences" and their inner peace and satisfaction with themselves, were consistently more deeply involved with others. They also appeared to be more concerned with improving the world, by choosing vocations that promoted justice, truth, compassion, and other values that Maslow considered "intrinsic" to self-actualization.

The idea that the discomfort of boredom, the yearning for expansion, and the unceasing pursuit of happiness are all resolved deep within the mind, at the source of thought, is one that has existed in many cultures besides ancient India's, and in many philosophies and psychologies. One recent approximation can be found in

*In fact, habituation to regular sensory input is also uniquely changed during the experience, in that there is EEG alpha—indicating relaxed alertness—but no alpha blocking, or loss of alpha, in the face of stimuli; or else there is alpha blocking but it fails to habituate to the stimuli causing it (Banquet, 1973; Wallace, 1970; Williams & West, 1975).

**While some people do, of course, stop using the TM technique, studies of the causes do not usually report boredom as a major cause. TM teachers claim that the usual cause is failure to complete the full course of instruction—and thus, perhaps, a failure to experience pure consciousness (without which the TM technique would be no different than any other "limited" experience.)

Ellis's Rational-Emotive Therapy. One of the "irrational ideas" challenged by RET is that happiness is caused by external events. The solution? Behave on the assumption that happiness is caused by one's inner state of mind (Ard, 1976). Similarly, Crosby (1973) also emphasizes the idea—don't expect others to fulfill you—presenting it clearly in a chapter called "The Happiness Thing: Need Fulfillment in Marriage." The solution? Be self-actualized!

While the idea has been around a long time, the means to give people a "happy outlook" or "self-actualization" has not been so obvious. In fact, as happiness and self-actualization become the primary concerns of the otherwise satisfied, some (e.g., Etzioni, 1977) claim that this emphasis itself is to blame for the failure of many relationships, for society's ills, and even for the continuing lack of happiness in the "me generation."

However, it does seem that it is only the *search* for a truly satisfying means of self-expansion that drives people to desert their responsibilities. *Finding* it—perhaps in the pure consciousness experience—should let one get on with the task of developing loving relationships and a better world.

9

Obstacles to Expansion

INTRODUCTION

In this chapter we look at the problems that clinicians and counselors see most often. Unlike the problem discussed in the last chapter, relationships suffering from these problems—poor communication, incompatibility, and the like—are not usually experienced as boring, but they do limit expansion through the relationship. Thus P will be no more satisfied with the relationship than if he or she were bored (although, as always, the forces for maintenance described in Chapter 7 might still be enough to keep P and O together).

Again the most frequent example in our discussions will be the marriage relationship. What obstacles have married couples encountered? Greene (1970) asked 750 couples coming for counseling to describe their problems. The twelve most common problems were lack of communication, constant arguments, unfulfilled emotional needs, sexual dissatisfaction, financial disagreements, in-laws, infidelity, conflict over children, domineering spouse, suspicious spouse, alcoholism, and lack of physical attractiveness.

Of course, marital therapists frequently interpret such complaints as symptoms of deeper problems of structure and process. Lack of communication, for example, looks to Stuart (1969) "to be a euphemism for a failure to reinforce each other" (p. 676). To Segraves (1982) it is caused by markedly discrepant schemata, and to Nadelson (1978), a neurotic transference.

In the rest of this chapter we look at some of these theoretical orientations to problems in relationships, plus data and observations about the problems, and the proposed solutions—both those in current use and those suggested by the self-expansion approach. Starting with Greene's list of couples' problems, below is a condensed list that seems applicable to all relationships.

1. Ineffective communication and problem solving, or other skill deficits
2. Seemingly incompatible personalities, behaviors, or attitudes
3. Difficulty coping with change in the self, the other, or the relationship
4. O's poor mental or physical health

5. Stressors in the social environment
6. Alternatives to the relationship

INEFFECTIVE COMMUNICATION
AND PROBLEM SOLVING,
OR OTHER SKILL DEFICITS

In the research on the marriage relationship, adjustment and satisfaction have been found to be closely associated with communication and problem-solving skills (e.g., Cuber & Harroff, 1965; Gottman, 1979; Kahn, 1970; Margolin & Wampold, 1981; Markman, 1981; Navran, 1967).

That these skills *cause* high marital quality—and their lack causes divorce—is of course less clear. Happy marriages may foster good relationship skills or both may be products of some third factor. Nor are we talking of communication in general, or just a head-on attack to problems: Simple "leveling" about negative feelings appears to increase family violence (Straus, 1974) and decrease effective communication (Bienvenu, 1970).

However, most clinicians are strongly convinced that communication and conflict-resolution skills are central to marital success (e.g., Gottman, 1979; Raush et al., 1974). Markman (1981) found that the quality of communication before marriage predicted reported relationship satisfaction 5½ years later ($r = .59$). The study is one of the few pre- to post-marriage longitudinal studies to successfully predict marital satisfaction, and communication was the key. (However, Markman measured only the positive/negative impact of communication as perceived by the spouse—a point that becomes significant.)

Other skill or knowledge deficits also seem important. For example, Huston (1982) found that although couples claim to want to be intimate, they organize their lives in the very first year of marriage so as to make their goal almost impossible to achieve. Also, in an examination of the factors determining marital happiness of 2034 married persons, White (1983) found that marital satisfaction both determines and is determined by time spent together. In other words, despite good intentions couples may out of ignorance choose lifestyles that could cause their relationships to fail. Similarly, misunderstandings about child development probably contribute to many problems for the parent-child relationship.

Much of marriage and family counseling might best be characterized as individualized classes to develop the skills required to maintain family relationships—behavior modification techniques, budgeting, listening, decision making. These skills are being emphasized more and more, before their lack becomes a problem in a relationship. (For a discussion and brief review of relationship training programs, see Olson et al., 1980.)

For most theorists, lack of skill is a good enough explanation for ineffectiveness in relationships. However, apparently spouses sometimes *know* effective responses but do not use them in their marriages. Gottman (1979) compared spouses from very unhappily married "clinic" couples and from very happily married "nonclinic" couples and found them responding with equal skill to difficult situations with a stranger in the spouse role, but with their own spouses in such a situation "clinical" spouses failed to exhibit their skill. Segraves (1982) describes similar experiences from his practice.

Of course it comes as no surprise to psychodynamic theorists that possessing skills does not guarantee their use; they see most communication problems arising from deeper resistances or unconscious conflicts. Similarly, systems theorists feel that families often deny problems, resist change, and fail to employ communication skills in order to maintain their family system as it is (Haley, 1973; Selvini et al., 1978). Nevertheless, clinicians espousing both theories frequently begin marriage or family therapy by trying to teach some skills anyway, to make the relationship functional again and demonstrate their professional competence. Even for proceeding to "deeper things," communication skills seem essential (Segraves, 1982).

If there is a single key discovery about relationship skills, it is that the emotions that accompany communications are crucial, perhaps even more crucial than cognitions (Fincham & O'Leary, 1982). Markman (1981) found that it was the positive or negative emotional impact of the spouses' communications that predicted marital happiness 5½ years later. In addition, Gottman (1982), as part of his ongoing intensive study of the temporal patterns and emotional qualities of marital communciations, found that physiological indicators of emotion during communications account for 84% of the variance in couples' marital satisfaction!

Poorly adjusted couples tend to use punitive tactics on each other, especially when dealing with conflicts or complaints; well-adjusted couples do not (Birchler et al., 1975; Cousins & Vincent, 1983; Gottman, 1979). Poorly adjusted couples also reciprocate negative affect, which tends to have an escalating effect in the conflict-resolution process as well as making both partners less likely to try to resolve conflicts and express complaints in the future (Gottman, 1979; Markman, 1982). Gottman (1982) describes the biggest problem in marriage as the "triumph of negative affect." Couples appear to become "locked into destructive interactions" with each other (Levenson & Gottman, 1983, p. 596). In fact, in a study of 30 couples, Levenson and Gottman found that the number of periods when both spouses were showing strong affect on physiological measures ("physiological linkage") while discussing their marital problems explained 60% of the variance in marital satisfaction.

Kelling (1979) also suspects that negativity devastates relationships, whether they were initially happy or not. He reports a laboratory study in which couples were requested (and provoked) to engage in arguments. He found that the greater the argument's intensity, the weaker the relationship's strength immediately following the argument. The initial strength of the relationship did not reduce the detrimental effect of arguing. Thus Kelling suggests that in strong relationships, arguments are probably avoided, or settled before they arise; because once they do arise, no relationship can handle them well.

Overall, the unedited expression of negative affect, both verbally and nonverbally, in and out of conflicts, appears from the literature to be one of the most reliable differences between "clinical" or unhappy marriages and better-adjusted ones. (This may vary across cultures, however. Winkler and Doherty, 1983, found that verbal aggression predicted marital satisfaction for Jewish-American couples, but not for Israeli couples.) Negative communication has also been found to be more typical of the families of disturbed children than normals (Jacob, 1975).

Such behaviorists as Gottman (1979), Markman (1981), and Patterson (Wills et al., 1974) tidily explain the devastating effects of negativity: Experiences of frustration, anger, and fear are unrewarding. Worse, they are negatively reinforcing, and members of relationships who resort to arguments or other negative communication acts are violating a fundamental rule: Under most conditions, punishment is a poor way to shape another organism's behavior to the pattern you want (Skinner, 1938).

The expression of positive feelings, on the other hand, is strongly associated with happy marriages (e.g., Fiore & Swensen, 1977; Margolin & Wampold, 1981; or the review by Lewis & Spanier, 1979). It is also somewhat independent of negativity (and less important) in that some unhappy couples express more "positivity" than happy couples—but these unhappy spouses seem to give positive comments by rote and receive them with disbelief (Gottman, 1982). Whether feelings are expressed or not, two studies suggest that just viewing the spouse positively, even more positively than is "realistic," is typical of the happily married (Preston et al., 1952; Hall & Taylor, 1976).

While the causal relation between positivity or negativity of communication and marital satisfaction is unclear, the assumption (and hope) is maintained that one of the prime skills couples need to learn is how to communicate more positively and how to recognize and avoid negative interactions.

Many skills besides communicating well and being positive no doubt are associated with successful relationships. New parents, for example, adapt much better if they exhibited before the birth a realistic understanding of their role (Garrett, 1983). General education is also probably important. Locksley (1982) found education, but not occupation (that is, probably, not simply socioeconomic status) to be strongly associated with better relationships.

To summarize, communication and problem-solving skills, and the key wisdom of accentuating the positive and deescalating the negative, plus other skills and general knowledge—are all associated with and presumed to be a cause of successful relationships. However, there is some evidence that in marriage, at least, people may have this knowledge and not use it.

Suggested Solutions in the Literature

Skills training is the obvious solution. Training in communication or problem-solving skills typically involves instruction in listening, expressing needs and desires, negotiating conflicts, avoiding destructive communication patterns, and absorbing concepts and developing behaviors pertinent to the specific relationship ("marriage goes through certain stages," "adolescents need firmness plus freedom," etc.). Some training programs are an application to families and friendships of what has been learned to be effective in therapy, small groups, and business meetings. Other programs, like Gottman's (1979) and Markman's (1982; Markman et al., 1982 and 1983), are closely tied to their own studies of communication and problem solving in successful relationships.

Besides having the clearest theories about the problem of skill deficits, behaviorists also have the most specific remedial programs (for a review, see Segraves, 1982). Jacobson and Margolin (1979), for example, help couples learn to make their marriages more rewarding by increasing positive exchanges and focusing on the strengths of the relationship and each other's positive qualities. Couples are also taught communication and problem-solving skills, and how to set up "contingency contracts" to eliminate some behaviors and increase other (e.g., "Every night you come home on time, I'll avoid asking you how it went at the office"). The general goal is to teach how to increase positive behaviors through reinforcement.

This behaviorists' approach to "skill deficits" in communication, problem solving, sexual behaviors, and so forth can be seen, partially or entirely, in almost every system of marital therapy, though frequently in a less rigorous (and less jargon-rich) form. The same principles of reward theory have also been applied to parent-child communications—where they could be said to have actually originated, with Patterson's (1971) successful, pioneering application of learning theory to children with behavior problems, at the University of Oregon.

How successful are programs that teach relationship skills? This is a thorny question. If the training and outcome criteria are the same, these programs look fairly successful (Segraves, 1982). However, Gottman (1979) found wide variations among his subjects in just their intellectual absorption of concepts, despite a great deal of individualized help. When it comes to applying the actual skills, at home, with some regularity, and with a result being a feeling of satisfaction with the relationship—Markman et al. (1982) conclude in their review of the research that, "We simply do not yet know" (p. 258). Although there are a number of programs plus evaluation studies of them, only short-term effects have been measured, designs have frequently been poor, and still, results have been mixed. Certainly improvements will come, however, as these dedicated clinicians find the right formula for getting these skills absorbed and applied by the people who need them. However, Markman et al. (1982) also point out that "We have to be careful not to make the logical error . . . [of] arguing that if skill training prevents problems, then a lack of skill causes problems" (p. 259). (After all, skills training is in itself a form of self-expansion. If something about the relationship was limiting P's and O's expansion, training may increase their self-expansion by bypassing the obstacle, without necessarily affecting it, or it mattering!)

Above all, skills training is usually applied as a means of prevention or enrichment. Thus it may be a blessing that arrives too late for relationships that are troubled. Teaching couples to give up negative patterns seems especially difficult, as these "scripts" often serve complicated purposes (Segraves, 1982). Also, as Levenson and Gottman (1983) pointed out, they seem to get "locked into" the very physiology.

As for increasing positivity, learning a new skill and seeing how many times one can say or do nice things should at first generate its own positivity. It will be expanding not only because it is a learning activity, but as Blau (1964) points out, "The repeated experience of being rewarded by the increased attachment of a loved one after having done a variety of things to please him may have the effect that giving pleasure to loved ones becomes intrinsically gratifying" (p. 77).

It *may* have that effect. Still most distressed relationships presumably began with this positive exchange, and yet they have broken down. Most parents of abused children, for example, say that they love their children. Teaching P what behaviors are positive for O, and to behave that way, is obviously an important tool for helping people maintain relationships. We predict, however, that teaching this "skill" of being positive, in particular, can have only limited success. Under stress, positivity tends to evaporate. For example, Levenson and Gottman (1983) found that the various differences in negativity/positivity between distressed and non-distressed couples became more pronounced when the topic was a marital conflict. Negativity seems to be easily aroused, broadly associated, and hard to get out of, so training individuals to replace intense negative reactions with positivity may not be easy. We discussed in the previous chapter how a feeling of well-being is not associated for long with even the most positive events, but seems to be related to locus of control, satisfaction with self, and elusive changes in attitude, mood, and the overall physiological state.

Skills and Self-Expansion

Relationship members who are learning communication and negotiation skills face three difficult tasks: (a) learning the concepts and skills, (b) applying this learning in their actual relationship, and (c) specifically developing two independent but apparently crucial abilities—to increase positive and limit negative communications.

Skills instructors are well aware of these difficulties. Typically they make the "classroom" training as lifelike as possible and give plenty of homework, to be done in the target relationship. Still, as we said, people often do not learn the skills; and even if they do, frequently they do not apply them at the crucial time, or with a positive attitude.

Educators tend to think that the major variable in learning is the ability of the student (Bloom, 1976; Chadwick, 1979), but the question, of course, is how to improve the student.

We think that all three of the difficulties associated with learning skills are closely connected to the issue of expansion. The more expanded people are, the more they can (a) incorporate and integrate new skills, (b) recognize the appropriate times to use their skills and the consequences of failing to do so, and (c) maintain some perspective and general positivity. We have suggested, especially in the previous chapter, that expansion and the capacity to be expanded may be closely linked to physiology. That is, the special expansion experience of pure consciousness, at least, appears to lead to coherence of the nervous system, which in turn is associated with improved measurements of intelligence, creativity, cognitive flexibility, and the like—all probably important for learning and applying skills. The pure consciousness experience also appears to be directly associated (Orme-Johnson et al., 1981) with improved direct measurements of learning and of academic performance, as well as problem-solving ability.* Finally, it appears to increase positivity ("placidity" on the Freiburger Personality Inventory; Fehr et al., 1977).

We do not mean in any way to detract from the importance of teaching skills. We do fear, however, that therapists' and their clients' dependence on skills, like the dependence on empathy in the 1960s or insight and catharsis during the 1950s, is going to disappoint them until they take into account an individual's cognitive and even physiological readiness to integrate new expansion.

INCOMPATIBILITY

When conflicts are chronic in a relationship and skillful communication only

---

*In fact, an entire university has been founded on the assumption that filling students with knowledge is only half the job, and the other half is expanding the container of knowledge—improving the student's learning capacity by increasing EEG coherence (through the pure consciousness experience). One 4-year longitudinal study of its students found significantly greater increases in intelligence and maturity test scores than are typical for the college years (Aron, Orme-Johnson, & Brubaker, 1981)—a promising (though hardly conclusive) finding.

seems to clarify, not resolve them, there is a temptation to conclude that the members are basically incompatible. "Temptation," because psychodynamicists and systems theorists, with their subtle attunement to hidden agenda, are quick to insist that there are few accidents in relationships—that, for example, chronic conflicts mean that "unconscious contracts" to meet each other's neurotic needs are being fulfilled (Sager, 1976). Further, little connection has been found between personalities at the time of marriage, whether compatible or incompatible, and later marital happiness (Udry, 1974)—with two possible exceptions: Marriages may be less stable when the husband is more introverted than the wife (Cattell & Nesselroade, 1967); and when he is more internal than the wife (Doherty, 1981), or similarly, more field independent (Sabatelli et al., 1983).

Nevertheless, even reward theorists, who usually make very little of individual differences, use them to explain some marital problems. For example, Jacobson and Margolin (1979) feel that individual differences in the "reward value of intimacy" can strongly determine marital outcome, and Burns (1973) suggests that cognitive orientations to be self-oriented, benevolent, and so forth can strongly influence marital outcome.

It probably seems safest, and kindest, to conclude that there are *some* true incompatibilities—and to let the two parties go their ways in peace. At the same time, many relationships undoubtedly are formed to meet unconscious, neurotically compatible needs, and these could be resolved or unlearned with the right approach (at which point, hopefully, the couple's healthier compatibilities would assert themselves).

Besides initial incompatibility and neurotic pseudo-incompatibility, another source of this problem could be that differences between members in a relationship start out seeming attractive and become unappealing later. As we have seen, differences can be one of the strongest causes of attraction. However, those differences in O that P cannot integrate during the actual formation and maintenance of a relationship may become "aversive" for P (Ables & Brandsma, 1977; Jacobson & Margolin, 1979).

Suggested Solutions in the Literature

How should one deal with seriously troublesome differences? Behaviorists would, of course, try to enhance conflict resolution skills, with perhaps a bit of positive emphasis on similarities and a little contingency contracting to reduce the aversive behaviors.

Psychoanalysts would analyze the "incompatibility" to gain insight into the neurotic needs being met—the transference underlying the marriage.

Segraves (1982) offers an interesting link between these two traditions, using the language of cognitive and social psychology as the bridge. He feels that chronic marriage disorders are due to one or both spouses' applying to the other schemata about the opposite sex that are markedly discrepant from the other's true personality (a distillation of the idea of transference). These wrong schemata come from previous experiences with the opposite sex—especially with the appropriate parent, but also with opposite sexed siblings or previous spouses. The failure to discriminate the differences between one's spouse and previous opposte-sex partners is said to be due to low levels of cognitive complexity (in Kelly's, 1955, sense), so that the spouse is viewed as one example of the opposite sex generally, rather than as an individual.

Thus personalities become incompatible, according to Segraves, because P perceives O as similar to one or more incompatible, upsetting O's previously in the life of P. They remain incompatible because P resists seeing how O differs from that previous O—and resists changes in O that make O any more different—because P would then have to change certain schemata (e.g., "he's lazy," "she's dumb"). These schemata are especially precious to P because in the past they have served to protect P from highly threatening O's.

The solution is to present P with characteristic behaviors of O that violate the schemata about O. To accomplish this, behavior modification techniques can be as useful as analysis; "Transference distortions can be disproved as well as modified by interpretation" (Segraves, 1982, p. 188).

One final solution to basic incompatibility comes from Guggenbuhl-Craig (1977/1981): Accept it as growthful.

> *A marriage works only if one opens himself to exactly that which he would never ask for otherwise. Only through rubbing oneself sore and losing oneself is one able to learn about oneself, God, and the world. . . . Marriage is hard and painful. . . . Dante did not get to Heaven without traversing Hell (p. 45).*

However, even Guggenbuhl-Craig admits divorce can sometimes be necessary in cases of incompatibility.

Incompatibility and Self-Expansion

To begin, we would apply here to incompatibility what we have already said about relationship skills. Segraves' approach, or the spirit of sacrifice suggested by Guggenbuhl-Craig, would be very good solutions—if P can manage them. This accomplishment, we have suggested, depends on P's capacity to expand, which is in turn largely determined by how expanded P is already.

More specifically, an expanded self might mitigate the problem of incompatibility in four ways.

First, incompatible relationships are less likely to be entered into.

Second, qualities that could become sources of incompatibility are not experienced as incompatible. In Chapter 5 we discussed data suggesting that an emotionally "mature" and confident P is more likely to enter a relationship with an O who is different from P. We interpreted these data as evidence for the desire to expand through relationships. We also think that a mature, expanded P is more likely to *remain* tolerant of these differences in O—out of appreciation for the expansion they have brought and/or continue to bring to P.

Third, if the relationship is tending to seem incompatible, as Segraves (1982) pointed out, professional help and adequate levels of cognitive complexity can still save the day. Cognitive complexity seems to be a very close approximation of our concept of degree of expansion. A cognitively complex person is "a flexible explorer of his world" who is "capable of entertaining and processing alternative explanations of an event and seeks diversity" (Crouse et al., 1968). According to Segraves, cognitive complexity permits the perception of important, subtle differences between what may have been in the past completely intolerable (e.g., P's mother's nagging) and something in the present, which may really only be mildly annoying (O's fussiness) or even enjoyable (O's protectiveness). Segraves feels that adequate levels of cognitive complexity can allow P to uncover and change the unconscious mechanisms making P and O feel "incompatible." That is, in our terms, the more expanded, the greater the capacity to expand—in this case by seeking rather than resisting dissimilarities and by being eager to let O become dissimilar to any past O and turn into someone new.

Fourth, we would agree with Guggenbuhl-Craig (1977/1981) that with a *broad enough* perspective (perhaps that of a Gandhi, a Francis of Assisi, or a Buddha) P might come to accept any kind of difference in O. Deviations from one's own values by loved ones are always the most threatening: An alcoholic parent is not just any alcoholic; a deceitful friend, not just any liar; a daughter who has broken the law, not just any criminal. However, difficult relationships such as these can sometimes develop our character.

As usual, we think that the pure consciousness experience might help promote these four solutions, since studies suggest that it may improve reasoning and cognitive discrimination (e.g., Dillbeck, 1982), tolerance (e.g., Shecter, 1978), cognitive complexity (e.g., Orme-Johnson, 1981; Miskiman, 1977), field independence (e.g., Pelletier, 1974) and breadth of moral reasoning (e.g., Nidich, 1976).

On the other hand, from the self-expansion perspective or from any other, there certainly may be times when the best route is through the exit.

DIFFICULTY COPING WITH CHANGE

Reviewing the literature on the decline of marital quality over the lifespan, Udry (1974) quotes Pineo's conclusion from one study to cover the entire literature: "We feel that it is unforeseen *changes* in the situation, personality, or behavior which contribute most to the disenchantment" (Pineo, 1961, p. 7, Udry's emphasis).*

The literature on the life cycle of the family certainly reinforces this impression. The birth of children and their entry into adolescence are both usually associated with downturns in marriage quality (see Rollins and Feldman, 1970).

Udry suggests that the reason personality and marital-role expectations do not predict marital happiness is that *"It is not some preexisting relationship between two people which determines the course of their marriage, but the responses of each to their interaction with each other"* as they and the relationship change with time (Udry, 1974, p. 229, Udry's italics), That is, the quality of response to the changing relationship best predicts marital happiness.

Some studies have suggested that, at least prior to the 1970s, success in marriage especially depended on the wife's flexibility and changes in personality (Uhr, 1957; Kieren & Tallman, 1972). Swensen and his associates (1981) found that flexibility was important for both partners when they studied couples in the last two major life cycle changes (children leaving home and husband retiring). Couples in these stages who showed flexibility (on a measure of ego development) rather than rigid conformity scored higher on measures of marital satisfaction.

After studying optimal families, Beavers (1976; Beavers & Voeller, 1983) also

---

*In the previous chapter we emphasized that this disenchantment was more likely from getting tired of the other, and getting tired of the other was often due to nothing but habituation or lack of change. However, change itself can also cause P to get tired of O: O can change to become less interesting, P can become dulled by unsuccessful expansion or integration attempts and thus less attentive to the expansion opportunties O offers, and so forth.

concluded that the *response* to change is all-important. In healthy families one sees "the miracle of life—'negentropy'—the utilization of energy to develop structure and fight the inexorable downhill pull found in any closed system" (p. 47). Families need to be "open to growth and change, and responsive to new stimulation" (p. 48).

Still more evidence for the importance of the response to change comes from a study by Kessler and Essex (1982). Using 2300 self-reports on stress and coping strategies, they replicated the well-documented finding that married people are less affected by stressors. They also found, however, that their married respondents were being exposed to as many stressors as the unmarried—that is, marriage was no shield—but that on the average, married persons coped better. Married persons without stress-coping skills such as flexibility showed no advantage over non-marrieds, which leads to the possible conclusion that the ability to cope with change may be the cause of both suffering less under stress and being successful in entering and maintaining a marriage—rather than the conclusion that had been drawn by previous theorists, that married life is inherently less stressful. (The same reasoning may hold for the research on friendships and support networks too.)

Looking for the effects of change on other relationships, we said in our discussion of the problem of "getting tired of the other" that the parent-child relationship has the advantage, at least for the parent, of the highest level of novelty and change in the other. The constant change of the child also makes this one of the most difficult relationships.

Friendships are also typically extremely vulnerable to changes in one member of the relationship (Dickens & Perlman, 1981; Reisman, 1979). Obviously moves to other locales frequently spell the end of a friendship (Parlee, 1979), but changes in marital status (Shulman, 1975) or socioeconomic status (Verbrugge, 1977) do also.

Suggested Solutions in the Literature

Proposed solutions to coping with change, including change in relationships, have in recent years been conceptualized almost exclusively in terms of the "stress" construct. Thus the solutions considered in this section are taken from the stress literature. They are four: Avoid change, don't see it as a stress, cope with it, and recover well from its effects.

Avoid Change

Too much change does indeed seem to be a stressor. Holmes and Rahe (1967) summed life change events as a rough measure of stress and found that high scores predicted stress-related illness. However, in our growth- and achievement-oriented culture, avoidance of such changes as career advancement or travel by one or both members of the relationship may be as good a way to destroy a relationship as to save it, in the long run (Foote, 1956/1963).

Don't See Change as a Stress

A more popular approach is to try to perceive change as a challenge rather than a threat (e.g., Lazarus & Launier, 1978) and life itself as a growth process to be relished (Beavers, 1976; Maslow, 1971; Rogers, 1961). The role of perception is especially brought home by Lazarus (1974), who maintains that the General Adaptation Syndrome described by Selye (1956) is in fact entirely the result of the psychological appraisal of threat or injury, citing the lack of this response in patients who are anesthetized during surgery or persons who are injured but unconscious.

On the topic of change in relationships, common sense, popular advice, and the research (e.g., Beavers, 1976; Lewis et al., 1976) all dictate that P must not only accept change in O, but support it, and even rejoice over it. Doing otherwise may be the surest way to lose O.

However, since all people have their limits in accepting change in those very close to them—especially if the change threatens self-esteem and/or maintenance of the relationship—the next two approaches are frequently necessary.

Cope

A number of researchers have surveyed the coping methods of adults and categorized them. Pearlin and Schooler (1978), for example, interviewed 2300 men and women in Chicago about their life stresses and strains (continuing stresses), their coping repertoire, and their emotional state. Findings from these studies suggest that coping mechanisms include personal strengths such as self-esteem and nonpassivity (Pearlin & Schooler, 1978), internality and "hardiness" (Kobasa, 1979; Kobasa et al., 1982); psychological "mechanisms" such as rationalization, denial, and revaluing (Pearlin & Schooler, 1978; Rahe & Arthur, 1978); knowledge and skills (suggested by the reliance in stress management courses on didactic instruction, and also by the superior coping of those with more education; Pearlin & Schooler, 1978); active behaviors such as assertiveness, effective communication, and alternative-seeking (Pearlin & Schooler, 1978); and external resources such as income, social status, marital status, social networks, community services and preventive medication or health care (Caplan, 1974; Pearlin & Schooler, 1978).

Interestingly, Pearlin and Schooler found that different mechanisms were important for coping with the stresses created by different relationships. In general, though, facing problems, not seeking outside advice, and making frequent positive comparisons were tactics associated with better coping with the stresses of both marital and parent-child relationships. Not surprisingly, men, the better educated, and the wealthier seemed to cope better. However, the most important factor seemed to be a varied repertoire: "The sheer richness and variety of responses and resources that one can bring to bear in coping with life-strains may be more important . . . than any single coping element" (p. 14-15).

Recover Well from Stress

This approach includes methods to recover from, to regulate, or to reduce (by preparing for) the effects of unavoidable stressors. Their usual aim is to keep one's physiology within acceptable ranges of the perceptible stress indicators such as rapid heartbeat, trembling, addictive behaviors, insomnia, moodiness, and feelings of anxiety. Typical techniques are rest (including meditation, biofeedback, relaxation techniques, vacationing, sleeping late, taking a day off, listening to music, etc.), medication, and restoring balance by doing something that produces a contrasting state (such as exercise after mental exertion).

Coping with Change and Self-Expansion

All four of the solutions to the problem of stressful change in a relationship or elsewhere can be enhanced to some degree by instruction (and are the elements of a typical stress management course). To the extent that they are teachable, what we already said about skills training applies; but the idea of expansion and the capacity to expand has some special, additional relevance to the problem of dealing with change.

Of the four approaches to avoiding the stress of change, the self-expansion approach makes us least enthusiastic about avoiding change itself. On that point we have the agreement of Hans Selye, who introduced us all to the idea of stress. He defined stress as "the nonspecific response of the body to any demand made upon it" (1974, p. 14). In other words, Selye equated the stress response with the physical response to any change. He added that when we say someone is "under stress," we "actually mean under excessive stress or distress . . . [because] stress is not something to be avoided. In fact, it is evident from the definition . . . that it can't be avoided" (p. 19). "The majority of people would suffer just as much from the boredom of purposeless existence . . . . The majority of people equally dislike a lack of stress and an excess of it" (p. 68).

This can be put in our own terms as follows. People seek to expand themselves by experiencing as much change and novelty as is comfortable—but no more. Avoiding change is an especially poor approach to life because, as we have said, past experience with change (past expansion) increases our capacity to be comfortable with change and expand from it in the future. To enjoy change, one must be expanded. To be expanded, one must enjoy, or at least be open to change—not avoid it.

Nowhere is this analysis more apt than in relationships. People want change in their relationships. It keeps a relationship alive, by promising new opportunities for self-expansion. Yet members of relationships are naturally also fearful of change, and even though they know that trying to avoid it only invites a backlash, they must resist it if they feel threatened. This brings us to the second solution—not perceiving change as a stress.

Cofer and Appley (1964) define psychological stress as a perceived threat to the integrity of the self. Lazarus (1974) reemphasizes the point by citing evidence that even the response to physical trauma is decided by the psychological interpretation of it. These explain the tremendous variation in the response of different people to the "same" event—for example, a spouse's bad mood or a child's misconduct.

From the self-expansion perspective, the appropriateness of one's response to change is mainly determined by one's capacity to integrate it. Capacity to integrate can vary with where one is in the expansion-integration cycle, e.g., if one is already overwhelmed with one or more expansion experiences yet to be integrated, integration of yet another change may be hampered. However, most of one's capacity to integrate (and thus make an appropriate response) would appear to depend on having varied and flexible cognitive structures near the surface of one's cognitive hierarchy, plus deeper structures that are relatively untouched by change. Both types of structures would seem to be the result of a great deal of past expansion.

This general factor, degree of experience at integrating novelty, has been suggested by Piaget (1963), among others. It is also suggested by the data on general education and a *variety* of coping mechanisms being most useful for coping with stress (Pearlin & Schooler, 1978).

The importance of this general factor for relationships is suggested by the apparent association of education (but not occupation) with marital satisfaction

(Locksley, 1982); and the apparent importance for marital outcome of cognitive complexity (Segraves, 1982; Crouse et al., 1968), ego development (Swensen et al., 1981), and intelligence (Terman & Oden, 1959). All these general indicators of what we would call expansion and expansion capacity involve, again, ample experience on the basis of deep stability, so that the self can expand with and integrate a new experience rather than fear that the change will de-expand or disintegrate the self.

Once again we must add that the basic capacity to expand also seems to be enhanced by the pure consciousness experience. This is sometimes described by experiencers as an experience of the "nonchanging, unchangeable self" (Maharishi, 1969). Thus to the degree that one can maintain this experience in the face of change, one views change with deep equanimity. The deepest aspect of the self (the "I") cannot be threatened because it cannot be changed, in any way. At levels closer to the surface there may be sadness, anger, fear, cool logic, empathy, or whatever response is most appropriate, according to the requirements of the environment; but the deepest aspect of the self is untouched. This is what Socrates meant by being a philosopher. When one *knows* the unchanging forms, especially the most central, the Form of the Good—one fears nothing, not even the hemlock.

A third way to avoid the stress associated with change was to enhance coping mechanisms, and, to the extent that coping is a skill, what we said about the self-expansion approach in relation to communication and relationship skills applies here. To the extent that coping mechanisms are more like personality traits, they are affected by one's level of expansion and capacity to integrate new expansion and then act, from a broader knowledge base.

As for the fourth solution, preparing for and recovering from the effects of stressful changes, this too requires enough breadth of awareness, through self-expansion, to be aware of the effects of stress and what ameliorates them. Maddi (1982), as part of his research with Kobasa on "hardiness" (Kobasa et al., 1982), has found that healthy, creative, successful people—the type of people who are often more expanded—tend to exercise more and in other ways protect themselves better from stress, both physiologically and psychologically.

However, one of the most strikingly effective ways of applying this fourth solution seems to be (again!) the pure consciousness experience. Hans Selye (1975) described its physiological correlates to be "exactly opposite to those . . . characteristic of the effort to meet the demands of stress," and said its strongest therapeutic effects "are most evident in those conditions known as 'diseases of stress' or diseases of adaptation' (especially mental, cardiovascular, gastrointestinal, and hypersensitivity ailments)" (p. ix-x). Other reviews of the TM research literature point to the same conclusion (Aron & Aron, 1979; Kanellakos, 1978).

One concern sometimes voiced about Eastern viewpoints is they may encourage a passive approach to stressors, i.e., acceptance, indifference, and letting everything remain the same. According to Vedic psychology, however, this passive attitude is not only an obstacle to the growth of consciousness, but an impossible goal. "Not by abstaining from action does one achieve non-action; nor by mere renunciation does one attain to perfection. No one, indeed, can exist for an instant without performing action; for everyone is helplessly driven to activity . . . Action is indeed superior to inaction" (Bhagavad-Gita, Ch. 3, vv 5-8).

Still, there appears to have been considerable passivity in the East—in the past, at least. One explanation is that it came from that natural human desire to expand.

People decided to imitate how they thought those with inner experiences of stability in the midst of change would probably act, speak, eat, and even breathe! In particular, they thought that such an inner equanimity must arise from not caring about or responding to the outer world. In fact, it does not, according to the research we have been citing and according to Vedic psychology. This misunderstanding has had unfortunate results: In Maharishi's (1969) words, this trained detachment "has helped to bring dullness, artificiality, and tension to life. . . . It has spoiled the brilliance of many a genius in every generation for centuries past. As a consequence, there has grown up in intelligent levels of society throughout the world a kind of fear of the spiritual life" (p. 156). Such a fear is sad, but understandable.

THE OTHER'S POOR
MENTAL OR PHYSICAL HEALTH

O's lack or loss of mental or physical health may create nearly insurmountable barriers to P's expansion through O if it eliminates or makes unavailable the valued aspects of O. O's disability may close avenues of expansion outside the relationship as well. Examples are alcoholism, senility, physical illness or handicap, retardation, psychoses, and neuroses (extremely low self-esteem, overdependence or fear of dependence, obsessive-compulsive behavior, unrealistic jealousy, etc.). Besides the stress these situations produce for both P and O, they often strongly motivate P, the nondisabled member, to leave even the most normatively involuntary relationship.

Suggested Solutions in the Literature

We are aware of no very interesting theories, much less good solutions to these types of obstacles. P simply needs O's recovery. If this is impossible, few professionals care to venture to make the decision—a very personal, moral one—as to whether the healthy member should stay or go.

Characteristically, Guggenbuhl-Craig (1977/1981) reminds us that these situations may provide an opportunity to make sacrifices:

> The willingness to sacrifice, the joy of sacrifice, the readiness to sacrifice have all taken on, in certain circles, an obscene connotation. This does not change the fact that the sacrifice of something very dear to us appears to be indispensable for individuation, for the salvation of the soul. (p. 109)

> Many marriages break up because the idea of sacrifice is rejected, and in this connection many analyses and psychotherapies have profoundly disturbing effects on marriage. In the name of the full development of the individual personality, of individual wholeness, the individuation marriage is sacrificed. (pp. 111–112)

Disabilities in the Other and Self-Expansion

Once again, we would apply everything we have said so far to this problem: the importance of skills, learned and applied by an expanded person; and the importance of cognitive complexity, moral development, and the like—all qualities that we have associated with being expanded. Within the broader vision of an expanded self, change—even tragedy, as in Brickman et al.'s (1978) study of paralyzed accident victims–has a better chance of being integrated, or somehow accepted at some level, as part of the changing world, which can never truly touch the deepest self within.

We would only add, with our usual optimism, that there is some promising evidence that if the affected O can and will experience pure consciousness, some disabilities might be ameliorated. The experience has been associated with reductions in alcoholism and drug addiction (Aron & Aron, 1980); neuroticism (Dick, 1974; Ferguson & Gowan, 1976); psychoses (Glueck & Stroebel, 1975); stress-related illnesses (E. Aron & A. Aron, 1979); and the aging process itself (Wallace et al., 1982).

In conclusion, if P chooses to stay in a relationship with a disabled O, P is going to need the patience, tolerance, and breadth of vision that would seem to come with an expanded self. If P chooses to leave, on the other hand, P may need almost as much of the same qualities.

SOCIAL STRESSORS

The list is long–discrimination, poverty, neighborhood crime, overcrowded housing, violent social and political upheavals, unpleasant or dangerous working conditions, unemployment, pollution, cultural disintegration, and social norms that conflict with one's personality.

Poverty and dicrimination probably strain relationships the most. Being poor and/or of a minority is particularly associated with low marital satisfaction (Renne, 1970), and friendship for such a person tends to be forced into a more utilitarian mold (Allan, 1977). Even the number of parent-child relationships becomes more a matter of practicality than preference (Hoffman & Hoffman, 1973).

Suggested Solutions in the Literature

The solutions most frequently offered involve changes in society to make it less stressful and more supportive of relationships, especially of family life (Etzioni, 1977). Examples are better housing, health care, and education; more jobs; a higher minimum wage; and various social services. In addition it is frequently suggested that the entire social structure must change, or at least the attitude of society towards the family and other close relationships, if these relationships are to survive.

Obviously, societies are finding that adequate amounts of any of these solutions are too elusive or too costly, even if long-term costs in some cases may prove to be higher. Thus, many of the stressors in this category remain for the individuals involved to deal with, calling forth the current solutions to problems of stress mentioned in the section under changes in relationships. One can learn to avoid stress, relish it, manage it, or recover from it quickly. Clearly among individuals and relationships there are many casualties.

Social Stressors and Self-Expansion

There is a disheartening circularity to social problems: Those not under stress (because they cope so well, are so expanded) already possess the qualities necessary to cope with stress, while the same qualities elude those who most need them.

One way to break this cycle lies in the less stressed helping the more stressed. Those who are more expanded do seem to do this: Maslow (1968) found self-actualized people to be more humanitarian, and according to Vedic psychology, the experience of pure consciousness makes a person's actions more and more "in response to the needs of the time; they fulfill the demands of their surroundings; [they arise from a] desire for 'the welfare of the world' " (Maharishi, 1969, p. 218).

Vedic psychology also suggests two other ways to break this vicious social stressor cycle. One, of course, is to provide the experience of pure consciousness to those segments of society most stuck in this cycle. While one might think they would be the least likely to enjoy or benefit from meditation, studies of juvenile offenders (e.g., Aron & Aron, in press) and of prisoners (e.g., Abrams & Siegel, 1978) indicate that they are highly motivated to continue the practice, they improve on objective measures, and they reduce their maladaptive attitudes and behaviors.

Another Vedic approach to social problems is for more people—any people—to have the experience. There is some very provocative evidence that the pure consciousness experience, if experienced by as little as 1% of a community, may actually have measurable positive effects on social problems (e.g., A. Aron & E. Aron, 1981; Dillbeck, Landrith & Orme-Johnson, 1981).

External stressors are definitely obstacles to expansion in relationships, and their effects cannot be ignored. Expansion requires resources, and the distribution of resources is not perfect, to say the least. Whatever the system, its success is largely determined by the quality of people making the decisions—their expansion, their breadth of vision, their coherence. Given that the decision makers are not yet all enjoying these qualities, there are going to be social obstacles to expansion. These must be removed by whoever can do it. The greater one's self-expansion, the more creative will be one's assaults on the barriers to human expansion.

ALTERNATIVES TO THE RELATIONSHIP

Alternative relationship partners, or activities (such as career pursuits), or life-styles (such as singleness) are frequent reasons for the ending of relationships. The importance of this factor is suggested by results of a two-year longitudinal study by Udry (1981) of 400 urban white couples. For these couples, a spouse's belief that if the relationship ended he or she would do as well or better with a different partner or lifestyle was a better predictor of subsequent breakup than marital satisfaction.

Similarly, Duck (1982) has found that members of a relationship consider alternatives constantly, and especially when there is trouble in the relationship.

No doubt the consideration of alternatives is usually the result, not the cause of trouble; but perhaps not always. Relationships seem to be more successful as well as longer lasting when social norms of loyalty to friends, family, and dependents are strong, so that barriers to even the consideration of alternatives are high. For example, among those who consider themselves religious (and presumably feel more constrained about alternatives because of their marriage vows), divorces are not only fewer, but marriages and families are experienced (Campbell, 1981) and judged by others (Stinnett & Sauer, 1977) to be happier.

Of course, the opportunity to expand through an alternative does not always conflict with maintaining a relationship. However, even adult friendship, probably the most voluntary and least exclusive "loving" relationship in our culture, may develop into a commitment, with the added expectations of loyalty and some degree of exclusivity. As Reisman (1979) found in reviewing most of those writing on the topic of friendship over the centuries, there is a strong feeling that an individual can only have one truly close friend at a given time.

Suggested Solutions in the Literature

The traditonal solution to the problem of alternatives is strong social norms against opting for them.

A more modern, "open market" solution is for the existing relationship to compete with alternatives: Spouses work to make themselves more fascinating; family life is portrayed as more rewarding than the single life; old friends are "gold" and new ones only "silver," to quote a children's song.

One can also personally choose to avoid contact with alternatives. Much as an alcoholic might avoid bars, caretakers of infants might simply choose to avoid college catalogs or employment want ads for a year or two.

Yet another proposed solution is to maintain both the alternative and the present relationship. At a younger age, children are found to insist upon exclusivity in their friendships; at an older age they do not (Reisman, 1979). Such a "maturing" is also suggested as possible for adults in marriage (O'Neill & O'Neill, 1972), although "open marriage" does not appear to be very successful in our culture (for a review, see Hatfield & Walster, 1978).

As for alternatives besides other relationships, a few people seem to manage two or more of what for many would be complete lifestyles: marriage, career, parent, athlete, artist, aesthete, world traveler—the possibilities in this culture are very rich. In some cases this Renaissance-person, smorgasbord approach seems to work, but there is evidence that marriage, at least, requires considerable concentration to achieve the current cultural ideal of happiness, intimacy, and mutual support of, for instance, Cuber & Harroff's (1965) "total" and "vital" marriages. In fact, those few marriages in the Burgess and Wallin (1953) data that did not decline in satisfaction with time were those in which the husband had *lost* money within the last 15 years and *dropped out* of community activities (Dizard, 1968).

Alternatives and Self-Expansion

When barriers are put between individuals and possible opportunities to expand, individuals tend to circumvent those barriers. There may be some attendant guilt, but Cuber and Harroff's (1965) couples illustrate the point. Even among their sample of mainly "pillars of the community," there were many private affairs and public divorces, and much neglect of spouses for the sake of careers.

Perhaps an ideal solution to alternatives, and one of the major plots of movies and novels, is that P test the alternatives and still prefer O. (Stereotypically, O is a sweet, wholesome, upright individual, while the alternative is steamy and sophisticated.) The plot is almost as satisfying when P finds the alternative to be better, and goes for it—while O and the others left behind bear P no hard feelings (or deserved to be hurt anyway). The home-is-best solution is the favorite, however, because there usually *are* hard feelings. Also, it is traditionally felt that one can anticipate more satisfaction and expansion (and avoid de-expansion) in the long run by valuing one's "sweetheart" and family over mere pleasure or success, and by developing qualities of loyalty, trustworthiness, commitment, responsibility, and the like.

So the preferred plot involves a heroic P who comes to value as good what is socially right. P then *wants* to do what has to be done and what the other people involved want and need done. The movie *Casablanca*, with perhaps one of the best-loved plots in our culture, involves just such a bittersweet solution.

How can one achieve this outcome when the alternative rears its attractive head? We emphasize, again, the importance of being expanded and the resulting greater capacity for expansion. In this case, the greater competence would serve to enhance the ability to consciously evaluate alternatives in light of one's long-term goals. A broad vision of one's life over time makes one spontaneously delay gratification, and when one has included many aspects of many others into the self, one spontaneously takes friends, family, community, and world into account in making decisions. An understanding and experience of an inner source of happiness and fulfillment (pure consciousness) might put alternatives still more into perspective.

Why does the romantic ideal seem to be that P test the alternative—either mentally or, to make a good story, by having an adventure or affair—and then return to O? Because this process results in P's greatest expansion (knowledge) of P's self and social environment. The audience knows from experience that the solution will last longer than one caused by external prohibitions. The same point is made by research on the "inoculation effect" of presenting both sides of an argument to create a lasting attitude, resistant to change (McGuire, 1964), even though presenting only one side creates the quickest initial change when the recipient is unaware of alternatives.

Relevant here is a study (Aron & Aron, 1983) of the processes that might account for the well-documented association of the pure consciousness experience with reduced drug use (for a review, see Siegel, 1981). In this study, most meditators described a gradual decline in their use of alcohol, tobacco, and prescribed and nonprescribed drugs. For some the decline took place over months and sometimes years, during which time they experimented by comparing how they felt with and without the substances in their bodies. Their final level of use (usually non-use) was based, they felt, on an internal, physical sensitization to the detrimental effects of the drugs, which had developed gradually with their continued TM practice. (A number of factors ruled out social influence as an important cause for most respondents.) This process strikingly contrasts with the "cold-turkey"-under-social-pressure approach so often employed to control addictions, including addictions to alternative relationships!

Of course relationships are not drugs—though some say they are addictive—but the study by Duck (1982) did suggest that we frequently review our relationships and weigh them against alternatives, much as these meditators seemed to have weighed their various internal physical states. When a choice is made on the basis of noticing the subtle inner effects of alternatives rather than on the basis of social or physical threats of de-expansion, it seems likely that it will be a more satisfying and lasting decision.

One final note: Sometimes, despite P's awareness of the costs, the alternative is better; or at least it appears to be, as P comprehends the situation. Then, in light of the self-expansion motive, we predict that P will choose the alternative. Inevitably, we want more and more for ourselves. If the result is pain for O and many others, then our best hope is that our tastes as to what we want more of will be based, in time, on broader perceptions of what our self includes.

10

Optimal Relationships

INTRODUCTION

Throughout this book we have discussed data, observations, and speculations about happy, satisfying relationships—perhaps not enough, but some. This chapter reviews these, plus additional ideas and data, in order to put together a picture of optimal loving relationships. We realize that using an image of any ideal can be unrealistic and irrelevant, as well as frustrating. On the other hand, descriptions of limiting or ideal cases can provide important theoretical and practical insights; so here goes.

First we review those few studies that have focused on trying to identify and understand optimal relationships, mostly strong families and happy marriages. Then we consider studies that have found single variables that distinguish happy relationships from the less happy. Next we turn to theories of optimal relationships, and finally we look at optimal relationships in the light of the idea of self-expansion.

STUDIES OF OPTIMAL RELATIONSHIPS

The study of optimal relationships began with large-scale questionnaire studies of "marital adjustment" and "marital happiness" (e.g., Burgess & Cottrell, 1939; Kirkpatrick, 1937; Locke, 1951; Terman, 1938). It also received an impetus from clinical psychology with the efforts to distinguish the families of disturbed children from those of normals (for reviews, see Jacob, 1975; Lytton, 1971; Riskin & Faunce, 1972). Finally, more recently, a few studies have focused on those relationships that stood out as optimal in the opinion of clinicians or other professionals.

Stinnett and Sauer (1977) administered questionnaires to 99 "strong families" identified by Oklahoma's county extension service home economists. The selection criteria were apparent high degrees of happiness in both the husband-wife and parent-child relationships as judged by the home economicsts, and ratings of "satisfactory" or "very satisfactory" for these relationships by the family members themselves.

From responses to the open-ended questions, Stinnett and Sauer distilled four main characteristics of these families: "(a) expression of appreciation of each other, (b) willingness to spend time together and participate in activities together, (c) good communication patterns, and (3) commitment to a religious life style" (p. 9).

Lewis et al. (1976) began by studying differences between families with and without psychiatrically labeled children. The families were rated by trained clinicians making blind observations from videotapes of the families' interaction while carrying out a variety of structured tasks. This procedure was then later applied to an extensive comparison of six families identified by the clinicians as "optimal" and six families judged "adequate." Ten characteristics were said to distinguish optimal families:

1. There is "not a single thread. . . . Competence must be considered a tapestry, reflecting differences in degrees along many dimensions" (p. 206).
2. Caring and trust.
3. "Respect for subjective views . . . free to be open and honest in agreement or disagreement and they did not speak for each other" (p. 207).
4. "Belief in complex motivations" (p. 208), as shown by flexibility in the pattern of problem-solving approaches and in the power structure.
5. "High levels òf initiative" (p. 208).
6. Power structure that included a strong (but internally egalitarian) parental coalition with clear leadership qualities, and "closeness," "respectful negotiation," and general flexibility about the distribution of power. Although they did not use the term, their description of the relation to children is similar to Baumrind's (1971) "authoritative parents."
7. High levels of "personal autonomy."
8. "A family mythology" congruent with reality.
9. Open expression of affection.
10. Many other variables, e.g., "spontaneity," "humor," "involvement."

Mudd and Taubin (1982) have reported a 20-year, ongoing questionnaire study of 100 "successful" families. As of 1979, 59 families, then in late middle age, responded to follow-up and showed qualities of pragmatic flexibility, an egalitarian marital relationship, democratic family structure, close friendships outside the home, community involvement, satisfaction with marriage and family life, and optimism about the future.

Finally, Cuber and Harroff's (1965) study of stable marriages among the affluent identified and described a minority, alas, of what they called intrinsic (as opposed to utilitarian) marriages. These could be called optimal in that they seemed to fulfill the cultural ideal of marriage as an intimate, loving, deeply committed and involving relationship. They were described with great enthusiasm by their members. (However, some of the couples in the more utilitarian marriages—the passive-congenials in particular—reported that their relationships were also optimal, for their needs.)

Among the intrinsic marriages, Cuber and Harroff described two types, which seemed to vary mostly in degree of intimacy. In the "vital" marriages, "the mates are intensely bound together psychologically in important life matters." There is an "exciting mutuality of feelings. . . . An activity is flat and uninteresting if the spouse is not part of it" (p. 39). The "total" relationship is simply even "more multifaceted. . . . In some cases all of the important life foci are vitally shared" (p. 40). "It is as if neither spouse has, or has had, a truly private existence" (p. 41).

Taken together, the various studies of successful marriages and families suggest relationships characterized by deep involvement, plus caring and appreciation. Otherwise, there is very little overlap among the descriptions; or as Lewis et al. (1976) wrote, "There is no single thread" (p. 206).

In the area of friendship, Reisman (1979) has reviewed not only recent data but traditional descriptions of friendships. He distinguishes reciprocal, receptive (when P looks up to O), and associative (formed through work or other nonvoluntary exposure to O) friendships. In most cultures the reciprocal friendship is the ideal: "An enduring relationship based on mutual respect and affection, within which there is a freedom to speak one's mind that is singular" (p. 59).

We know of no empirical studies of optimal friendships. Reisman points out differences in ideals for friendships across the lifespan and in different cultures. From his own questionnaire studies and reviews of the other scattered research on friendship, Reisman found friendship in the United States to be greatly affected by mobility. He felt that his respondents held the usual ideal of a close, reciprocal friendship, but seldom achieved it, at least in their middle years. However, Campbell (1981) found in his quality-of-life surveys that five out of six people had a "confidante," a friend (or relative not living with them) with whom they "would feel comfortable discussing just about any private problem. . . no matter how personal it might be" (pp. 105–106). When asked about their friendships generally, fewer than one in ten were dissatisfied with the quality of their friendships.

We know of only one study of any variables distinguishing satisfying friendships from less satisfying ones: Reis (1982) found that personal interactions by either sex with a woman are associated with less loneliness than interactions by either sex with a man. (The opportunities for debate here are too numerous for us to even begin to explore!)

The studies of optimal parent-child relationships are usually evaluated in terms of outcome, not satisfaction. For example, Baumrind (1971) does not focus on how satisfying it is for parent or child to be in a permissive, authoritarian, or authoritative relationship!

Therefore, to get from the available data a picture of optimal, enduring relationships, we are again left with studies of marriage.

COMPARISONS
ON ONE VARIABLE

There are many, many studies of the interpersonal correlates or predictors of marital happiness, and they have revealed a wide variety of variables that discriminate significantly between happy and unhappy couples. In a review of this literature, Lewis and Spanier (1979) summarized the findings under five general attributes associated with marital quality: positive regard, emotional gratification, effective communication, role fit, and amount of interaction.

We cannot attempt to consider all of this literature, but we have selected a few of the stronger studies in order to try, from this angle, to get a feeling for the nature of better relationships.

The communication of happy couples is more pleasant and, interestingly, less predictable (less like a script). For example, Gottman (1979, 1982; Levenson &

Gottman, 1983)—using various systems of coding interaction sequences, facial expressions, and psychophysiological changes—has compared the communication pattern of couples scoring high on a marital satisfaction measure and not reporting marital problems to that of unsatisfied couples "having difficulty." He has found less negativity and also less "negative reciprocity" (responding to a negative expression with another negative) in the happy group, as well as much less predictability in the sequencing of statements. Physiological indicators are very different, with happier couples showing less "linkage" (simultaneous variation or inverse variation).

Gottman has also found that all these differences are accentuated when couples discuss their problems. Describing the overall affect of communications, Gottman (1982) concluded very succinctly that "unhappy marriages are nastier." Also, people in happy marriages seem happy to talk to each other.

Lewis et al. (1976) also noted both positivity and unpredictability in the communications of their "optimal families."

Markman (1981) found that more positive communications before marriage predicted happier marriages five years later. Very many other studies have found good communication skills related to marriage happiness.

The communication of affection seems especially important. For example, Fiore and Swensen (1977) compared satisfied, nonclinic couples with dissatisfied, clinic couples and found that the latter group scored lower on all six of Swensen's categories of love behaviors except unexpressed feelings. (Interestingly, the two groups did not differ in their expectations for love in marriage, but only in the degree to which their expectations were being fulfilled.)

Many have noted that happy couples handle conflicts better (e.g., Gottman, 1979; Levenson & Gottman, 1983; Margolin & Wampold, 1981, Yelsma, 1981).

Besides evidence for positive communication, evidence for overall positivity in optimal relationships creeps into almost all results. There is more positivity in speech and gestures (e.g., Margolin & Wampold, 1981; Noller, 1982); about life (Yelsma, 1981); in response to each other's troubles and complaints (Cousins & Vincent, 1983); about how well each thinks he or she knows the other's thoughts (Siegel, 1982); and about each other's personalities—even to the point of being "unrealistic" (Hall & Taylor, 1976; Preston et al., 1952). There is also more perceived consensus (Arias & O'Leary, 1981; Pineo, 1961).

Lack of negativity is yet another, apparently independent factor, which may be even more important than positivity (e.g., Cousins & Vincent, 1983; Gottman, 1979).

All of these factors tend to describe the qualities of the relationship as much or more than the qualities of the members, although they certainly are not usually independent. Personality differences among happy and unhappy spouses as groups are not very clear, except that, as we mentioned in the previous chapter, certain patterns may be incompatible.

However, Crouse et al. (1968) pointed out that the failure to find personality differences between the happily and unhappily married may be due to focusing too much on the content of personality (traits, attitudes, etc.), when actually the structure of personality may be what matters. Structure, in their research, was defined as "integrative complexity," or cognitive "adaptivity," which makes a person "a flexible explorer of his world. . . . He does not close fast under uncertainty and is attuned, adaptive, and sensitive to environmental change. He is capable of entertaining and processing alternative explanations of an event and seeks diversity and discrepant information in his information processing" (p.643).

Crouse et al. studied 42 couples who, as Princeton University faculty members and spouses, were "fairly homogeneous with respect to intelligence" (p. 644) and education. They found that marital satisfaction was significantly higher for those couples in which both spouses scored high on a measure of integrative complexity, compared to couples in which both scored low on the measure.

Using another measure that may assess personality "structure," Swensen et al. (1981) found that couples at the retirement stage of the life cycle who were also at a post-conformist level of ego-development, as measured by Loevinger and Wessler's (1970) scale, were happier than conformist couples at that stage—and nearly as happy as newlyweds.

As for the other, nonpsychological variables on which differences predict marital satisfaction—satisfaction is lower for minorities, the poor, and the less well educated (Renne, 1970), although these variables account for less variance than many have expected (Campbell, 1981). Nor does this mean there are large numbers of optimal marriages among wealthy, well-educated whites. Cuber and Harroff (1965) found very few intrinsically happy marriages among the affluent, even if after ten years the spouses had claimed to have never considered divorce. Lewis and Spanier (1979) proposed that socioeconomic factors probably contribute only according to the couple's satisfaction with their life style and with their achievements in the area of income and occupation. Finally, that the relation of income to marital satisfaction is not simple is pointed up by Dizard's (1968) finding that the few couples in Burgess and Wallin's (1953) data who became happier over time were those whose income (and the husband's involvement in community organizations) had declined.

Finally, Terman and Oden (1959) found in Terman's longitudinal study of a gifted group of Californians (those scoring high on intelligence tests while in school) that of those who had married by midlife, 85% scored above average on a test of marital happiness.

Thus far, in looking at specific variables, we have found that satisfying relationships are characterized by positive and unpredictable communication, skill at conflict resolution, communication of affection, general positivity, and a lack of negativity. As for the individuals in these relationships, they tend to be more cognitively complex, ego-developed, and intelligent.

Optimal relationships also appear to flourish among individuals labeled with yet another optimal trait—self-actualization. In the process of studying this characteristic, Maslow (1950/1973) looked at the relationships (marriage, kin, and friendship) of self-actualizing people and reported, "They are capable of more fusion, greater love, more perfect identification, more obliteration of the ego boundaries than other people would consider possible." However, this may be possible because "the opposite members in these relationships are ordinarily (about two-thirds of the cases) also self-actualizing persons. There is high selectiveness here considering the small proportion of such people in the general population." Finally, Maslow notes that "self-actualizing people have these especially deep ties with rather few individuals" (p. 192). We will consider Maslow's ideas about the cognitive basis of optimal relationships when we turn to theories of optimal relationships.

Mahrer (1982) seems to capture the flavor of the relationships of self-actualizing individuals with special eloquence: "The ability to fuse or blend with another person is a mark of the highest plateau of intimacy, from the perspective of humanistic thinking. . . . No longer are such persons constrained within fixed boundaries or static domains" (pp. 150–151).

However, with this type of description (obviously so close to our own thinking about self-expansion) we begin to move from data to the theory of what is really going on inside the most satisfying long-term relationships.

THEORIES

In applying general systems theory to the family, Speer (1970), Buckley (1967), and Beavers (1976) have all suggested that the healthy family is open and interactive, as well as stable and having clear boundaries. Speer quotes Sonne as saying that a social system "which is not growing is as if dead" (p. 270). According to Beavers, the healthiest families have a "clear and flexible" structure.

From the psychodynamic viewpoint, Reik (1949) says that a satisfying, long-term love relationship occurs if and when both partners move gracefully beyond the passion of falling in love (which is bound to end once reality breaks down P's idealization of O—or, in Reik's terms, the projection of P's ego ideal). If anything is left after the burning passion, it will be "an afterglow," from which a "new kind of companionship" arises, based on reality and characterized by "ease and harmony." There is a "mutual identification and common experiences, joy and grief that bind two people more intimately together than romance ever did" (p. 92).

Other psychoanalytic theorists (e.g., Segraves, 1982) also see the transference phenomenon as a sort of mirage standing in the way of couples getting to their real goal, but it is hard for them to describe what the basis of this better, enduring relationship might be. Jung (1925/1959) said that it can only occur in the second half of life, when one is no longer the slave of biological and social demands. At this point some individuals, but not all, will begin on the "inner integration" of the conscious and unconscious. The marriage both benefits from and helps in this interaction. However, the process is not easily described, much less taught: "The secret of psychic development can never be betrayed, simply because that development is a question of individual capacity" (p. 544).

The other Jungian we have been citing, Guggenbuhl-Craig (1977/1981), said that successful marriage today requires understanding the nature of marriage as a path to "salvation" rather than mere "well-being." Those interested in such a path should know that great determination and sacrifice will be required of the optimal married couple, but the benefits will be great.

Reward or social exchange theories imply that an optimal relationship would maximize both members' rewards and minimize their costs. Further, for both members, relationship outcomes would exceed their internal comparison of the relationship to their ideal, and also to their alternatives.

Role theory implies that an optimal relationship would involve minimal role conflicts. That is, members would be in roles that were not internally contradictory as defined by society and that did not conflict with their other roles, with society's expectations, or with their own personalities, goals, or abilities.

Some ideas about optimal relationships can also be found in studies of cognitive processes. Both Crouse et al. (1968) and Segraves (1982) suggested the centrality of cognitive complexity for marital happiness, and cognitive explanations are also found in the humanistic viewpoint of Rogers (1972). In fact, the major theory about the basis of optimal loving relationships comes from the humanistic-cognitive theory of Abraham Maslow (1962).

Maslow posits two cognitive styles: "Being-motivated" (B-cognition) and "Deficiency-motivated" (D-cognition). In relationships, these give rise to B- versus D-love. In B-love, P loves O for O's qualities—it is almost an aesthetic appreciation of O. In D-love, P loves O for what O can provide P. Maslow provides a long list of differences between the two kinds of love, which we have summarized below.

B-love	D-love
gets stronger	is eventually sated
is nonpossessive	is possessive
is always good for O	produces some anxiety or hostility
allows P to really see O	is blind
is richer, "higher," more valuable	

Yet another inspired description of love comes from Lee's (1977) *agape* love, one of the six types he has identified. Agape love is said to be always patient and kind, never demanding anything in return. It is described in all the major religions, but, according to Lee, he never found it in its pure form among the Americans, Canadians, and Britons he interviewed!

On the whole, in our opinion, the standard theories about relationships—social exchange theory, role theory, systems theory, and psychodynamic theories—are rather uninspired on the topic of the optimal relationship. Perhaps this is because of a lack of data, perhaps a lack of optimism, or perhaps it comes from kindness. For the most striking thing about optimal relationships is that, even if a Maslow or Lee describes the ideal, *no one* volunteers to instruct us how to achieve it. True, the data suggest that, at a minimum, communication needs to be positive and affectionate, and the relationship needs to be central to the lives of those involved. However, is a happy relationship the result of people wanting to be together and communicating positively? Or does the happy relationship cause them to be positive and involved? Or is it that the positive behaviors and intimate feelings arise from the individuals themselves, because they are intelligent, cognitively complex, self-actualized, or whatever? And if individuals make the difference, how in heck do they get like that?

Berscheid and Walster (1978) expressed the frustration nicely: "While all of us can aspire to love another simply for the other's 'being' rather than for the satisfactions the other provides, only very few exceptional, 'self-actualized' individuals may ever actually experience such love" (pp. 156–157).

Another possibility is that all our ideals about how we ought to love one another are really only instruments of self-torture. As Guggenbuhl-Craig (1977/1981) said about marriage and the family,

If, using great psychological acuity, one were to dream up a social institution that would be unable to function in every case and which was meant to torment its members, one would certainly invent the contemporary marriage and the institution of today's family. (pp. 9-10)

OPTIMAL RELATIONSHIPS AND SELF-EXPANSION

The Nature of Love

Trying to feel B-love and trying to stay married until "death do us part" may well be torture—but these are still very widespread human ideals. In that sense if in no other, the ideals are real. When we think of close, loving relationships—when we think of love—we think of acting spontaneously and joyously on the other's behalf, whatever our personal sacrifice.

Who fulfills these ideals of love? Apparently very few. The question then is, why did humans develop these ideals, these monstrous sources of frustration and guilt? Of what use are they when, as we have said throughout this book, humans also have an insatiable desire to expand the self—one's own self only—and to have more and more until one has *everything*. Is there any way to span this gulf between what one does for oneself and one's ideals about doing for others?

The answer, we think, is that there is no gulf at all. Self-expansion subsumes both "selfish" D-love and "self-actualizing" B-love, because both are for the self. To love for our own self-expansion seems to be the universal reason for all kinds of love. This idea should not be a great shock; even saints serve others and do penance to God out of a desire to save their own souls. (They certainly do not think that God's welfare, or the ultimate welfare of their fellow humans, depends on their own mortal efforts.)

Furthermore, far from being "bad," the self-expansion motive seems to be the most efficient way of arranging that humans grow in their "unselfish" concern for each other. As P includes more and more aspects of O, P eventually begins to think of O as an extension of P's self. P finds that when O is happy, successful, and so forth, P feels happier and more successful. P does not think of O's welfare *instead* of P's, but rather *as an extension of P's own.*

Thus P comes to consider O as almost the same as P's self, but as we described in Chapter 8 (on "getting tired of the other") P's desire to expand does not stop here. Although P may still be expanding through O, eventually this expansion will slow down. P does not want to hurt O (who is now almost like P's own self) or de-expand by leaving the relationship, therefore P—especially after having found this expansion with O to be so successful and satisfying—seeks to expand in still other ways. And other ways. And O does too, so as a result P finds O to be a "new" source for P's self-expansion; and the growth continues in the relationship. However, P *still* wants more.

We said that according to Vedic psychology P is actually working toward an end state in which each O, and everything, is felt to be included in the self. Vedic psychology calls this "unity consciousness." We also ventured to suggest that this state develops through repeated experiences of pure consciousness, or "tastes" of this oneness, and that even these tastes give P a feeling of unlimited expansion, and therefore of fulfillment. In addition, we cited evidence in Chapter 8 for the growth in meditators of the qualities that the literature associated with satisfying relationships. In part, the experience probably improves relationship satisfaction through the increases in intelligence, cognitive flexibility, and so forth, which it appears to develop. However, we think that in large part the experience optimizes a relationship merely by increasing P's inner happiness, so the relationship becomes a place to enjoy fulfillment, rather than to find it.

So perhaps Maslow was right—B-love is possible. In unity consciousness, when the self is fully "actualized," one does love the other for the other's essential Being—that Being being the same as one's own.

The Nature of Optimal Relationships

If love is something that grows through self-expansion, and relationships are substantial means of self-expansion, then relationships probably ought to be places where people can grow towards B-love—rather than suffer over its absence. Thus an optimal relationship is one in which growth is happening.

Looking again at the data on optimal relationships, we see a great deal of variation among these relationships (Lewis et al.'s 1976, "no single thread"), because people are different, and people make relationships. Some prefer to be very intimate, others more autonomous; some prefer to delve into each other's minds, others to share an active life. While the content or behaviors of an optimal relationship must vary according to the individuals involved, describing the form or process may be easier, which we will try here.

We think optimal relationships must develop three processes: a means of harmonizing differences, a means for both members to continue to feel expanded, and a means for each to develop a very broad, expanded perspective about their lives and relationship. While these processes probably arise most often in the early, middle, and later periods of a relationship, respectively, we think that all three need to be present to some degree during all phases. Also, the first probably depends most on the qualities of the individuals involved and the last probably receives a major input from the continued expansion provided by the relationship.

Concerning the first process: The very fact that all individuals differ implies much about the form and process necessary for an optimal relationship. To be attracted to O and to keep being attracted, P must sense differences or novel aspects to O that P can include into P's self and thereby enjoy self-expansion. *However,* there will be other differences that P definitely does not find attractive or cannot integrate, and these will have to be dealt with. In some relationships there will be fewer of these, and optimal relationships will often involve individuals who are to a high degree initially compatible. Nevertheless, every pair will have some differences to resolve, therefore an optimal relationship also must involve at least one member who is either good at communicating and resolving conflicts—or has the sense to get help. (In these ways optimal relationships avoid the problems, discussed in Chapter 9, of poor skills, of incompatibility, and, to some extent, of poor coping with change in each other. They also will have weathered the storms of high costs described by exchange theorists and of role conflicts described by role theorists.)

Second, with all their interesting differences thoroughly explored and their aversive differences somehow harmonized—and just when, as we have already said, P has come to love O almost as if O were P's own self—P almost inevitably feels bored with the relationship. Ah, the irony of it. P does need to expand, however, and apparently the relationship presents no more opportunities.

To overcome this difficulty, P and O will need to develop one or more of the solutions discussed in Chapter 8. In fact, optimal couples will probably discover all of them in time. They will continue to uncover subtle aspects of the other, to grow and offer new aspects to the other, and to appreciate all expansion experiences to a greater extent because of the other's presence. Above all, they will begin to recognize that no one and nothing can offer complete fulfillment. In order to be in a relationship, each must accept this limit with a person, eventually, and look *inside* for the abilities, understandings and/or experience that will maximize the self-expansion. They will recognize this fact not with bitterness, but with joy, for happiness is under their own control after all.

The consequences are great when the members of a long-term relationship are able to develop processes that resolve the immense problem of their desire for infinite self-expansion within a finite experience. In particular, only when people feel that they are expanding maximally will their attitude and behavior take on that elusive positive quality so much associated with successful relationships. (In addition to solving the problem of boredom, this second process, if it is achieved by lessening dependence on external events for happiness, will also help solve the problems of alternatives, social stressors, and ill health in the other.)

The third form or process found in optimal relationships is most elusive and undoubtedly most important for an optimal and *lasting* relationship—that somehow the members keep and grow in their perspective. The bigger this perspective, the better they are able to cope with change, with stress, with the seductiveness of alternatives, and with ill health, economic loss, whatever. We also think that the evidence on happiness and well-being suggests that the bigger the perspective, the greater the feeling of satisfaction with life.

We think that it is this expanded perspective in optimal relationships that is really being described by Stinnett and Sauer's (1977) factor of "appreciation" and "commitment to a religious lifestyle"; by Lewis et al.'s (1976) emphasis on "respect," "belief in complex motivations," and "a family mythology congruent with reality"; and by so many researchers' findings of flexibility, cognitive complexity, and ego development among the most satisfied members of relationships. Above all, we think that the more this process of expanding one's perspective achieves its effects, the closer P comes to B-love; to *agape* love; to Maher's description of "a lack of constraint"; to Reik's "new companionship," which binds people more intimately "than romance ever did"; to Jung's mysterious inner integration; and to Guggenbuhl-Craig's "salvation." This is heady stuff.

These three processes of optimal relationships—the integration of differences, the discovery of ways to expand maximally, and the growth of an expanded and expanding perspective—are already at work in expanded individuals. In short, we think that optimal relationships are made up of optimal (expanded) individuals. The relationship itself can contribute to this expansion. Flexibility, cognitive or integrative complexity, ego development, EEG coherence—they each touch on different causes/effects of expansion. It seems to us that if individuals and professionals want to do something more about creating optimal relationships, they may want to think more in terms of self-expansion, and do whatever is necessary to make this expansion process as rapid as possible.

References

Ables, B. S., & Brandsma, J. M. (1977). *Therapy for couples*. San Francisco: Jossey-Bass.

Abrams, A. I. (1977). The effects of meditation on elementary school students (Doctoral dissertation, University of California, 1976). *Dissertation Abstracts International, 37,* 5689A.

Abrams, A. I., & Siegel, L. M. (1978). The Transcendental Meditation program and rehabilitation at Folsom State Prison: A cross-validation study. *Criminal Justice and Behavior, 5,* 3-20.

Adams, J. S. (1965). Inequity in social exchange. In L. Berkowitz (Ed.), *Advances in experimental social psychology* (Vol. 2, pp. 267-299). New York: Academic Press.

Adey, W. R., Walter, D. O., & Hendrix, C. E. (1961). Computer techniques in correlation and spectral analyses of cerebral slow waves during discriminative behavior. *Experimental Neurology, 3,* 501-524.

Alexander, C. N. (1981, August). *Transcendental Meditation effects on ego development and personality validated in prisoners*. Paper presented at the annual convention of the American Psychological Association, Los Angeles.

Allan, G. (1977). Class variation in friendship patterns. *British Journal of Sociology, 28,* 389-393.

Alston, W. P. (1977). What is human agency? In T. Mischel (Ed.), *The self: Psychological and philosophical issues* (pp. 103-135). Totowa, NJ: Rowman & Littlefield.

Anderson, N. (1968). Likeableness ratings of 555 personality-trait words. *Journal of Personality and Social Psychology, 9,* 272-279.

Anderson, S. A., Russell, C. S., & Schumm, W. R. (1983). Perceived marital quality and family life-cycle categories: A further analysis. *Journal of Marriage and the Family, 45,* 127-138.

Aranya, S. H. (1963). *Yoga philosophy of Patanjali* (P. N. Mukerji, Trans.). Calcutta: Pooran Press.

Archer, R. L., & Burleson, J. A. (1980). The effects of timing of self-disclosure on attraction and reciprocity. *Journal of Personality and Social Psychology, 38,* 120-130.

Ard, B. N., Jr. (1976). The rational-emotive approach to marriage counseling. In B. N. Ard, Jr., & C. C. Ard (Eds.), *Handbook of marriage counseling* (2nd ed., pp. 103-108). Palo Alto CA: Science & Behavior Books.

Arias, I., & O'Leary, K. D. (1981, November). *Prediction accuracy, perceived similarity, and actual similarity in marital satisfaction*. Paper presented at the 15th annual convention of the Association for Advancement of Behavior Therapy, Toronto, Ontario.

Aron, A. (1970). *Relationship variables in human heterosexual attraction*. Unpublished doctoral dissertation, University of Toronto, Ontario.

Aron, A., Ain, R., Anderson, J. A., Burd, H., Filman, G., McCallum, R., O'Reilly, E., Rose, A., Stichmann, L., Tamari, Z., Wawro, J., Weinberg, L., & Winesauker, J. (1974). Relationships with opposite-sexed parents and mate choice. *Human Relations, 27,* 17-24.

Aron, A., & Aron, E. N. (1980). The Transcendental Meditation program's effect on addictive behavior. *Addictive Behaviors, 5,* 3–12.

Aron, A., & Aron, E. N. (1981). Evidence from Transcendental Meditation research for a social field. In W. J. Reckmeyer (Ed.), *General systems research and design: Precursors and futures* (pp. 316–322). Louisville, KY: Society for General Systems Research.

Aron, A., & Aron, E. N. (in press). Rehabilitation of juvenile offenders through the Transcendental Meditation program: The first controlled study. *Journal of Crime and Justice.*

Aron, A., & Dutton, D. G. (1983, April). *Falling in love: Personal accounts of recently experienced strong attractions.* Paper presented at the 75th annual meeting of the Southern Society for Philosophy and Psychology, Atlanta, GA.

Aron, A., Orme-Johnson, D., & Brubaker, P. (1981). The Transcendental Meditation program in the college curriculum: A four-year longitudinal study of effects on cognitive and affective functioning. *College Student Journal, 15,* 140–146.

Aron, E. N., & Aron, A. (1979). The Transcendental Meditation program for the reduction of stress-related conditions. *Journal of Chronic Diseases and Therapeutics Research, 3,* 11–21.

Aron, E. N., & Aron, A. (1981). Psychology's progress and the psychologist's personal experience. *Journal of Mind and Behavior, 2,* 397–406.

Aron, E. N., & Aron, A. (1982). Transcendental Meditation program and marital adjustment. *Psychological Reports, 51,* 887–890.

Aron, E. N., & Aron, A. (1983). The patterns of reduction of drug and alcohol use among Transcendental Meditation participants. *Bulletin of the Society of Psychologists in Addictive Behaviors, 2,* 28–33.

Aronson, E. (1969). The theory of cognitive dissonance: A current perspective. In L. Berkowitz (Ed.), *Advances in experimental social psychology* (Vol. 4, pp. 1–34). New York: Academic Press.

Aronson, E., Helmreich, R., & LeFan, J. (1970). To err is humanizing–sometimes: Effects of self-esteem, competence, and a pratfall on interpersonal attraction. *Journal of Personality and Social Psychology, 16,* 259–264.

Aronson, E., & Linder, D. (1965). Gain and loss of esteem as determinants of interpersonal attraction. *Journal of Experimental Social Psychology, 1,* 156–171.

Aronson, E., Willerman, B., & Floyd, J. (1966). The effect of a pratfall on increasing interpersonal attractiveness. *Psychonomic Science, 4,* 157–158.

Aronson, E., & Worchel, P. (1966). Similarity vs. liking as determinants of interpersonal attractiveness. *Psychonomic Science, 5,* 157–158.

Bahr, S. J., Chappell, C. B., & Leigh, G. K. (1983). Age at marriage, role enactment, role consensus, and marital satisfaction. *Journal of Marriage and the Family, 45,* 795–803.

Bank, S. P., & Kahn, M. D. (1982). The sibling bond. New York: Basic Books.

Banikiotes, P. G., & Neimeyer, G. J. (1981). Construct importance and rating similarity as determinants of interpersonal attraction, *British Journal of Social Psychology, 20,* 259–263.

Banquet, J. P. (1973). Spectral analysis of the EEG in meditation. *Electroencephalography and Clinical Neurophysiology, 35,* 143–151.

Banquet, J. P., & Sailhan, M. (1977). Quantified spectral analysis of sleep and Transcendental Meditation. In D. W. Orme-Johnson & J. T. Farrow (Eds.), *Scientific research on the Transcendental Meditation program: Collected papers* (Vol. 1, pp. 182–186). Livingston Manor NY: MIU Press.

Banta, T. J., & Hetherington, M. (1963). Relations between needs of friends and fiances. *Journal of Abnormal and Social Psychology, 69,* 401–404.

Basham, A. L. (1959). *The wonder that was India.* New York: Grove Press.

Bataille, G. (1962). *Eroticism* (M. Dalwood, Trans.). London: Calder.

Baumrind, D. (1971). Current patterns of parental authority. *Developmental Psychology Monograph, 4*(1, Pt. 2).

Beach, F. A., Le Boeuf, B. J. (1967). Coital behavior in dogs. 1. Preferential mating in the bitch. *Animal Behaviour, 15,* 546–558.

Beavers, W. R. (1976). A theoretical basis for family evaluation. In J. Lewis, R. W. Beavers, J. T Gossett, & V. A. Phillips, *No single thread* (pp. 46–81). New York: Brunner/Mazel.

Beavers, W. R., & Voeller, M. N. (1983). Family models: Comparing and contrasting the Olson Circumplex Model with the Beavers Systems Model. *Family Process, 22,* 85–98.

Bennett, J. E., & Trinder, J. (1976). Hemispheric laterality and cognitive style associated with Transcendental Meditation. *Psychophysiology, 14,* 293–296.

Bergler, E. (1946). *Unhappy marriage and divorce: A study of neurotic choice of marriage partners.* New York: International Universities Press.

Berl, E. (1924). *The nature of love* (F. Rothwell, Trans.). London: Chapman & Hall.

Berlyne, D. E. (1960). *Conflict, arousal, and curiosity.* New York: McGraw-Hill.
Berlyne, D. E. (1973). The vicissitudes of aplopathematic and thelematoscopic pneumatology (or the hydrography of hedonism). In D. E. Berlyne & K. B. Madsen (Eds.), *Pleasure, reward, and preference* (pp. 1–33). New York: Academic Press.
Bernstein, W. M., Stephenson, B. O., Snyder, M. L., & Wicklund, R. A. (1983). Causal ambiguity and heterosexual affiliation. *Journal of Experimental Social Psychology, 19,* 78–92.
Berscheid, E. (1983). Emotion. In H. H. Kelley, E. Berscheid, A. Christensen, J. H. Harvey, T. L. Huston, G. Levinger, E. McClintock, L. A. Peplau, & D. R. Peterson (Eds.), *Close Relationships* (pp. 110–168). New York: Freeman.
Berscheid, E., Dion, K., Walster, E., and Walster, G. W. (1971). Physical attractiveness and dating choice: A test of the matching hypothesis. *Journal of Experimental Social Psychology, 7,* 173–189.
Berscheid, E., & Walster, E. H. (1978). *Interpersonal attraction* (2nd ed.). Reading, MA: Addison-Wesley.
Bienvenu, J., Sr. (1970). Measurement of marital communication. *Family Coordinator, 19,* 26–31.
Binet, A. (1887). Le fetischisme dans l'amour [Fetishism in love]. *Revue philosophique, 24,* 260.
Birchler, G. R., Weiss, R. L., & Vincent, J. P. (1975). A multimethod analysis of social reinforcement exchange between maritally distressed and non-distressed spouse and stranger dyads. *Journal of Personality and Social Psychology, 31,* 349–360.
Bischof, N. (1975). A systems approach toward the functional connections of attachment and fear. *Child Development, 46,* 801–817.
Blau, P. (1964). *Exchange and power in social life.* New York: Wiley.
Bloom, B. (1976). *Human characteristics and school learning.* New York: McGraw-Hill.
Bloomfield, H. H., Cain, M. P., & Jaffe, D. T. (1975). *TM: Discovering inner energy and overcoming stress.* New York: Delacorte.
Bowen, M. (1976). The use of family theory in clinical practice. In B. N. Ard, Jr., & C. C. Ard (Eds.), *Handbook of marriage counseling* (2nd ed., pp. 109–138). Palo Alto, CA: Science & Behavior Books.
Bowlby, J. (1958). The nature of the child's tie to his mother. *International Journal of Psycho-Analysis, 39,* 350–373.
Brehm, J., Gatz, M., Goethals, G., McCrimmon, J., & Ward, L. (1978). Physiological arousal and interpersonal attraction. *JSAS: Catalogue of Selected Documents in Psychology, 8,* 63. (ms. #1724)
Brickman, P., Coates, D., & Janoff-Bulman, R. (1978). Lottery winners and accident victims: Is happiness relative? *Journal of Personality and Social Psychology, 36,* 917–927.
Bridges, J. W. (1935). *The meaning of love: A psychological analysis and interpretation.* Cambridge: Sci-Art.
Brink, J. H. (1977). Effect of interpersonal communication on attraction. *Journal of Personality and Social Psychology, 35,* 783–790.
Brockner, J., & Swap, W. C. (1976). Effects of repeated exposure and attitudinal similarity on self-disclosure and interpersonal attraction. *Journal of Personality and Social Psychology, 33,* 531–540.
Broderick, C., & Smith, J. (1979). The general systems approach to the family. In W. R. Burr, R. Hill, F. I. Nye, & I. L. Reiss (Eds.), *Contemporary theories about the family* (Vol. 2, pp. 112–129). New York: Free Press.
Bucke, R. M. (1969). *Cosmic consciousness: A study in the evolution of the human mind.* New York: Dutton. (Original work published 1901)
Buckley, W. (1967). *Sociology and modern systems theory.* Englewood Cliffs, NJ: Prentice-Hall.
Burgess, W. W., & Cottrell, L. S. (1939). *Predicting success or failure in marriage.* New York: Prentice-Hall.
Burgess, E. W., Locke, H. J., Thomes, M. M. (1963). *The Family.* New York: American Book.
Burgess, E. W., & Wallin, P. (1953). *Engagement and marriage.* Philadelphia: Lippincott.
Burns, T. (1973). A structural theory of social exchange. *Acta Sociologica, 16,* 188–208.
Burr, W. R. (1970). Satisfaction with various aspects of marriage over the life cycle: A random middle class sample. *Journal of Marriage and the Family, 32,* 29–37.
Burr, W. R., Leigh, G. K., Day, R. D., & Constantine, J. (1979). Symbolic interaction and the family. In W. R. Burr, R. Hill, F. I. Nye, & I. L. Reiss (Eds.), *Contemporary theories about the family* (Vol. 2, pp. 42–111). New York: Free Press.
Byrne, D. (1971). *The attraction paradigm.* New York: Academic Press.

Byrne, D., & Clore, G.L., Jr. (1966). Predicting interpersonal attraction toward strangers presented in three different stimulus modes. *Psychonomic Science, 4*, 239-240.

Byrne, D., Ervin, C. R., & Lamberth, J. (1970). Continuity between the experimental study of attraction and "real life" computer dating. *Journal of Personality and Social Psychology, 16*, 157-165.

Byrne, D., & Griffitt, W. (1966). Similarity versus liking: A clarification. *Psychonomic Science, 6*, 295-296.

Byrne, D., Griffitt, W., Hudgins, W., & Reeves, K. (1970). Attitude similarity-dissimilarity and attraction: Generality beyond the college sophomore. *Journal of Social Psychology, 79*, 155-162.

Byrne, D., Griffitt, H., & Stefaniak, D. (1967). Attraction and similarity of personality characteristics. *Journal of Experimental Social Psychology, 2*, 98-107.

Byrne, D., & Lamberth, J. (1971). Cognitive and reinforcement theories as complementary approaches to the study of attraction. In B. Murstein (Ed.), *Theories of attraction and love.* New York: Springer.

Cameron, P. (1972). Stereotypes about generational fun and happiness vs. self-appraised fun and happiness. *Gerontologist, 12*, 120-123, 190.

Cameron, P., Titus, D. G., Kostin, J., & Kostin, M. (1973). The life satisfaction of nonnormal persons. *Journal of Counseling and Clinical Psychology, 41*, 207-214.

Campbell, A. (1981). *The sense of well-being in America.* New York: McGraw-Hill.

Caplan, G. (1974). *Support systems and community mental health.* New York: Behavioral Publications.

Carrington, P., & Ephron, H. S. (1975). In S. Arieti & G. Chrzanowski (Eds.), *New dimensions in psychiatry: A world view.* New York: Wiley.

Cash, T. F., & Darlega, V. J. (1978). The matching hypothesis: Physical attractiveness among same-sexed friends. *Personality and Social Psychology Bulletin, 4*, 240-243.

Casler, L. (1973). Towards a re-evaluation of love. In M. E. Curtin (Ed.), *Symposium on love.* New York: Behavioral Publications.

Cattell, R. B., & Nesselroade, J. B. (1967). Likeness and completeness theories examined by sixteen personality factor measures on stably and unstably married couples. *Journal of Personality and Social Psychology, 7*, 351-361.

Chadwick, C. (1979). Why educational technology is failing (and what should be done to create success). *Educational Technology, 19*(1), 7-19.

Cialdini, R. B., & Mirels, H. L. (1976). Sense of personal control and attributions about yielding and resisting persuasion targets. *Journal of Personality and Social Psychology, 33*, 395-402.

Clark, M. S. (1982). A role for arousal in the link between feeling states, judgments, and behavior. In M. S. Clark & S. T. Fiske (Eds.), *Affect and cognition: The 17th annual Carnegie Symposium on cognition.* Hillsdale, NJ: Erlbaum.

Clark, M. S., Milberg, S., & Erber, R. (1984). Effects of arousal on interpreting other people's emotions. *Journal of Personality and Social Psychology, 46*, 551-560.

Clark, M. S., Milberg, S., & Ross, J. (1983). Arousal cues arousal-related material in memory: Implications for understanding effects of mood on memory. *Journal of Verbal Learning and Verbal Behavior, 22*, 633-649.

Clark, M. S., & Mills, J. (1979). Interpersonal attraction in exchange and communal relationships. *Journal of Personality and Social Psychology, 37*, 12-24.

Clore, G. L. (1977). Reinforcement and affect in attraction. In S. Duck (ed.), *Theory and practice in interpersonal attraction.* London: Academic Press.

Clore, G. L., & Gormly, J. B. (1974). Knowing, feeling, and liking: A psychophysiological study of attraction. *Journal of Research in Personality, 8*, 218-230.

Cofer, C. N., & Appley, M. H. (1964). *Motivation: Theory and research.* New York: Wiley.

Cohn, A. R. (1976). Self concept and role perceptions as correlates of marital satisfaction. *Dissertation Abstracts International 36*, 3569B. (University Microfilms No. 73-3,000)

Coleman, A. D., & Coleman, L. L. (1975). *Love and ecstasy.* New York: Seabury.

Cooley, C. H. (1902). *Human nature and the social order.* New York: Scribner's.

Cousins, P. D., & Vincent, J. P. (1983). Supportive and aversive behavior following spousal complaints. *Journal of Marriage and the Family, 45*, 679-682.

Cronbach, L. J. (1960). *Essentials of psychological testing.* New York: Harper & Row.

Crosby, J. F. (1973). *Illusion and disillusion: The self in love and marriage.* Belmont, CA: Wadsworth.

Crouse, B., Karlins, M., & Schroder, H. (1968). Conceptual complexity and marital happiness. *Journal of Marriage and the Family, 30*, 643-646.

Cuber, J. F., & Harroff, P. B. (1965). *The significant Americans.* New York: Appleton-Century.

Darley, J. M., & Berscheid, E. (1967). Increased liking as a result of the anticipation of personal contact. *Human Relations, 20,* 29-40.

Dashiell, J. F. (1925). A quantitative demonstration of animal drive. *Journal of Comparative Psychology, 5,* 205-208.

Davis, D. (1981). Implications for interaction versus effectance as mediators of the similarity-attraction relationship. *Journal of Experimental Social Psychology, 17,* 96-116.

Davis, K. E., & Todd, M. J. (1982). Friendship and love relationships. In K. E. Davis & T. O. Mitchell (Eds.), *Advances in Descriptive Psychology* (Vol. 2, pp. 79-122). Greenwich, CT: JAI Press.

Day, B. R. (1961). A comparison of personality needs of courtship couples and same sex friendships. *Sociology and Social Research, 45,* 435-440.

Dean, A., & Lin, N. (1977). The stress-buffering role of social support. *Journal of Nervous and Mental Disease, 165,* 403-417.

Deaux, K. (1972). To err is humanizing: But sex makes a difference. *Representative Research in Social Psychology, 3,* 20-28.

Deci, E. L. (1975). *Intrinsic motivation.* New York: Plenum Press.

Dember, W. N., & Earl, R. W. (1957). Analysis of exploratory, manipulatory, and curiosity behaviors. *Psychological Review, 64,* 91-96.

Dember, W. N., & Penwell, L. (1980). Happiness, depression and the Polyanna principle. *Bulletin of the Psychonomic Society, 15,* 321-323.

Dick, L. D. (1974). A study of meditation in the service of counseling. (Doctoral dissertation, University of Oklahoma, 1974). *Dissertation Abstracts International, 8,* 4037B.

Dickens, W. J., & Perlman, D. (1981). Friendship over the life-cycle. In S. Duck & R. Gilmour (Eds.) *Personal relationships: Vol. 2. Developing personal relationships* (pp. 91-122). New York: Academic Press.

Dillbeck, M. C. (1982). The effects of Transcendental Meditation technique on visual perception and verbal problem solving. *Memory and Cognition, 10,* 207-215.

Dillbeck, M. C., & Bronson, E. C. (1981). Short-term longitudinal effects of the Transcendental Meditation technique on EEG power and coherence. *International Journal of Neuroscience, 14,* 147-151.

Dillbeck, M. C., Landrith, G., & Orme-Johnson, D. W. (1981). The Transcendental Meditation program and crime rate change in a sample of forty-eight cities. *Journal of Crime and Justice, 4,* 25-46.

Dillbeck, M. C., Orme-Johnson, D. W., & Wallace, R. K. (1981). Frontal EEG coherence, H-reflex recovery, concept learning, and the TM-Sidhi program. *International Journal of Neuroscience, 15,* 151-157.

Dion, K., Bersheid, E., & Walster, E. (1972). What is beautiful is good. *Journal of Personality and Social Psychology, 24,* 285-290.

Dizard, J. (1968). *Social change in the family.* Chicago: University of Chicago Press.

Doherty, W. J. (1981). Locus of control differences and marital dissatisfaction. *Journal of Marriage and the Family, 43,* 369-377.

Domash, L. H. (1977). Introduction. In *Scientific research on the Transcendental Meditation program: Collected papers* (Vol. 1, pp. 13-31). Livingston Manor, NY: MIU Press.

Douvan, E. (1977). Interpersonal relationships: Some Questions and observations. In G. Levinger & H. L. Raush (Eds.), *Close relationships: Perspectives on the meaning of intimacy.* Amherst: University of Massachusetts Press.

Driscoll, R., Davis, K. E., & Lipitz, M. E. (1972). Parental influence and romantic love: The Romeo and Juliet effect. *Journal of Personality and Social Psychology, 24,* 1-10.

Duck, S. W. (1973). Similarity and perceived similarity of personal constructs as influences on friendship choice. *British Journal of Social and Clinical Psychology, 12,* 1-6.

Duck, S. W. (1977). Inquiry, hypothesis, and the quest for validation: Personal construct systems in the development of acquaintance. In S. W. Duck (Ed.), *Theory and practice in interpersonal attraction* (pp. 379-404). New York/London: Academic Press.

Duck, S. W. (1982). A topography of relationship disengagement and dissolution. In S. Duck (Ed.), *Personal relationships: Vol. 4. Dissolving personal relationships* (pp. 1-30). London: Academic Press.

Dutton, D. (1979, June). *The arousal-attraction link in the absence of negative reinforcement.* Paper presented at the annual convention of the Canadian Psychological Association, Toronto.

Dutton, D. G., & Aron, A. P. (1974). Some evidence for heightened sexual attraction under conditions of high anxiety. *Journal of Personality and Social Psychology, 30,* 510–517.

Easterlin, R. (1973). Does money buy happiness? *The Public Interest, 30,* 3–10.

Ellis, H. (1935). *Psychology of sex: A manual for students.* New York: Emerson.

Ellis, H. (1936). *Studies in the psychology of sex.* New York: Random House.

Emery, D., & Dindia, K. (1982, July). *Relational rejuvenation and maintenance: Or "no sex until you do X".* Paper presented at the International Conference on Personal Relationships, Madison, WI.

Epstein, S. (1973). The self-concept revisited: Or a theory of a theory. *American Psychologist, 28,* 404–416.

Erikson, E. H. (1950). *Childhood and society.* New York: Norton.

Etzioni, A. (1977). The family: Is it obsolete? *Journal of Current Social Issues, Winter,* 4–9.

Farrow, J. T. (1977). Physiological changes associated with transcendental consciousness, the state of least excitation of consciousness. In D. W. Orme-Johnson & J. T. Farrow (Eds.), *Scientific research on the Transcendental Meditation program: Collected papers (Vol. I)* (pp. 108–133). Livingston Manor, NY: MIU Press.

Farrow, J. T., & Hebert, J. R. (1982). Breath suspension during the Transcendental Meditation technique. *Psychosomatic Medicine, 44,* 133–153.

Fehr, T., Nerstheimer, U., & Torber, S. (1977). Study of personality changes resulting from the Transcendental Meditation program: Freiburger Personality Inventory. In D. W. Orme-Johnson & J. T. Farrow (Eds.), *Scientific research on the Transcendental Meditation program: Collected papers* (Vol. 1, pp. 420–424). Livingston Manor, NY: MIU Press.

Ferguson, P. C., and Gowan, J. C. (1976). TM: Some preliminary findings. *Journal of Humanistic Psychology, 16,* 51–60.

Ferguson, T. J., Rule, B. G., & Carlson, D. (1983). Memory for personally relevant information. *Journal of Personality and Social Psychology, 44,* 251–261.

Festinger, L. (1957). *A theory of cognitive dissonance.* Evanston, IL: Row, Peterson.

Festinger, L., Schachter, S., & Back, K. (1950). *Social pressures in informal groups: A study of human factors in housing.* New York: Harper & Row.

Fincham, F., & O'Leary, K. D. (1982, August). *Affect in the eighties: A new direction in behavioral marital therapy.* Paper presented at the meeting of the American Psychological Association, Washington, DC.

Fiore, A., & Swensen, C. H. (1977). Analysis of love relationships in functional and dysfunctional marriages. *Psychological Reports, 40,* 707–714.

Fitzgerald, R. V. (1973). *Conjoint family therapy.* New York: Jason Aronson.

Foa, U. G. (1971). Interpersonal and economic resources. *Science, 171,* 345–351.

Foa, U. G., & Foa, E. B. (1974). *Societal structures of the mind.* Springfield, IL: Charles C Thomas.

Folkes, V. S. (1982). Forming relationships and the matching hypothesis. *Personality and Social Psychology Bulletin, 8,* 631–636.

Foote, N. N. (1963). Matching of husband and wife in phases of development. In M. B. Sussman (Ed.), *Sourcebook in marriage and family* (pp. 15–21). Boston: Houghton-Mifflin. (Original work published 1956)

Ford, C. S., & Beach, F. A. (1951). *Patterns of sexual behavior.* New York: Harper & Row.

Freud, S. (1927). Some psychological consequences of anatomical distinction between the sexes. *International Journal of Psycho-Analysis, 8,* 133–142.

Freud, S. (1961). *Civilization and its discontents* (J. Strachey, Trans.). New York: Norton. (Original work published 1930)

Freud, S. (1951). *Group psychology and the analysis of the ego* (J. Strachey, Trans.). New York: Liveright. (Original work published 1921)

Freud, S. (1953). Three essays on sexuality. In J. Strachey (Ed.), *The standard edition of the complete works of Sigmund Freud* (Vol. 7). London: Hogarth. (First German edition, 1905)

Freud, S. (1959). *Beyond the pleasure principle* (J. Strachey, Trans.). New York: Bantam. (Original work published 1920)

Frumkin, R. M. (1961). Beauty. In A. Ellis & A. Abarbanel (Eds.), *The encyclopedia of sexual behavior* (Vol. 1, pp. 216–227). New York: Hawthorn.

Gallup, G. (1977). Human needs and satisfaction: A global survey. *Public Opinion Quarterly, 40,* 459–467.

Garrett, E. T. (1983, August). *Women's experiences of early parenthood: Expectation vs reality.* Paper presented at the annual convention of the American Psychological Association, Anaheim, CA.

Gebhard, P. H. (1965). Situational factors affecting human sexual behavior. In F. A. Beach (Ed.), *Sex and behavior* (pp. 483-495). New York: Wiley.

Gergen, K. J. (1977). The social construction of self-knowledge. In T. Mischel (Ed.), *The self: Psychological and philosophical issues* (pp. 139-169). Totowa, NJ: Rowman & Littlefield.

Glueck, B. C., & Stroebel, C. F. (1975). Biofeedback and meditation in the treatment of psychiatric illness. *Comprehensive Psychiatry, 16,* 303-321.

Glueck, B. C., & Stroebel, C. F. (1977). Physiological correlates of relaxation. In A. A. Sugarman and R. E. Tarter (Eds.), *Expanding Dimensions of Consciousness.* New York: Springer.

Goldman, W., & Lewis, P. (1977). Beautiful is good: Evidence that the physically attractive are more socially skillful. *Journal of Experimental Social Psychology, 13,* 125-130.

Goldstein, J. W., & Rosenfeld, H. (1969). Insecurity and preferences for persons similar to oneself. *Journal of Personality, 37,* 253-268.

Goleman, D. & Schwartz, G. (1976). Meditation as an intervention in stress-reactivity. *Journal of Consulting and Clinical Psychology, 44,* 456-466.

Gollwitzer, P. M., Wicklund, R. A., & Hilton, J. L. (1982). Admission of failure and symbolic self-completion: Extending Lewinian theory. *Journal of Personality and Social Psychology, 43,* 358-371.

Goodwin, H. M., & Mudd, E. H. (1976). Marriage counseling: Methods and goals. In B. N. Ard, Jr., & C. C. Ard (Eds.), *Handbook of marriage counseling* (2nd ed., pp. 71-83). Palo Alto, CA: Science & Behavior Books.

Gottman, J. M. (1979). *Marital interaction: Experimental investigations.* New York: Academic Press.

Gottman, J. M. (1982, July). *Temporal form: Toward a new scientific language for describing relationships.* Paper presented at the International Conference on Personal Relationships, Madison, WI.

Gowan, J. C. (1974). *The development of the psychedelic individual.* Buffalo, NY: Creative Education Foundation.

Gowan, J. C. (1980). *Operations of increasing order.* Westlake Village, CA: Author (1426 Southwind Circle).

Grant, V. W. (1957). *The psychology of sexual emotion; The basis of selective attraction.* New York: Longmans, Green.

Grant, V. W. (1976). *Falling in love: The psychology of the romantic emotion.* New York: Springer.

Graziano, W., Brothen, T., & Berscheid, E. (1978). Height and attraction: Do men and women see eye-to-eye? *Journal of Personality, 46,* 128-145.

Greene, B. L. (1970). *A clinical approach to marital problems.* Springfield, IL: Charles C Thomas.

Greenwald, A. G. (1980). The totalitarian ego: Fabrication and revision of personal history. *American Psychologist, 35,* 603-618.

Griffitt, W., & Veitch, R. (1974). Preacquaintance attitude similarity and attraction revisited: Ten days in a fall-out shelter. *Sociometry, 37,* 163-173.

Gross, A. E., & Crofton, C. (1977). What is good is beautiful. *Sociometry, 40,* 85-90.

Guerney, B. G. (1977). *Relationship enhancement.* San Francisco, CA: Jossey-Bass.

Guggenbuhl-Craig, A. (1981). *Marriage: Dead or alive* (M. Stein, Trans.). Dallas: Spring. (Original work published 1977)

Hahn, H. (1975). *The effects of Transcendental Meditation on three factors of personal discontentment: Hostility, anxiety, and depression.* Unpublished master's thesis, California State University, Haywood.

Haley, J. (1973). *Uncommon therapy.* New York: Norton.

Hall, C. S., & Lindzey, G. (1970). *Theories of personality* (2nd ed.). New York: Wiley.

Hall, C. S., & Lindzey, G. (1978). *Theories of personality* (3rd ed.). New York: Wiley.

Hall, C. S., & Nordby, V. J. (1973). *A primer of Jungian psychology.* New York: Taplinger.

Hall, J. A., & Taylor, S. E. (1976). When love is blind: Maintaining idealized images of one's spouse. *Human Relations, 29,* 751-761.

Hamilton, G. V. (1929). *A research in marriage.* New York: Albert & Charles Boni.

Hansen, D. A. (1982). Review of *Interpersonal relations: A theory of interdependence. Journal of Marriage and the Family, 84,* 246-248.

Harlow, H. F. (1953). Motivation as a factor in the acquisition of new responses. *Nebraska symposium on motivation, 1,* 24-49.

Harvey, O. J., Hunt, D., & Schroder, H. (1961). *Conceptual systems and personality organization.* New York: Wiley.

Hatfield, E. (1982). Passionate love, companionate love, and intimacy. In M. Fisher & G. Stricker (Eds.), *Intimacy.* New York: Plenum Press.

Hatfield, E. (1984). *Physical attractiveness in social interaction.* Unpublished manuscript.
Hatfield, E. (in press). The dangers of intimacy. In V. Derlaga (Ed.), *The development of intimate relationships.* New York: Praeger.
Hatfield, E., Traupmann, J., Sprecher, S., Utne, M., & Hay, J. (1984). Equity in intimate relations: recent research. In W. Ickes (Ed.), *Compatible and incompatible relationships* (pp. 1–27). New York: Springer-Verlag.
Hatfield, E., Utne, M. K., & Traupmann, T. L. (1979). Equity theory and intimate relationships. In R. L. Burgess & T. L. Huston (Eds.), *Social exchange in developing relationships* (pp. 99–103). New York: Academic Press.
Hatfield, E., & Walster, G. W. (1978). *A new look at love.* Reading, MA: Addison-Wesley.
Heider, F. (1958). *The psychology of interpersonal relations.* New York: Wiley.
Hilgard, E. R. (1949). Human motives and the concept of the self. *American Psychologist, 4,* 374–382.
Hjelle, L. A. (1974). Transcendental meditation and psychological health. *Perceptual and Motor Skills, 39,* 623–628.
Hochberg, J. E. (1964). *Perception.* Englewood Cliffs, NJ: Prentice-Hall.
Hoffman, L. W., & Hoffman, M. L. (1973). The value of children to parents. In J. T. Fawcett (Ed.), *Psychological perspectives on population* (pp. 19–76). New York: Basic Books.
Holman, T. B., & Burr, W. R. (1980). Beyond the beyond: The growth of family theories in the 1970s. *Journal of Marriage and the Family, 42,* 729–741.
Holmes, T. H., & Rahe, R. H. (1967). The social readjustment rating scale. *Journal of Psychosomatic Research, 11,* 213–218.
Homans, G. (1958). Social behavior as exchange. *American Journal of Sociology, 63,* 597–606.
Hudson, W. W., & Murphy, G. J. (1980). The non-linear relationship between marital satisfaction and stages of family life cycle: An artifact of type I errors? *Journal of marriage and the Family, 42,* 263–267.
Huesmann, L.R. (1980). Toward a predictive model of romantic behavior. In K. S. Pope et al. (Eds.), *On love and loving* (pp. 152–171). San Francisco, CA: Jossey-Bass.
Hull, C. L. (1943). *Principles of behavior.* New York: Appleton-Century.
Huston, T. L. (1973). Ambiguity of acceptance, social desirability, and dating choice. *Journal of Experimental Social Psychology, 9,* 32–42.
Huston, T. L. (1974). A perspective on interpersonal attraction. In T. L. Huston (Ed.), *Foundation of interpersonal attraction* (pp. 3–28). New York: Academic Press.
Huston, T. L. (1982, July). *A topography of marriage: A longitudinal study of changes in husband-wife relationships over the first year.* Presented at the International Conference on Personal Relationships, Madison, WI.
Izard, C. E. (1963). Personality similarity and friendship: A follow-up study. *Journal of Abnormal and Social Psychology, 66,* 598–600.
Jackson, R. M., Fischer, C. S., & Jones, L. M. (1977). The dimensions of social networks. In C. S. Fischer (Ed.), *Networks and places: Social relations in the urban setting.* New York: Free Press.
Jacob, T. (1975). Family interaction in disturbed and normal families: A methodological and substantive review. *Psychological Bulletin, 82,* 33–65.
Jacobsohn, P., & Matheny, A. (1962). Mate selection in open marriage systems. *International Journal of Comparative Sociology, 3,* 98–123.
Jacobson, N. S., & Margolin, G. (1979). *Marital therapy: Strategies based on social learning and behavior exchange principles.* New York: Brunner/Mazel.
James, W. (1948). *Psychology.* Cleveland: Fine Editions Press. (Original work published 1890)
Johnston, T. L., & Jaremko, M. E. (1979). Correlational analysis of suggestibility, self-preoccupation, styles of loving, and sensation seeking. *Psychological Reports, 45,* 23–26.
Jones, E. E., Bell, L., & Aronson, E. (1972). The reciprocation of attraction from similar and dissimilar others: A study in person perception and evaluation. In C. G. McClintock (Ed.), *Experimental social psychology* (pp. 142–179). New York: Holt, Rinehart.
Jung, C. G. (1940). *The integration of personality* (S. M. Dell, Trans.). London: Kegan Paul.
Jung, C. G. (1959). Aion: Researches into the phenomenology of the self. In *Collected works* (Vol. 9). New York: Pantheon. (Original work published 1951)
Jung, C. G. (1959). Marriage as a psychological relationship. In V. S. DeLaszlo (Ed.), *The basic writings of C. G. Jung* (R. F. C. Hull, Trans.; pp. 531–544). New York: Modern Library. (Original work published 1925)
Jung, C. G. (1965). *Memories, dreams and reflections* (A. Jaffe, Ed.). New York: Vintage.
Kagan, J. (1972). Motives and development. *Journal of Personality and Social Psychology, 22,* 51–66.

Kahn, M. (1970). Nonverbal communication and marital satisfaction. *Family Process, 9,* 449–456.

Kammann, R. (1982). *Personal circumstances and life events as poor predictors of happiness.* Paper presented at the annual convention of the American Psychological Association, Washington, DC.

Kammann, R., & Campbell, K. (1982). Illusory correlation in popular beliefs about the causes of happiness. *New Zealand Psychologist, 11,* 56–63.

Kanellakos, D. P. (1978). Transcendental consciousness: Expanded awareness as a means of preventing and eliminating the effects of stress. In C.D. Spielberger & I. G. Sarason (Eds.), *Stress and anxiety* (Vol. 5, pp. 261–315), Washington, DC: Hemisphere.

Kelley, H. H. (1983). Love and commitment. In H. H. Kelley, E. Berscheid, A. Christensen, J. H. Harvey, T. L. Huston, G. Levinger, E. McClintock, L. A. Peplau, & D. R. Peterson (Eds.), *Close Relationships* (pp. 265–314). New York: Freeman.

Kelley, H. H., & Thibaut, J. W. (1978). *Interpersonal relations: A theory of interdependence.* New York: Wiley.

Kelling. G. W. (1979). *Blind mazes: A study of love.* Chicago: Nelson-Hall.

Kelman, H. (1958). Compliance, identification and internalization: Three processes of attitude change. *Journal of Conflict Resolution, 2,* 51–60.

Kelly, G. A. (1955). *The psychology of personal constructs.* New York: Norton.

Kenrick, D. T., & Cialdini, R. B. (1977). Romantic attraction: Misattribution versus reinforcement explanations. *Journal of Personality and Social Psychology, 35,* 381–391.

Kenrick, D. T., Cialdini, R., & Linder, D. (1979). Misattribution under fear producing circumstances: Four failures to replicate. *Personality and Social Psychology Bulletin, 5,* 329–334.

Kerckhoff, A. C. (1974). The social context of interpersonal attraction. In T. L. Huston (Ed.), *Foundations of interpersonal attraction.* New York: Academic Press.

Kerckhoff, A. C., & Davis, K. E. (1962). Value consensus and need complementarity in mate selection. *American Sociological Review, 27,* 295–303.

Kessler, R. C., & Essex, M. (1982). Marital status and depression: The importance of coping resources. *Social Forces, 61,* 484–507.

Kieren, D., & Tallman, I. (1972). Spousal adaptability: An assessment of marital competence. *Journal of Marriage and the Family, 34,* 247–256.

Kiesler, C. A., & Baral, R. (1970). The search for a romantic partner: The effects of self-esteem and physical attractiveness on romantic behavior. In K. Gergen & D. Marlowe (Eds.), *Personality and social behavior.* Reading, MA: Addison-Wesley.

Kinch, J. W. (1963). A formalized theory of the self-concept. *American Journal of Sociology, 68,* 481–486.

Kirkpatrick, C. (1937). Community of interest and the measurement of marriage adjustment. *Family, 18,* 133–137.

Kobasa, S. C. (1979). Stressful life events, personality, and health: An inquiry into hardiness. *Journal of Personality and Social Psychology, 37,* 1–11.

Kobasa, S. C., Maddi, S. R., & Kahn, S. (1982). Hardiness and health: A prospective study. *Journal of Personality and Social Psychology, 42,* 168–177.

Kohlberg, L. (1969). Stage and sequence: The cognitive-developmental approach to socialization. In D. A. Goslin (Ed.), *Handbook of socialization and research* (pp. 347–480). Chicago: Rand McNally.

Koffka, K. (1935). *Principles of Gestalt psychology.* New York: Harcourt, Brace.

Krech, D., Crutchfield, R. S., & Ballachey, E. L. (1962). *Individual in society: A textbook of social psychology.* New York: McGraw-Hill.

Kuhn, M. H., & McPartland, T. S. (1954). An empirical investigation of self-attitudes. *American Sociological Review, 19,* 68–76.

Kuhn, T. S. (1962). *The structure of scientific revolutions.* Chicago: University of Chicago Press.

Kukulan, J., Aron, A., & Abrams, A. I. (in press). The Transcendental Meditation program and children's personality. In *Scientific research on the Transcendental Meditation program: Collected papers* (Vol. 3). Rheinweiler, West Germany: MIU Press.

Lamberth, J. (1980). *Social psychology.* New York: Macmillan.

Lasswell, T. E., & Lasswell, M. E. (1976). I love you but I'm not in love with you. *Journal of Marriage and Family Counseling, 2,* 211–224.

Layton, B. D., & Insko, C. A. (1974). Anticipated interaction and the similarity-attraction effect. *Sociometry, 37,* 149–162.

148   REFERENCES

Lazarus, R. S. (1974). Cognitive and coping processes in emotion. In B. Weiner (Ed.), *Cognitive views of human motivation.* New York: Academic Press.
Lazarus, R. S., & Launier, R. (1978). Stress-related transactions between person and environment. In L. A. Pervin (Ed.), *Perspectives in interactional psychology.* New York: Plenum Press.
Lee, J. A. (1976). *The colors of love.* New York: Prentice-Hall, 1976.
Lee, J. A. (1977). A typology of styles of loving. *Personality and Social Psychology Bulletin, 3,* 173–182.
Levenson, H., & Harris, C. N. (1980). Love as a process of reducing uncertainty–cognitive theory. In K. S. Pope et al. (Eds.), *Love and the Search for Identity* (pp. 266–281). San Francisco: Jossey-Bass.
Levenson, R. W., & Gottman, J. M. (1983). Marital interaction: physiological linkage and affective exchange. *Journal of Personality and Social Psychology, 45,* 587–597.
Levine, P. H. (1976). The coherence spectral array (COSPAR) and its application to the studying of spatial ordering in the EEG. *Proceedings of the San Diego Biomedical Symposium, 15,* 237–247.
Levine, P. H., Hebert, R., Haynes, C. T., & Strobel, U. (1977). EEG coherence during the Transcendental Meditation technique. In D.W. Orme-Johnson & J. T. Farrow (Eds.), *Scientific research on the Transcendental Meditation program: Collected papers* (Vol. 1, pp. 187–207). Livingston Manor, NY: MIU Press.
Levinger, G. (1974). A three-level approach to attraction: Toward an understanding of pair relatedness. In T. L. Huston (Ed.), *Foundations of interpersonal attraction.* New York: Academic Press.
Levinger, G., & Breedlove, J. (1966). Interpersonal attraction and agreement: A study of marriage partners. *Journal of Personality and Social Psychology, 3,* 367–372.
Levinger, G., & Snoek, J. D. (1972). *Attraction in relationship: A new look at interpersonal attraction.* Morristown, NJ: General Learning Press.
Lewin, K. (1936). *Principles of topological psychology.* (F. Heider & G. M. Heider, Trans.). New York: McGraw-Hill.
Lewis, J., Beavers, R., Gossett, J. T., & Phillips, V. A. (1976). *No single thread.* New York: Brunner/Mazel.
Lewis, R. A., & Spanier, G. B. (1979). Theorizing about the quality and stability of marriage. In W. R. Burr, R. Hill. F. I. Nye, & I. L. Reiss (Eds.), *Contemporary theories about the family* (Vol. 1, pp. 268–294). New York: Free Press.
Lewis, T. (1976). Cited in H. H. Bloomfield & R. B. Corey, *Happiness: The TM program, psychiatry, and enlightenment.* New York: Dawn Press/Simon & Schuster.
Linton, R. (1936). *The study of man.* New York: Appleton-Century.
Litwak, E., Count, G., & Haydon, E. M. (1960). Group structure and interpersonal creativity as factors which reduce errors in the prediction of marital adjustment. *Social Forces, 38,* 308–315.
Livingston, K. R. (1980). Love as a process of reducing uncertainty–Cognitive theory. In K. S. Pope et al. (Eds.), *On love and loving* (pp. 133–151). San Francisco, CA: Jossey-Bass.
Locke, H. J. (1951). *Predicting adjustment in marriage: A comparison of a divorced and a happily married group.* New York: Holt, Rinehart.
Locksley, A. (1982). Social class and marital attitudes and behavior. *Journal of Marriage and the Family, 44,* 427–440.
Loevinger, J., & Wessler, R. (1970). *Measuring ego development* (Vol. 1). San Francisco, CA: Jossey-Bass.
Lombardo, J. P., Weiss, R. F., & Buchanan, W. (1972). Reinforcing and attracting functions of yielding. *Journal of Personality and Social Psychology, 21,* 359–368.
Lombardo, J. P. Weiss, R. F., & Stich, M. H. (1973). Effectance reduction through speaking in reply and its relation to attraction. *Journal of Personality and Social Psychology, 28,* 325–332.
Lott, A. J., & Lott, B. E. (1974). The role of reward in the formation of positive interpersonal attitudes. In T. L. Huston (Ed.), *Foundations of interpersonal attraction* (pp. 171–189). New York: Academic Press.
Lukenbach, A. (1978, August). *Qualitative differences in psychophysiology with different states of consciousness: A new approach to research using the Science of Creative Intelligence.* Paper presented at the 86th annual convention of the American Psychological Association, Toronto, Ontario.

Lytton, H. (1971). Observation studies of parent-child interaction: A methodological review. *Child Development, 42,* 651-684.

Maddi, S. R. (1982, August). *Creativity and Health: Do the gods give two good things to one person?* Paper presented at the meeting of the American Psychological Association, Washington, DC.

Maharishi Mahesh Yogi (1969). *Bhagavad-Gita: A new translation and commentary: Chapters 1-6.* New York: Penguin.

Maharishi Mahesh Yogi (1972). *The science of creative intelligence.* Livingston Manor, New York: MIU Press.

Maharishi Mahesh Yogi (1977). Foreword. In D. W. Orme-Johnson & J. T. Farrow (Eds.), *Scientific research on the Transcendental Meditation program: Collected papers* (Vol. 1, pp. 1-4). Livingston Manor, NY: MIU Press.

Mahrer, A. R. (1982). Humanistic approaches to intimacy. In M. Fisher & G. Stricker (Eds.), *Intimacy* (pp. 141-159). New York: Plenum.

Malinowski, B. (1932). *The sexual life of savages in northwestern Melanesia* (3rd ed.). London: Routledge.

Mangus, A. R. (1936). Relationships between the young woman's conception of her intimate male associates and her ideal husband. *Journal of Social Psychology, 7,* 368-373.

Margolin, G., & Wampold, B. E. (1981). Sequential analysis of conflict and accord in distressed and nondistressed marital partners. *Journal of Consulting and Clinical Psychology, 49,* 554-567.

Markman, H. J. (1981). Prediction of marital distress: A 5-year follow-up. *Journal of Consulting and Clinical Psychology, 49,* 760-762.

Markman, H. J. (1982, July). *The short-term results of cognitive-behavioural program for premarital couples designed to prevent marital distress.* Paper presented at the International Conference on Personal Relationships, Madison, WI.

Markman, H. J., Floyd, F., & Dickson-Markman, F. (1982). Towards a model for the prediction and primary prevention of marital and family distress and dissolution. In S. Duck (Ed.), *Personal relationships: Vol. 4. Dissolving personal relationships* (pp. 233-261). London: Academic Press.

Markman, H. J., Jamieson, K. J., & Floyd, F. J. (1983). The assessment and modification of premarital relationships: Preliminary findings on the etiology and prevention of marital and family distress. *Advances in Family Intervention, Assessment and Theory, 3,* 41-89.

Markus, H. (1977). Self-schemata and processing information about the self. *Journal of Personality and Social Psychology, 35,* 63-78.

Markus, H. (1980). The self in memory and thought. In D. M. Wegner & R. R. Vallacher (Eds.), *The self in social psychology* (pp. 102-130). New York: Oxford University Press.

Maslow, A. H. (1962). *Toward a psychology of being.* Princeton, NJ: Van Nostrand.

Maslow, A H. (1967). A theory of metamotivation: The biological rooting of the value-life. *Journal of Humanistic Psychology, 7,* 93-127.

Maslow, A. H. (1968). *Toward a psychology of being* (2nd. ed.). Princeton, NJ: Van Nostrand

Maslow, A. H. (1970). *Motivation and personality.* New York: Harper & Row.

Maslow, A. H. (1971). *The farther reaches of human nature.* New York: Penguin.

Maslow, A. H. (1973). Self-actualizing people: A study of psychological health. In R. J. Lowry (Ed.), *Dominance, self-esteem, self-actualization: Germinal papers of A. H. Maslow* (pp. 177-193). Monterey, CA: Brooks/Cole. (Original work published 1950)

Maulsby, R. (1971). An illustration of emotionally evoked theta rhythm in infancy: Hedonic hypersyncrony. *Electroencephalography and Clinical Neurophysiology, 31,* 157-165.

McCall, G. J. (1974). A symbolic interactionist approach to attraction. In T. L. Huston (Ed.), *Foundations of interpersonal attraction.* New York: Academic Press.

McCall, G. J. (1977). The social looking glass: A sociological perspective on self-development. In T. Mischel (Ed.), *The self: Psychological and philosophical issues* (pp. 274-287). Totowa, NJ: Rowman & Littlefield.

McClelland, D. C., Atkinson, J. W., Clark, R. W., & Lowell, E. L. (1953). *The achievement motive.* New York: Appleton-Century.

McClintock, C. (1972). Social motivation—A set of propositions. *Behavioral Sciences, 17,* 438-454.

McDonald, G. W. (1981). Structural exchange and marital interaction. *Journal of Marriage and the Family, 43,* 825-839.

McDonald, P. J., Harris, S. G., & Maher, J. E. (1983). Arousal-induced self-awareness: An artifactual relationship? *Journal of Personality and Social Psychology, 2,* 285-289.

McGuire, W. J. (1964). Inducing resistance to persuasion: Some contemporary approaches. In L. Berkowitz (Ed.), *Advances in experimental social psychology* (Vol. 1, pp. 192–229). New York: Academic Press.

Mead, G. H. (1934). *Mind, self, and society.* Chicago: University of Chicago Press.

Mednick, A. (1962). The associative basis of the creative process. *Psychological Review, 69,* 220–227, 232.

Meeker, B. (1971). Decisions and exchange. *American Sociological Review, 36,* 485–495.

Mettee, D. R., & Aronson, E. (1974). Affective reactions to appraisal from others. In T. L. Huston (Ed.), *Foundations of interpersonal attraction* (pp. 235–283). New York: Academic Press.

Mill, J. S. (1904). *A system of logic, ratiocinative and inductive: Being a connected view of the principles of evidence and the methods of scientific investigation.* London: Longmans, Green.

Miller, H. L., & Siegel, P. S. (1972). *Loving: A psychological approach.* New York: Academic Press.

Miller, N., Campbell, D. T., Twedt, H., & O'Connell, E. J. (1966). Similarity, contrast, and complementarity in friendship. *Journal of Personality and Social Psychology, 3,* 3–12.

Mischel, T. (1977). Conceptual issues in the psychology of the self: An introduction. In T. Mischel (Ed.), *The self: Psychological and philosophical issues* (pp. 3–28). Totowa, NJ: Rowman & Littlefield.

Mischel, W. (1968). *Personality and assessment.* New York: Wiley.

Miskiman, D. E. (1977). The effect of the Transcendental Meditation program on the organization of thinking and recall (secondary organization). In D. W. Orme-Johnson & J. T. Farrow (Eds.), *Scientific research on the Transcendental Meditation program: Collected papers* (Vol. 1, pp. 385–392). Livingston Manor, NY: MIU Press.

Mitroff, I. J. (1974). *The subjective side of science.* New York: Elsevier.

Montgomery, K. C. (1954). The role of exploratory drive in learning. *Journal of Comparative and Physiological Psychology, 47,* 60–64.

Morse, D., Martin, J., Furst, M., & Dubin, L. (1977). A physiological and subjective evaluation of meditation, hypnosis, and relaxation. *Psychosomatic Medicine, 39,* 304–324.

Morse, D., Martin, J., Furst, M., & Dubin, L. (1979a). A physiological and subjective evaluation of neutral and emotionally-charged words for meditation (part 1). *Journal of the American Society of Psychosomatic Dentistry and Medicine, 26,* 31–38.

Morse, D., Martin, J., Furst, M., & Dubin, L. (1979b). A physiological and subjective evaluation of neutral and emotionally-charged words for meditation (part 2). *Journal of the American Society of Psychosomatic Dentistry and Medicine, 26,* 56–62.

Mudd, E. H., & Taubin, S. (1982). Success in family living—does it last? A twenty-year follow-up. *American Journal of Family Therapy, 10,* 59–67.

Murch, G. M. (1973). *Visual and auditory perception.* Indianapolis: Bobbs-Merrill.

Murdock, G. P. (1949). *Social structure.* New York: Macmillan.

Murray, H. (1938). *Explorations in personality.* New York: Oxford University Press.

Murstein, B. I. (1971a). Critique of models of dyadic attraction. In B. I. Murstein (Ed.). *Theories of attraction and love* (pp. 1–31). New York: Springer.

Murstein, B. I. (1971b). A theory of marital choice and its applicability to marriage adjustment. In B. I. Murstein (Ed.), *Theories of attraction and love.* New York: Springer.

Murstein, B. I. (1976). *Who will marry whom? Theories and research in marital choice.* New York: Springer.

Murstein, B. I. (1977). The Stimulus-Value-Role (SVR) theory of dyadic relationships. In S. Duck (Ed.), *Theory and practice in interpersonal attraction.* New York: Academic Press.

Murstein, B. I. (1980). Mate selection in the 1970s. *Journal of Marriage and the Family, 42,* 777–792.

Murstein, B. I., Cerreto, M., & MacDonald, M. (1977). A theory and investigation of the effect of exchange-orientation on marriage and friendship. *Journal of Marriage and the Family, 39,* 543–548.

Mussen, P., Honzik, M. P., & Eichorn, D. H. (1982). Early adult antecedents of life satisfaction at age 70. *Journal of Gerontology, 37,* 316–322.

Nadelson, C. C. (1978). Marital therapy from a psychoanalytic perspective. In T. J. Paolino & B. S. McCrady (Eds.), *Marriage and marital therapy.* New York: Brunner/Mazel.

Nahemow, L., & Lawton, M. P. (1975). Similarity and propinquity in friendship formation. *Journal of Personality and Social Psychology, 32,* 204–213.

Navran, L. (1967). Communication and adjustment in marriage. *Family Process, 6,* 173–184.

Neimeyer, G. J., & Neimeyer, R. A. (1981). Functional similarity and interpersonal attraction. *Journal of Research in Personality, 15*, 427–435.

Newcomb, T. M. (1956). The prediction of interpersonal attraction. *American Psychologist, 11*, 575–586.

Newcomb. T. M. (1961). *The acquaintance process*. New York: Holt, Rinehart.

Nidich, S. I. (1976). A study of the relationship of Transcendental Meditation to Kohlberg's stages of moral reasoning. (Doctoral dissertation, University of Cincinnati, 1975) *Dissertation Abstracts International, 36*, 4361A–4362A.

Nidich, S., Seeman, W., & Dreskin, T. (1973). Influence of transcendental meditation: A replication. *Journal of Counseling Psychology, 20*, 565–566.

Nimkoff, M. (1947). *Marriage and the family*. Boston: Houghton Mifflin.

Nissen, H. W. (1930). A study of exploratory behavior in the white rat by means of the obstruction method. *Journal of Genetic Psychology, 37*, 361–376.

Noller, P. (1982). Channel consistency and inconsistency in the communications of married couples. *Journal of Personality and Social Psychology, 43*, 732–741.

Nystul, M. S., & Garde, M. (1977). Comparison of self-concepts of Transcendental Meditators and nonmeditators. *Psychological Reports, 41*, 303–306.

Olson, D. H., Russell, C. S., & Sprenkle, D. H. (1980). Marital and family therapy: A decade review. *Journal of Marriage and the Family, 42,*

Olson, D. H., Russell, C. S., & Sprenkle, D. H. (1983). Circumplex model of marital and family systems: VI. Theoretical update. *Family Process, 22*, 69–83.

O'Neill, N., & O'Neill, G. (1972). *Open marriage*. New York: Avon.

Orme-Johnson, D. W. (1973). Autonomic stability and Transcendental Meditation. *Psychosomatic Medicine, 35*, 341–349.

Orme-Johnson, D. W. (1977). Experimental evidence that the Transcendental Meditation technique produces a fourth and fifth state of consciousness in the individual and a profound influence of orderliness in society. In D. W. Orme-Johnson & J. T. Farrow (Eds.), *Scientific research on the Transcendental Meditation program: Collected papers (Vol. I)* (pp. 671–691). Livingston Manor, NY: MIU Press.

Orme-Johnson, D. W. (1981, August). *Behavioral correlates of EEG phase coherence.* Paper at the meeting of the American Psychological Association, Los Angeles (see also below).

Orme-Johnson, D. W., Dillbeck, M. C., Alexander, C. N., Van den Berg, W., & Dillbeck, S. L. (in press). Unified-field based psychology: The Vedic psychology of Maharishi Mahesh Yogi–the fulfillment of modern psychology. In R. A. Chalmers, G. Clements, H. Shenkluhn, & M. Weinless (Eds.), *Scientific research on the Transcendental Meditation and TM-Sidhi programme: Collected papers* (Vol. 4). Rheinweiller, West Germany: MERU Press.

Orme-Johnson, D. W., & Farrow, J. T. (1977). *Scientific research on the Transcendental Meditation program: Collected papers (Vol. I).* Livingston Manor, NY: MIU Press.

Orme-Johnson, D. W., & Haynes, E. T. (1981). EEG phase coherence, pure consciousness, creativity, and TM-Sidhi experiences. *International Journal of Neuroscience, 13*, 211–217.

Orme-Johnson, D. W., Wallace, R. K., Dillbeck, M. C., Ball, O., & Alexander, C. N. (1981, August). *Behavioral correlates of EEG phase coherence.* Paper presented at the annual convention of the American Psychological Association, Los Angeles.

Osgood, C. E., & Tannenbaum, P. H. (1955). The principle of congruity in the prediction of attitude change. *Psychological Review, 62*, 42–55.

Ossorio, P. G. (1981). Outline of descriptive psychology for personality theory and clinical applications. In K. E. Davis (Ed.), *Advances in descriptive psychology* (Vol. 1). Greenwich, CT: JAI Press.

Pagano, R. R., & Frumkin, L. R. (1977). The effect of Transcendental Meditation on right hemispheric functioning. *Biofeedback and Self-Regulation, 2*, 407–415.

Parlee, M. B. (1979). The friendship bond. *Psychology Today, 13*, 43–54.

Patterson, G. R. (1971). Behavioral intervention procedures in the classroom and in the home. In A. E. Bergin & S. L. Garfield (Eds.), *Handbook of psychotherapy and behavior change: An empirical analysis.* New York: Wiley.

Pearlin, L. I., & Schooler, C. (1978). The structure of coping. *Journal of Health and Social Behavior, 19*, 2–21.

Peeke, H. V. S., & Herz, M. J. (1973). *Habituation.* New York: Academic Press.

Pelletier, K. R. (1974). Influence of Transcendental Meditation upon autokinetic perception. *Perceptual and Motor Skills, 39*, 1031–1034.

Perls, F. S., Hefferline, R. F., & Goodman, P. (1951). *Gestalt therapy.* New York: Julian Press.

Piaget, J. (1963). *The origins of intelligence in children* (M. Cook, Trans.). New York: Norton. (Original work published 1952)

Pineo, P. C. (1961). Disenchantment in the later years of marriage. *Marriage and Family Living*, *23*, 3–11.

Pirot, M. (1977). The effects of the Transcendental Meditation technique upon auditory discrimination. In D. W. Orme-Johnson and J. T. Farrow (Eds.), *Scientific research on the Transcendental Meditation program: Collected papers* (Vol. 1, pp. 331–334). Livingston Manor, NY: MIU Press.

Plutchik, R. (1967). Marriage as dynamic equilibrium: Implications for research. In H. L. Silverman (Ed.), *Marital counseling: Psychology, ideology, science* (pp. 347–367). Springfield, IL: Charles C Thomas.

Posavac, E. (1971). Dimensions of trait preferences and personality type. *Journal of Personality and Social Psychology*, *19*, 274–281.

Preston, M. G., Peltz, W. L., Mudd, E. H., & Froscher, H. B. (1952). Impressions of personality as a function of marital conflict. *Journal of Abnormal and Social Psychology*, *47*, 326–336.

Rahe, R. H., & Arthur, R. A. (1978). Life change and illness studies. *Journal of Human Stress*, *4*, 3–15.

Raush, H. L., Barry, W. A., Hertel, R. K., & Swain, M. A. (1974). *Communication, conflict and marriage*. San Francisco, CA: Jossey-Bass.

Reader, N., & H. B. English (1947). Personality factors in adolescent female friendships. *Journal of Consulting Psychology*, *11*, 212–220.

Reik, T. (1944). *A psychologist looks at love*. New York: Farrar & Rinehart.

Reik, T. (1949). *Of love and lust: On the psychoanalysis of romantic and sexual emotions*. New York: Farrar, Straus & Giroux.

Reis, H. T. (1982, July). *Determinants, consequences and characteristics of social relationships*. Paper presented at the International Conference on Personal Relationships, Madison, WI.

Reis, H. T., Wheeler, L., Spiegel, N., Kernis, M. H., Nezlek, J., & Perri, M. (1982). Physical attractiveness in social interaction: 2. Why does appearance affect social experience? *Journal of Personality and Social Psychology*, *43*, 979–996.

Reisman, J. M. (1979). *Anatomy of friendship*. New York: Irvington.

Reisman, J. M. (1981). Adult friendships. In S. Duck & R. Gilmour (Eds.), *Personal relationships: Vol. 2. Developing personal relationships* (pp. 205–230). New York: Academic Press.

Renne, K. S. (1970). Correlates of dissatisfaction in marriage. *Journal of Marriage and the Family*, *32*, 54–67.

Richardson, H. M. (1939). Studies of marital resemblance between husbands and wives and between friends. *Psychological Bulletin*, *36*, 104–120.

Riddle, A. (1979). Effects of selected elements of meditation on self-actualization, locus of control, and trait anxiety. (Doctoral dissertation, University of South Carolina, 1979). *Dissertation Abstracts International*, *40*, 3419A.

Riordan, C. A., & Tedeschi, J. T. (1983). Attraction in aversive environments: Some evidence for classical conditioning and negative reinforcement. *Journal of Personality and Social Psychology*, *44*, 683–692.

Riskin, J., & Faunce, E. E. (1972). An evaluative review of family interaction research. *Family Process*, *11*, 365–455.

Rogers, C. R. (1947). Some observations on the organization of personality. *American Psychologist*, *2*, 358–368.

Rogers, C. R. (1959). A theory of therapy, personality, and interpersonal relationships, as developed in the client-centered framework. In S. Koch (Ed.), *Psychology: A study of a science* (Vol. 3, pp. 184–256). New York: McGraw-Hill.

Rogers, C. R. (1961). *On becoming a person: A therapist's view of psychotherapy*. Boston: Houghton Mifflin.

Rogers, C. R. (1969). *Freedom to learn*. Columbus: Charles E. Merrill.

Rogers, C. R. (1972). *Becoming partners: Marriage and its alternatives*. New York: Delacorte.

Rollins, B. C., & Feldman, H. (1970). Marital satisfaction over the life cycle. *Journal of Marriage and the Family*, *32*, 20–28.

Rosenman, M. F. (1978). Liking, loving, and styles of loving. *Psychological Reports*, *42*, 1243–1246.

Rothbaum, F., Weisz, J. R., & Snyder, S. S. (1982). Changing the world and changing the self: A two-process model of perceived control. *Journal of Personality and Social Psychology*, *42*, 5–37.

Rotter, J. B. (1966). Generalized expectancies for internal versus external control of reinforcement. *Psychological Monographs*, *80*, (1, Whole No. 609).

Rubin, Z. (1970). Measurement of romantic love. *Journal of Personality and Social Psychology*, *10*, 265-273.

Rubin, Z. (1973). *Liking and loving: An invitation to social psychology*. New York: Holt, Rinehart.

Rubin, Z. (1974). From liking to loving: Patterns of attraction in dating relationships. In T. L. Huston (Ed.), *Foundations of interpersonal attraction*. New York: Academic Press.

Ryder, R. G. (1973). Longitudinal data relating marriage satisfaction and having a child. *Journal of Marriage and the Family*, *35*, 604-606.

Sabatelli, R. M., Dreyer, A., & Buck, R. (1983). Cognitive style and relationship quality in married dyads. *Journal of Personality*, *51*, 192-201.

Safilios-Rothschild, C. (1976). A macro- and micro-examination of family power and love: An exchange model. *Journal of Marriage and the Family*, *38*, 355-362.

Sager, C. J. (1976). *Marriage contracts and couple therapy: Hidden forces in intimate relationships*. New York: Brunner/Mazel.

Sarbin, T. R. (1952). A preface to a psychological analysis of the self. *Psychological Review*, *59*, 11-22.

Sarbin, T. R., & Allen, V. L. (1968). Role theory. In G. Lindzey & E. Aronson (Eds.), *Handbook of social psychology* (2nd ed., Vol. 1, pp. 488-567). Reading MA: Addison-Wesley.

Schachter, S. (1959). *The psychology of affiliation*. Stanford, CA: Stanford University Press.

Schachter, S., & Singer, J. (1962). Cognitive, social and physiological determinants of emotional state. *Psychological Review*, *69*, 379-399.

Schiller, B. (1932). A quantitative analysis of marriage selection in a small group. *Journal of Social Psychology*, *3*, 297-318.

Sears, D. O. (1983). The personal-positivity bias. *Journal of Personality and Social Psychology*, *44*, 233-250.

Seeman, W., Nidich, S., & Banta, T. (1972). Influence of transcendental meditation on self-actualization. *Journal of Counseling Psychology*, *19*, 184-187.

Segal, M. W. (1974). Alphabet and attraction: An unobtrusive measure of the effect of propinquity in a field setting. *Journal of Personality and Social Psychology*, *30*, 654-657.

Segraves, R. T. (1982). *Marital therapy: A combined psychodynamic-behavioral approach*. New York: Plenum Press.

Seligman, M. E. P. (1975). *Helplessness*. San Francisco, CA: Freeman.

Selvini, M., Palazzoli, M. S., Boscolo, L., Cecchin, G., & Prata, G. (1978). *Paradox and counterparadox*. New York: Jason Aronson.

Selye, H. (1956). *The stress of life*. New York: McGraw-Hill.

Selye, H. (1974). *Stress without distress*. New York: New American Library.

Selye, H. (1975). Foreword. In H. H. Bloomfield, M. P. Cain & D. T. Jaffe, *TM: Discovering inner energy and overcoming stress* (pp. ix-xii). New York: Delacorte.

Selye, H. (1978). On the real benefits of eustress. *Psychology Today*, *10*, 60-64.

Selye, H. (1980). The stress concept today. In I. L. Kutash & L. B. Schlesinger (Eds.), *Handbook of stress and anxiety* (pp. 127-143). San Francisco: Jossey-Bass.

Shanteau, J., & Nagy, G. F. (1979). Probability of acceptance in dating choice. *Journal of Personality and Social Psychology*, *37*, 522-533.

Shapiro, J. S. (1975). The relationship of selected characteristics of Transcendental Meditation to measures of self-actualization, negative personality characteristics, and anxiety (Doctoral dissertation, University of California, 1975). *Dissertation Abstracts International*, *36*, 137A.

Shecter, H. (1978). *The Transcendental Meditation Program in the classroom*. Unpublished doctoral dissertation, York University, Toronto, Ontario.

Shelly, M. W. (1973a). *The counter-evolution*. Lawrence, KS: University of Kansas Press.

Shelly, M. W. (1973b). *Sources of satisfaction*. Lawrence, KS: University of Kansas Press.

Shrauger, J. S., & Schoeneman, T. J. (1979). Symbolic interactionist view of self-concept: Through the looking glass darkly. *Psychological Bulletin*, *65*, 549-573.

Shulman, N. (1975). Life-cycle variations in patterns of close relationships. *Journal of Marriage and the Family*, *37*, 813-921.

Siegel, D. (1982, July). *Attributional bias in close relationships: 'Mind reading' in couples*. Paper presented at the International Conference on Personal Relationships, Madison, WI.

Siegel, L. M. (1981). The Transcendental Meditation program and the treatment of drug abuse. In J. H. Lowinson & P. Ruiz (Eds.), *Substance abuse: Clinical problems and perspectives*. Baltimore: Williams & Wilkins.

Sigall, H., & Landy, D. (1973). Radiating beauty: The effects of having a physically attractive partner on person perception. *Journal of Personality and Social Psychology*, *28*, 218-224.

Skinner, B. F. (1938). *The behavior or organisms.* New York: Appleton-Century.

Smith, M. B. (1978). Perspectives on selfhood. *American Psychologist, 33,* 1053–1063.

Snyder, M., Tanke, E. D., & Berscheid, E. (1977). Social perception and interpersonal behavior: On the self-fulfilling nature of social stereotypes. *Journal of Personality and Social Psychology, 35,* 656–666.

Snyder, R. A. (1979). Individual differences and the similarity/attraction relationship: Effects of level of similarity-dissimilarity. *Perceptual and Motor Skills, 49,* 1003–1008.

Snygg, D., & Combs, A. W. (1949). *Individual behavior.* New York: Harper & Row.

Solomon, M. R., & Schopler, J. (1978). The relationship of physical attractiveness and punitiveness: Is the linearity assumption out of line? *Personality and Social Psychology Bulletin, 4,* 483–486.

Solomon, R. L. (1980). The opponent-process theory of acquired motivation: The costs of pleasure and the benefits of pain. *American Psychologist, 35,* 691–712.

Solomon, S., & Saxe, L. (1977). What is intelligent, as well as attractive, is good. *Personality and Social Psychology Bulletin, 3,* 670–673.

Solovyev, V. (1947). *The meaning of love* (J. Marshall, Trans.). New York: International University Press.

Spanier, G. B., & Lewis, R. A. (1980). Marital quality: A review of the seventies. *Journal of Marriage and the Family, 42,* 825–839.

Speer, D. C. (1970). Family systems: Morphostasis and morphogenesis, or "is homeostasis enough?" *Family Process, 9,* 259–278.

Steck, L., Levitan, D., McLane, D., & Kelley, H. H. (1982). Care, need, and conceptions of love. *Journal of Personality and Social Psychology, 43,* 481–491.

Steffen, J. J., McLaney, M. A., & Hustedt, T. K. (1982). *The development of a measure of limerence.* Paper presented at the annual convention of the American Psychological Association, Washington, DC.

Stekel, W. (1943). *Frigidity in women* (Vol. 1). New York: Liveright.

Stendahl (Marie-Henri Beyle) (1927). *On love* (H. B. V., Trans.). New York: Boni & Liveright.

Stinnett, N. & Sauer, K. (1977). Relationship patterns among strong families. *Family Perspective, 11,* 3–11.

Straus, M. A. (1974). Leveling, civility, and violence in the family. *Journal of Marriage and the Family, 36,* 13–24.

Strauss, A. (1946). The influence of parent-image upon marital choice. *American Sociological Review, 11,* 554–559.

Stroebe, W., Insko, C. A., Thompson, V. D., & Layton, B. D. (1971). Effects of physical attractiveness, attitude similarity, and sex on various aspects of interpersonal attraction. *Journal of Personality and Social Psychology, 18,* 79–91.

Stroebel, C. F., & Glueck, B. C. (1978). Passive meditation: Subjective, clinical, and electrographic comparison with biofeedback. In G. E. Schwartz & D. Shapiro (Eds.), *Consciousness and self-regulation: Advances in research and theory* Vol. 2, pp. 401–428). New York: Plenum Press.

Stuart, R. B. (1969). Operant-interpersonal treatment for marital discord. *Journal of Consulting and Clinical Psychology, 33,* 675–682.

Suarez, V. M. (1976). *The relationship of the practice of Transcendental Meditation to subjective evaluations of marital satisfaction and adjustment.* Unpublished master's thesis, University of Southern California, Los Angeles.

Suttie, I. D. (1935). *The origins of love and hate.* London: Kegan Paul, Trench, Trubner.

Swann, W. B., & Hill, C. A. (1982). When our identities are mistaken: Reaffirming self-conceptions through social interaction. *Journal of Personality and Social Psychology, 43,* 59–66.

Swann, W. B., & Read, J. R. (1981). Self-verification processes: How we sustain our self-conceptions. *Journal of Experimental Social Psychology, 17,* 351–372.

Swensen, C. H., Jr. (1961). Love: A self-report analysis with college students. *Journal of Individual Psychology, 17,* 167–171.

Swensen, C. H. (1972). The behavior of love. In H. Otto (Ed.), *Love today: A new exploration.* New York: Association Press.

Swensen, C. H. (1973). A scale for measuring the behavior and feelings of love. In J. W. Pfeiffer & J. E. Jones (Eds.), *The 1973 annual handbook for group facilitators* (pp. 71–85). Iowa City: University Association.

Swensen, C. H., Eskew, R. W., & Kohlhepp, K. A. (1981). Stage of family life cycle, ego development, and the marriage relationship. *Journal of Marriage and the Family, 43,* 841–853.

Tedeschi, J. T. (1974). Attributions, liking, and power. In T. L. Huston (Ed.), *Foundations of interpersonal attraction*. New York: Academic Press.

Tennov, D. (1979). *Love and limerence: The experience of being in love*. New York: Stein and Day.

Teresa of Avila (1960). *The life of Teresa of Jesus: The autobiography of St. Teresa of Avila* (E. A. Peers, Trans. and Ed.). Garden City, NY: Image. (original work published 1583)

Terman, L. M. (1938). *Psychological factors in marital happiness*. New York: McGraw-Hill.

Terman, L. M., & Oden, M. H. (1959). *Genetic studies of genius: Vol. 5. The gifted group at mid-life*. Stanford, CA: Stanford University Press.

Tesser, A. (1980). Self-esteem maintenance in family dynamics. *Journal of Personality and Social Psychology, 39,* 77-91.

Thibaut, J. W., & Kelley, H. H. (1959). *The social psychology of groups*. New York: Wiley.

Tjoa, A. S. (1975). Meditation, neuroticism, and intelligence: A follow-up. *Gedrag: Tijdschrift voor Psychologie, 3,* 167-182.

Tolliver, D. (1977). Personality as a factor determining response to two different meditation techniques. (Senior thesis, Princeton University, 1976). Cited in P. Carrington, 1977, *Freedom in meditation*. New York: Anchor Press/Doubleday.

Traupmann, J., & Hatfield, E. (1981). Love and its effect on mental and physical health. In J. March, S. Kiesler, R. Fogel, E. Hatfield, & E. Shanas (Eds.), *Aging: Stability and change in the family* (pp. 253-274). New York: Academic Press.

Travis, F. (1979). The Transcendental Meditation technique and creativity: A longitudinal study of Cornell University undergraduates. *Journal of Creative Behavior, 13,* 169-180.

Triandis, H. C. (1977). *Interpersonal behavior*. Monterey, CA: Brooks/Cole.

Triandis, H. C., & Davis, E. (1965). Race and belief as determinants of behavioral intention. *Journal of Personality and Social Psychology, 2,* 715-725.

Tridon, A. (1920). *Psychoanalysis and behavior*. New York: Knopf.

Truch, S. (1977). *The Transcendental Meditation technique and the art of learning*. New York: Littlefield.

Udry, J. R. (1974). *The social context of marriage* (3rd ed.). Philadelphia: Lippincott.

Udry, J. R. (1981). Marital alternatives and marital disruption. *Journal of Marriage and the Family, 43,* 879-897.

Uhr, L. M.(1957). *Personality changes during marriage*. Unpublished doctoral dissertation, University of Michigan, Ann Arbor.

Van den Berg, W. P., & Mulder, B. (1976). Psychological research on the effects of the Transcendental Meditation technique on a number of personality variables. *Gedrag: Tijdschrift voor Psychologie, 4,* 206-218.

VanReken, M. K. (1977). An investigation of spouse's perceptions of the marital relationship over the family life cycle. (Unpublished doctoral dissertation, Purdue University). (Cited in Swensen, Eskew, & Kohlhepp, 1981)

Venditti, M. C. (1980). *How to be your own marriage counselor*. New York: Continuum.

Verbrugge, L. M. (1977). The structure of adult friendship choices. *Social Forces, 56,* 576-597.

Wallace, R. K. (1970). Physiological effects of Transcendental Meditation. *Science, 167,* 1751-1754.

Wallace, R. K., Dillbeck, M. C., Jacobe, E., & Harrington, B. (1982). The effects of the Transcendental Meditation and TM-Sidhi program on the aging process. *International Journal of Neuroscience, 16,* 53-59.

Walster, E. (1965). The effect of self-esteem on romantic liking. *Journal of Experimental Social Psychology, 1,* 184-197.

Walster, E. (1971). Passionate love. In B. I. Murstein (Ed.), *Theories of attraction and love*. New York: Springer.

Walster, E., Aronson, V., Abrahams, D., & Rottman, L. (1966). The importance of physical attractiveness in dating behavior. *Journal of Personality and Social Psychology, 4,* 508-516.

Walster, E., Berscheid, E., & Walster, G. W. (1976). New directions in equity research. In L. Berkowitz (Ed.), *Advances in experimental social psychology* (Vol. 9, pp. 1-42). New York: Academic Press.

Walster, E., & Walster, G. W. (1963). Effect of expecting to be liked on choice of associates. *Journal of Personality and Social Psychology, 67,* 402-404.

Walster, E., Walster, G. W., & Berscheid, E. (1977). *Equity: Theory and research*. Boston: Allyn & Bacon.

Walster, E., Walster, G. W., & Traupmann, J. (1978). Equity and premarital sex. *Journal of Personality and Social Psychology, 36,* 82-92.

Walster, E., Walster, G. W., Piliavin, J., & Schmidt, L. (1973). "Playing hard-to-get": Understanding an elusive phenomenon. *Journal of Personality and Social Psychology, 26,* 113-121.

Westermarck, E. (1921). *The history of human marriage* (5th ed.). London: Macmillan.

White, G. L. (1980). Physical attractiveness and courtship progress. *Journal of Personality and Social Psychology, 39,* 660-668.

White, G. L., Fishbein, S., & Rutstein, J. (1981). Passionate love and misattribution of arousal. *Journal of Personality and Social Psychology, 41,* 56-62.

White, L. K. (1983). Determinants of spousal interaction: Marital structure of marital happiness. *Journal of Marriage and the Family, 45,* 511-520.

White, R. W. (1959). Motivation reconsidered: The concept of competence. *Psychological Review, 66,* 297-333.

Whiting, J. W. M., & Child, I. L. (1953). *Child training and personality: A cross-cultural study.* New Haven, CT: Yale University Press.

Wiggins, J., Wiggins, N., & Conger, J. (1968). Correlates of heterosexual semantic preference. *Journal of Personality and Social Psychology, 10,* 82-89.

Williams, P., & West, M. (1975). EEG responses to photic stimulation in persons experienced at meditation. *Electroencephalography and Clinical Neurophysiology, 39,* 519-522.

Wills, T. A., Weiss, R. L., & Patterson, G. R. (1974). A behavioral analysis of the determinants of marital satisfaction. *Journal of Consulting and Clinical Psychology, 42,* 802-811.

Winch, R. F. (1958). *Mate-selection.* New York: Harper & Row.

Winkler, J., & Doherty, W. J. (1983). Communication styles and marital satisfaction in Israeli and American couples. *Family Process, 22,* 221-228.

Woodworth, R. S. (1918). *Dynamic psychology.* New York: Columbia University Press.

Wylie, R. C. (1974). *The self-concept.* Lincoln: University of Nebraska Press.

Wylie, R. C. (1979). *The self-concept: Vol. 2. Theory and research on selected topics.* Lincoln: University of Nebraska Press.

Yelsma, P. (1981). Conflict predispositions: Differences between happy and clinical couples. *American Journal of Family Therapy, 9,* 57-63.

Zajonc, R. B. (1968). Attitudinal effects of mere exposure. *Journal of Personality and Social Psychology Monograph Supplement, 9,* 1-27.

Zetterberg, H. L. (1966). The secret ranking. *Journal of Marriage and the Family, 28,* 134-142.

Zuckerman, M. (1979). *Sensation seeking: Beyond the optimal level of arousal.* Hillsdale, NJ: Erlbaum.

Author Index

Ables, B. S., 115
Abrahams, D., 38, 50, 51
Abrams, A. I., 15, 124, 102
Adams, J. S., 73
Adey, W. R., 106
Ain, R., 74
Alexander, C. N., 103–104
Allan, G., 123
Allen, V. L., 77–78
Allport, G., 75, 84
Alston, W. P., 10
Anderson, J. A, 74
Anderson, N., 38
Anderson, S. A., 96
Appley, M. H., 23–24, 120
Aranya, S. H., 107
Archer, R. L., 34
Ard, B. N., Jr., 108
Arias, I., 132
Aron, A., 3, 34, 37, 42, 49, 63–66, 74, 102, 121, 123–124, 126
Aron, E. N., 102, 121, 123, 124, 126
Aronson, E., 37–39, 44, 48, 50
Aronson, V., 38, 50, 51
Arthur, R. A., 119
Atkinson, J. W., 20
Augustine, 12, 14

Back, K., 36
Bahr, S. J., 78
Ball, O., 103–104, 114
Bank, S. P., 29, 89

Banikiotes, P. G., 35
Banquet, J.-P., 17, 103, 104, 107
Banta, T. J., 55, 105
Ballachey, E. L., 4, 33
Baral, R., 51
Barry, W. A., 110
Basham, A. L., 6
Bataille, G., 27, 38, 52
Baumrind, D., 130
Beach, F. A., 38
Beavers, W. R., 81, 82, 117–119, 130–132, 134, 137–138
Bell, L., 48
Bennett, J. E., 104, 105
Bergler, E., 79, 94
Berl, E., 27
Berlyne, D. E., 20, 22, 38, 65
Berntein, W. M., 33
Berscheid, E., 4, 5, 37–38, 47–48, 50–52, 56, 58, 59, 63, 65, 73, 135
Bienvenu, J., 110
Binet, A., 62
Birchler, G. R., 111
Bischof, N., 30
Blau, P., 73
Bloom, B., 114
Bloomfield, H. H., 13, 103
Boscolo, L., 111
Bowen, M., 89
Bowlby, J., 62
Brandsma, J. M., 115
Brothen, T., 50
Breedlove, J., 46

157

Brehm, J., 63
Brickman, P., 100, 101, 122
Bridges, J. W., 62
Brink, J. H., 50
Brockner, J., 36
Broderick, C., 82
Bronson, E. C., 15, 103
Brown, R., 4
Brubaker, P., 114
Buchanan, W., 50
Buck, R., 115
Bucke, R. M., 106
Buckley, W., 47, 134
Burd, H., 74
Burgess, E. W., 91, 92, 103, 125, 129, 133
Burleson, J. A., 34
Burns, T., 76, 115
Burr, W. R., 77-78, 81, 92
Byrne, D., 33, 35, 37, 42, 48

Cain, M. P., 13, 103
Cameron, P., 100
Campbell, A., 71, 92, 97, 100, 105, 124
    131, 133
Campbell, D. T., 35
Campbell, K., 100
Caplan, G., 29, 119
Carlson, D., 10
Carrington, P., 89
Cash, T. F., 51
Casler, L., 58
Cattell, R. B., 115
Cecchin, G., 111
Cerreto, M., 76
Chadwick, C., 114
Chappell, C. B., 78
Child, I. L., 39
Cialdini, R. B., 50, 64-65
Clark, M. S., 64, 67, 76
Clark, R. W., 20
Clore, G. L., 34, 35, 55
Coates, D., 100, 101, 122
Cofer, C. N., 23-24, 120
Cohn, A. R., 103
Coleman, A. D., 34
Coleman, L. L., 34
Combs, A. W., 11
Conger, J., 37
Constantine, J., 77-78
Cooley, C. H., 9
Cottrell, L. S., 129
Count, G., 103
Cousins, P. D., 111, 132

Crofton, C., 37
Cronbach, L. J., 105
Crosby, J. F., 108
Crouse, B., 103, 105, 116, 121, 132-134
Crutchfield, R. S., 4, 33
Cuber, J. F., 72, 77, 83, 86, 94, 96, 99,
    125, 130, 133

Darley, J. M., 47
Dashiell, J. F., 21
Davis, D., 36, 46
Davis, E., 39
Davis, K. E., 49, 52, 56-57, 59, 61
Day, B. R., 55
Day, R. D., 77-78
Dean, A., 29
Deaux, K., 39
Deci, E. L., 20-22
Dember, W. N., 20, 100
Derlega, V. J., 51
Dick, L. D., 123
Dickens, W. J., 92, 118
Dickson-Markman, F., 112, 113
Dillbeck, M. C., 6, 15, 103, 105-106, 117,
    123-124
Dillbeck, S. L., 6
Dindia, K., 95, 99
Dion, K., 37, 50-51
Dizard, J., 125, 133
Doherty, W. J., 111, 115
Domash, L. H., 14
Douvan, E., 52
Dreskin, T., 105
Dreyer, A., 115
Driscoll, R., 52
Dubin, L., 15, 107
Duck, S. W., 35, 46, 124, 126
Dutton, D., 37, 63-65

Earl, R. W., 20
Easterlin, R., 100
Ellis, H., 34, 47, 108
Emery, D., 95, 99
English, H. B., 35
Ephron, H. S., 89
Epstein, S., 10, 23-24
Erber, R., 64, 67
Erikson, E. H., 17, 94-95
Ervin, C. R., 33, 37
Eskew, R. W., 97, 98, 103, 117, 133
Essex, M., 29, 118
Etzioni, A., 108, 123

Farrow, J. T., 6-7, 14-15, 103, 106
Faunce, E. E., 129
Fechner, G., 13
Fehr, T., 114
Feldman, H., 91, 92, 96, 117
Ferguson, P. C., 89, 103, 123
Ferguson, T. J., 10
Festinger, L., 20, 36, 43, 55
Filman, G., 74
Fincham, F., 111
Fiore, A., 57, 112, 132
Fischer, C. S., 92
Fishbein, S., 64, 65
Fitzgerald, R. V., 79
Floyd, F., 112, 113
Floyd, J., 38, 39
Foa, E. B., 42, 74
Foa, U. G., 29, 42, 74
Folkes, V. S.,33
Foote, N. N., 29, 92, 95, 99, 118
Ford, C. S., 38
Freud, S., 11-13, 19-20, 27, 62, 79
Froscher, H. B., 112
Frumkin, R. M., 38
Frunkin, L. R., 104-105
Furst, M., 15, 107

Gallup, G., 100
Garde, M., 103
Garrett, E. T., 112
Gatz, M., 63
Gebhard, P. H., 62
Gergen K. J., 9, 11
Glueck, B. C., 15, 89, 104, 107, 123
Goethals, G., 63
Goldman, W., 50
Goldstein, J. W., 47
Goleman, D., 106
Gollwitzer, P. M., 9, 19
Goodman, P., 43
Goodwin, H. M., 95
Gormly, J. B., 34
Gossett, J. T., 119, 130-132, 137-138
Gottman, J. M., 34, 110-113, 131-132
Gowan, J. C., 13, 25, 75, 89, 103, 123
Grant, V. W., 27, 56, 62, 67, 79
Graziano, W., 50
Greene, B. L., 109
Greenwald, A. G., 9, 19, 23-24
Griffitt, W., 35-36, 48
Gross, A. E., 37
Guerney, B. G., 96
Guggenbuhl-Craig, A., 30-72, 80-81, 94-96, 116-117, 122, 134-135, 138

Hahn, H., 89
Haley, J., 81, 111
Hall, C. S., 6, 9, 11, 51, 63
Hall, J. A., 112, 132
Hamilton, G. V., 62
Hansen, D. A., 75, 78, 80, 84-85
Harlow, H. F., 20
Harrington, B., 103, 123
Harris, C. N., 90
Harris, S. G., 65
Harroff, P. B., 72, 77, 83, 86, 94, 96, 99, 125, 130, 133
Harvey, O. J., 26
Hatfield, E. (Walster), 4, 5, 27, 37-38, 42, 47, 49-52, 56, 58-60, 63, 66, 73-74, 76, 84, 89-90, 125, 135
Hatkoff, T. S., 58
Hay, J., 73
Haydon, E. M., 103
Haynes, E. T., 15, 17, 103, 106
Hebert, J. R., 7, 14-15, 103, 106
Hefferline, R. F., 43
Heider, F., 43-44
Helmreich, R., 39
Hendrix, C. E., 106
Hertel, R. K., 110
Herz, M. J., 92
Hetherington, M., 55
Hilgard, E. R., 10
Hill, C. A., 9
Hilton, J. L., 9, 19
Hjelle, L. A., 105
Hochberg, J. E., 43
Hoffman, L. W., 27, 92, 123
Hoffman, M. L., 27, 92, 123
Holman, T. B., 81
Holmes, T. H., 118
Homans, G., 73
Hudgins, W., 35
Hudson, W. W., 96
Huesmann, L. R., 25, 61, 93, 95
Hull, C. L., 19
Hunt, D., 26
Hustedt, T. K., 59
Huston, T. L., 33, 38, 51, 99, 110

Insko, C. A., 46, 51
Izard, C. E., 47

Jackson, D. D., 81
Jackson, R. M., 92
Jacob, T., 111, 129

Jacobe, E., 103, 123
Jacobsohn, P., 35
Jacobson, N. S., 93, 95, 112, 115
Jaffe, D. T., 13, 103
James, W., 11-12, 16
Janoff-Bulman, R., 100, 101, 122
Jaremko, M. E., 58
Johnston, T. L., 58
Jones, E., 48
Jones, L. M., 92
Jung, C. G., 4, 6, 13, 23-24, 27, 34, 51,
        62-63, 79, 81, 84-85, 89, 94-95,
        134, 138

Kagan, J., 20
Kahn, M., 110
Kahn, M. D., 29, 89
Kahn, S., 121
Kammann, R., 100
Kanellakos, D. P., 6, 121
Karlins, M., 103, 105, 116, 121, 132-134
Kelley, H. H., 41, 43, 56, 73, 75-76
Kelling, G. W., 27, 47, 52, 93, 95, 111
Kelman, H., 29
Kelly, G. A., 46, 115
Kenrick, D. T., 64-65
Kerckhoff, A. C., 39, 49
Kernis, M. H., 50
Kessler, R. C., 29, 118
Kieren, D., 117
Kiesler, S., 51
Kinch, J. W., 9
Kirkpatrick, C., 129
Kobasa, S. C., 121
Koffka, K., 42-44
Kohlberg, L., 75
Kohler, W., 43
Kohlhepp, K. A., 97, 98, 103, 117, 133
Kostin, J., 100
Kostin, M., 100
Krech, D., 4, 33
Kuhn, M. H., 11
Kuhn, T. S., 23
Kukulan, J., 102

Lamberth, J., 5, 33, 37, 42
Landrith, G., 124
Landy, D., 50
Lasswell, M. E., 58
Lasswell, T. E., 58
Launier, R., 118
Lawton, M. P., 48, 49
Layton, B. D., 46, 51

Lazarus, R. S., 118, 120
Le Boeuf, B. J., 38
Lee, J. A., 58, 135
LeFan, J., 39
Leigh, G. K., 77-78
Levenson, H., 90
Levenson, R. W., 34, 111, 113, 131-132
Levine, P. H., 15, 103
Levinger, G., 28, 46
Levitan, D., 56
Lewin, K., 4, 11, 17, 42
Lewis, J., 119, 130-132, 137-138
Lewis, P., 50
Lewis, R. A., 86, 96, 112, 131, 133
Lewis, T., 107
Lin, N., 29
Linder, D., 50, 64
Lindzey, G., 6, 9, 11
Linton, R., 58
Lipitz, M. E., 52
Litwak, E., 103
Livingston, K. R., 95
Locke, H. J., 92, 102, 129
Locksley, A., 112, 121
Loevinger, J., 17, 75, 97, 133
Lombardo, J. P., 50
Lott, A. J., 42, 66
Lott, B. E., 42, 66
Lowell, E. L., 20
Lukenbach, A., 27
Lytton, H., 129

Maddi, S. R., 121
MacDonald, M., 76
Maharishi Mahesh Yogi, 6, 7, 13, 16, 25,
        107, 121, 122, 124
Maher, J. E., 65
Mahrer, A. R., 133, 138
Malinowski, B., 38
Mangus, A. R., 62
Margolin, G., 93, 95, 110, 112, 115, 132
Markman, H. J., 71, 110-113, 132
Markus, H., 10
Martin, J., 15, 107
Maslow, A. H., 21, 22, 27, 103, 105, 107,
        118, 124, 133, 135, 136
Matheny, A., 35
Maulsby, R., 106
McCall, G. J., 9, 27
McCallum, R., 74
McClelland, D. C., 20
McClintock, C., 76
McCrimmon, J., 63
McDonald, G. W., 26, 76

McDonald, P. J., 65
McGuire, W. J., 126
McLane, D., 56
McLaney, M. A., 59
McPartland, T. S., 11
Mead, G. H., 9
Mednick, A., 103
Meeker, B., 76
Mettee, D. R., 37
Milberg, S., 64, 67
Mill, J. S., 12
Miller, H. L., 92
Miller, N., 35
Mills, J., 76
Mirels, H. L., 50
Mischel, T., 11
Mischel, W., 11
Miskiman, D. E., 105, 117
Montgomery, K. C., 20
Morse, D., 15, 107
Mudd, E. H., 95, 112, 130
Mulder, B. N., 89, 105
Murdock, G. P., 39
Murphy, G. J., 96
Murray, H., 19
Murstein, B. I., 37, 38, 42, 48, 49, 51,
    58, 76

Nadelson, C. C., 79, 109
Nagy, G. F., 38, 51
Nahemow, L., 48, 49
Navran, L., 110
Neimeyer, G. J., 35, 46
Neimeyer, R. A., 46
Nerstheimer, U., 114
Nesselroade, J. B., 115
Newcomb, T. M., 36, 42, 43
Nexlek, J., 50
Nidich, S. I., 105, 117
Nimkoff, M., 35
Nissen, H. W., 21
Noller, P., 132
Nordby, V. J., 51, 63
Nystul, M. S., 103

O'Connell, E. J., 35
Oden, M. H., 103, 121, 133
O'Leary, K. D., 111, 132
Olson, D. H., 82, 110
O'Neill, G., 125
O'Reilly, E., 74
Orme-Johnson, D. W., 6, 15, 17, 103–
    106, 114, 117, 124

Osgood, C. E., 43
Ossorio, P. G., 56

Pagano, R. R., 104, 105
Palazzoli, M. S., 111
Parlee, M. B., 118
Patanjali, 14
Patterson, G. R., 111, 113
Pearlin, L. I., 119, 120
Peeke, H. V. S., 92
Pelletier, K. R., 89, 105, 117
Peltz, W. L., 112
Penwell, L., 100
Perlman, D., 92, 118
Perls, F. S., 43
Perri, M., 50
Phillips, V. A., 119, 130–132, 137–138
Philo, 14
Piaget, J., 17, 23, 93, 120
Piliavin, J., 49
Pineo, P. C., 49, 91, 92, 96, 117, 132
Pirot, M., 105
Plato, 3, 12, 14, 25, 75
Plotinus, 14
Plutchik, R., 93
Posavac, E., 38
Prata, G., 111
Preston, M. G., 112
Proxmire, W., 5

Rahe, R. H., 118–119
Raush, H. L., 110
Read, J. R., 9
Reader, N., 35
Reeves, K., 35
Reik, T., 4, 27, 29, 56, 61, 66, 79, 94,
    134, 138
Reis, H. T., 50, 131
Reisman, J. M., 92, 118, 125, 131
Renne, K. S., 103, 123, 133
Richardson, H. M., 35
Riddle, A., 107
Riordan, C. A., 64, 65
Riskin, J., 129
Rogers, C. R., 11, 12, 25, 105, 118, 134
Rollins, B. C., 91, 92, 96, 117
Rose, A., 74
Rosenfeld, H., 47
Rosenman, M. F., 58
Ross, J., 64
Rothbaum, F., 29
Rotter, J. B., 47

Rottman, L., 38, 50, 51
Rubin, Z., 33, 52, 56, 58
Rule, B. G., 10
Russell, C. S., 82, 96, 110
Rutstein, J., 64, 65
Ryder, R. G., 148

Sabatelli, R. M., 115
Safilios-Rothschild, C., 74
Sager, C. J., 79, 115
Sailhan, M., 17, 103, 104
Sarbin, T. R., 10, 77-78
Satir, V., 81
Sauer, K., 124, 129, 130, 138
Saxe, L., 38
Schachter, S., 29, 33, 36, 63
Schiller, B., 62
Schmidt, L., 49
Schoeneman, T. J., 11
Schooler, C., 119, 120
Schopler, J., 37
Schroder, H., 26, 103, 105, 116, 121, 132-
    134
Schumm, W. R., 96
Schwartz, G., 106
Sears, D. O., 47
Seeman, W., 105
Segal, M. W., 36
Segraves, R. T., 79, 109-113, 115-116, 121,
    134
Seligman, M. E. P., 26, 99
Selvini, M., 111
Selye, H., 118, 120, 121
Shanteau, J., 38, 51
Shapiro, J. S., 89
Shecter, H., 89, 103, 105, 117
Shelly, M. W., 106
Shrauger, J. S., 11
Shulman, N., 118
Siegel, D., 132
Siegel, L. M., 124, 126
Siegel, P. S., 92
Sigall, H., 50
Singer, J., 63
Skinner, B. F., 112
Smith, J., 82
Smith, M. B., 10, 24
Snoek, J. D., 46
Snyder, M., 33, 38
Snyder, R. A., 48
Snyder, S. S., 29
Snygg, D., 11
Socrates, 12, 121

Solomon, M. R., 37
Solomon, R. L., 23
Solomon, S., 38
Solovyev, V., 27
Spanier, G. B., 86, 96, 112, 131, 133
Speer, D. C., 82, 134
Spiegel, N., 50
Sprecher, S., 73
Sprenkle, D. H., 82, 110
Steck, L., 56
Stefaniak, D., 35
Steffen, J. J., 59
Stekel, W., 62
Stendhal (Marie-Henri Beyle), 3, 50
Stephenson, B. O., 33
Stich, M. H., 50
Stichmann, L., 74
Stinnett, N., 124, 129, 130, 138
Straus, M. A., 110
Strauss, A., 62
Strobel, U., 103
Stroebe, W., 51
Stroebel, C. F., 15, 89, 104, 107, 123
Stuart, R. B., 100
Suarez, V. M., 102
Suttie, I. D., 56
Swain, M. A., 110
Swann, W. B., 9, 19, 29
Swap, W. C., 36
Swensen, C. H., Jr., 29, 57, 92, 97, 98, 103,
    112, 117, 132-133

Tallman, I., 117
Tamari, Z., 74
Tanke, E. D., 38
Tannenbaum, P. H., 43
Taubin, S., 130
Taylor, S. E., 112, 132
Tedeschi, J. T., 33, 64-65
Tennov, D., 59
Teresa of Avila, 12, 14, 105, 106
Terman, L. M., 103, 121, 129, 133
Tesser, A., 28, 76
Thibaut, J. W., 41, 73, 75-76
Thomes, M. M., 92
Thompson, V. D., 51
Titus, D. G., 100
Tjoa, A. S., 89
Todd, M. J., 56-57, 59, 61
Tolliver, D., 107
Torber, S., 114
Torrance, E. P., 103
Traupmann, J., 56-59, 73-74
Travis, F., 103

Triandis, H. C., 39, 46
Tridon, A., 62
Trinder, J., 104, 105
Truch, S., 6
Twedt, H., 35

Udry, J. R., 74, 87, 115, 117, 124
Uhr, L. M., 92, 117
Utne, M., 56, 73

Van den Berg, W. P., 6, 89, 105, 106
VanReken, M. K., 97
Veitch, R., 36
Venditti, M. C., 94
Verbrugge, L. M., 118
Vincent, J. P., 111, 132
Voeller, M. N., 82, 117–119

Wallace, R. K., 15, 103–104, 107, 114, 123
Wallin, P., 91, 92, 103, 125, 133
Walster, E. H. (*see* Hatfield, E. H.)
Walster, G. W., 38, 47, 49, 51–52, 58, 60, 73–74, 125
Walter, D. O., 106
Wampold, B. E., 110, 112, 132
Ward, L., 63
Watts, A., 6
Watzlawick, P., 81
Wawro, J., 74
Weakland, J., 81

Weinberg, L., 74
Weiss, R. F., 50
Weiss, R. L., 111
Weisz, J. R., 29
Wertheimer, M., 43
Wessler, R., 17, 75, 97, 133
West, M., 107
Westermarck, E., 4, 38
Wheeler, L., 50
White, G. L., 38, 64, 65
White, L. K., 110
White, R. W., 20–22, 24
Whiting, J. W. M., 39
Wicklund, R. A., 9, 19, 33
Wiggins, J., 37
Wiggins, N., 37
Wilkinson, 82
Willerman, B., 38, 39
Williams, P., 107
Wills, T. A., 111
Winch, R. F., 4, 35
Winesauker, J., 74
Winkler, J., 111
Woodworth, R. S., 20
Worchel, P., 48
Wylie, R. C., 9

Yelsma, P., 132

Zajonc, R. B., 36
Zetterberg, H. L., 38
Zuckerman, M., 20, 94

Subject Index

Academic achievement, 15, 114
Accommodation, 93
Adaptability, system, 82
Adaptation level, 101
Addictions, 119, 122–123, 126
Admirable characteristics (*see* Attraction
 prediction rules)
Affective-arousal-state-specific memory,
 64–65, 67
Affiliation, need for, 4, 29
Agape love, 58, 135, 138
Age and happiness, 100
Aging, 103, 125
Alternatives to a relationship, 76, 83–87,
 94, 110, 124–127, 138
 (*See also* Comparison level)
Ambivalence, 56
Anima/animus archetype, 4, 62–63, 79–80
Anxiety, 29, 102, 119, 135
Appearance, 37–38, 44
Appreciation, 130–131, 138
Archetype, 4, 11, 34, 62–63, 79–81, 94
Arousal, physiological, 20, 63, 93
 (*See also* Attraction, theories of)
Aspiration, level of, 75
Assimilation, 93
Attachment, 4, 27, 79
Attitude similarity, and attraction, 35–36,
 42, 44
Attraction:
 definitions of, 33–34, 52–53
 intensity of, 56
 prediction of (*see* Attraction prediction
  rules)

readiness in, 66
study of, 4–5
theories of: affective-arousal-state-
  specific memory, 64–65, 67
 attribution, 5, 43
 boundary breaking, 65
 cognitive balance and dissonance, 5, 43
 cues, specific, 62–63, 66, 67
 equity, 5
 exchange, 5, 41–42
 filtering model, 49
 Gestalt, 42–45
 labeling, 5
 misattribution of arousal (two-
  component), 64–65, 67
 reactance, 5
 readiness, 66
 relief from punishment (negative
  reinforcement), 65–67
 reward, 41–42, 44–45
 self-expansion and, 66–67
 social learning, 41
 stimulus-value-role, 49
 (*See also* Arousal, physiological;
  Relationships)
Attraction prediction rules:
 admirable characteristics as, 37–39, 42,
  44–48, 50–51
 appearance, 37–38, 44
 aspects of, 38, 44
 consistency of judgments of, 37
 importance, 37
 impressions, first, 38
 matching hypothesis, 37–39, 42–44

Attraction prediction rules (*Cont.*):
  and liking, reciprocal (being liked),
    36-37, 42, 45-50
  and norms and social context, 39, 42,
    44-48, 51, 124
  and propinquity, 36, 42, 44-49
  and similarity (and dissimilarity), 35-36,
    42, 44-49
    of attitudes, 35-36, 42, 44
    of cognitive structures, 35
    of personalities, 35
  and self-expansion, 45-52
Authoritarian or authoritative parent,
    130-131
Autonomic stability, 106

Beauty (*see* Attraction prediction rules)
Behavioral modification, 110, 116
Being (B) love, 135-138
Bhagavad-Gita, 6, 121
Biofeedback, 15, 107
Boredom, 91-109, 117, 137
Boundary breaking, 65
Breath suspension, 14, 16, 89
British school of psychoanalysis, 79

Capacity for intimate contact, 105
Cathexis, 83-84
Characteristics, admirable, 37-39, 42, 45-
    48, 50-51
Change, 22-23, 109, 117-122, 138
  (*See also* Stress)
Circumplex model of family-system
    qualities, 82-83
Classical conditioning, 66
Cognition theory for decline in satisfaction,
    93-94
Cognitive discrimination, 117
Cognitive flexibility and complexity, 15,
    103, 105, 114-117, 121-122, 132-
    135
Cognitive orientation, 76
Cognitive structure, 35, 46
Coherence, EEG, 14-16, 89, 103-105, 114,
    138
Commitment, 56, 97
  exchange based on, 76
Communication:
  good, 94, 109-114, 130-132, 135, 137
  negative/positive affect and, 110-115,
    132-133, 135
Companionship, 91
Companionate love, 5, 58, 61, 92, 94

Comparison level, 73-75, 93, 134
  of the alternative, 73-75, 134
  (*See also* Alternatives to a
    relationship)
Complementarity of needs, 4, 45
Complexity/uncertainty:
  reduction of, 20, 22
  optimal level of, 20-21
Conflict-habituated relationship, 72, 77-78
Conflict-resolution skills, 110, 115
Conformity, 89
Consciousness:
  pure (*see* Pure consciousness experience)
  states of, 16, 17
Contingency contracts, 112, 115
Continued expansion, 137
Coping, 118-122, 138
  (*See also* Stress)
Creativity:
  in marriage, 103
  and pure consciousness experience, 15,
    103, 105, 114
Crime as relationship stressor, 123
Crystallization, 3
Cues, specific, in attraction, 62-63, 66, 67

Decision theory, 93
Deexpansion and de-integration, 25-26,
    85-87, 97
Deficiency (D) love, 135-136
Delay of gratification, 126
Dependence/independence, 89, 122
Depression, 89
Descriptive psychology, 56
Detachment, 16
Determinism, 16
Devitalized relationship, 72, 78
Differences, 30
Differentiation, system, 82
Discrimination against minorities as
    relationship stressor, 123
Disengaged-enmeshed dimension of a
    system, 82
Dissimilarities (*see* Attraction prediction
    rules, and similarity)
Drives, 19-20, 84
Duty (level of motivation), 75, 78, 80, 84,
    86

Eastern psychology, 3, 6, 15, 25, 75
  (*See also* Vedic psychology)

Education, 100–101, 123
Effectance, potential, 21, 24–25, 50
Egalitarian marriage, 130
Ego:
    development of: conformist level of, 97
      and marital satisfaction, 117, 133
      and optimal relationships, 138
      and pure consciousness experience,
        103, 105
      post-conformity level of, 97
    distance of, 89
    Freudian, 81, 83
    ideal, 27, 94, 134
    integrity of, 17
    oriented psychologists, 79
    strength of, 89
Electroencephalogram (EEG):
    and alpha blocking, 107
    coherence of, 14–16, 89, 103–105,
      114, 138
Emotions, strong, 65
Empathy, 29
Empty nest, 97
Equity theory, 73–74, 76, 87–88
Eros love, 58
Evolution, 21
Expanded perspective, 137–138
Experiencer, 12, 16–17
Exchange theory, 73–77, 83–84, 86–87,
    94, 134–135, 137
Exclusiveness, 57, 125
Exploration, mastery, 19–21
    (*See also* Effectance, potential)
External stressors, 110, 123–124, 138

Family therapy, 81–82
Fantasy, 56
Fascination, 57
Fatalism, 16
Field independence, 89, 100, 117
Filtering model, 49
Financial disagreements, 109
First impressions, 38
    (*See also* Attraction prediction
      rules)
Flexibility, system, 82–83, 138
Formal operations, 17
Free will, 16
Friendship love, 56–58, 60
Friendship types, 131
Fulfillment, 26, 126, 138
Functional similarity, 46

General adaptation syndrome, 118–119
    (*See also* Stress; Coping)
General systems theory, 81–83, 86, 94,
    134–135, 137
Gestalt theory, 42–46
Goal-based exchange, 76
Grade point average and pure conscious-
    ness experience, 15, 114
Growth, 22, 29, 42, 81, 116, 118

Habituation, 92–93, 99, 101, 106–107, 117
    (*See also* Boredom)
Handicap, 122
Happiness, 99–101
    and age, 100
    and education, 100–101
    and health, 101
    and income, 100–101
    inner, 99, 126, 136, 138
    and pure consciousness experience,
      107–108
    as satisfaction with life, 106, 138
    set, 100–101
    as well-being, 99, 101, 113, 138
    (*See also* Satisfaction)
Hardiness, 119
Harmonizing differences, 137
Health and happiness, 101
Height, 50
Homeostasis, 19–22, 75, 78, 81
Honesty, 130
Housing, 123

"I," 11–13, 15–18, 24–25, 106
Id, 81, 83
Idealization, 56
Identification, 17–18
Impressions, first, 38
    (*See also* Attraction prediction rules)
Incompatibility, 109, 114–117
Independence/dependence, 89, 122
Individual differences, 22, 26–27, 78,
    83, 86, 94, 115–116
Information theory, 47
Inherited tendencies, 11, 27
Initiative, 130
Inoculation effect, 126
Instincts, 19, 79
Instrumental conditioning, 66
Integral ego, 17

Integration, in self-expansion process,
    22–25, 88, 90, 94
Intelligence:
    and attractiveness, 38
    and capacity to expand, 26
    and general competence, 105
    inherited, 27
    and marital satisfaction, 113, 133, 135,
        138
    and pure consciousness experience, 15,
        113, 114
Internal locus of control, 100–102, 105,
    113–114, 119
Internalization, 84
Interpersonal Judgment Scale (IJS), 34, 35
Intrinsic relationship, 72, 86, 94, 96–97
    99, 130
Introversion, 115
Isolation, 65

Jealousy, 122

Knowledge:
    domain of, 22
    as resource, 24

Learned helplessness, 26, 99
Learning theory for decline in satisfaction,
    92–93
Leveling, 110
Libido, 19, 41
Life cycle, 96–98, 117
Life instinct, 20
Life satisfaction (see Satisfaction)
Life space, 11, 17
Liking:
    vs. loving, 55, 61
    reciprocal (being liked), 36–37, 42,
        45–50
    (See also Attraction prediction rules)
    Scale, 52
Limerence, 59
Love:
    Eastern (Vedic) study of, 6–7, 13–18
    falling in, 3, 37, 60
    at first sight, 62
    vs. liking, 55
    possession in, 56
    scale, 32
    theories of (see Attraction, theories of;
        Relationships, theories of)

types of: agape, 58, 135, 138
    being (B), 135–138
    companionate, 5, 58, 61, 92, 94
    deficiency (D), 135–136
    eros, 58
    friendship, 56–58, 60
    generative, 94
    limerence, 59
    ludus, 58
    mania, 58, 59
    mature, 94
    passionate, 5, 27, 58–61, 63, 92,
        94
    practical, 58
    pragma, 58
    romantic, 5, 30, 56–59, 95
    saintly, 58
    salvation-oriented, 94
    selfless, 7
    storge, 58
    (See also Relationships, types of)
Western study of: anthropological, 3, 4
    in clinical psychology, 4
    historical, 3, 4
    interdisciplinary, 5
    in literature, 3
    philosophical, 3
    psychiatric, 4
    psychoanalytic, 4
    social psychological, 4–5
    sociological, 4
Ludus love, 58

Maintaining relationships (see
    Relationships)
Major intersection, 28
Mania love, 58, 59
Marriage, 29–30
    satisfaction in, 4, 102
    (See also Relationship, satisfaction in)
Marriage encounter, 96
Mastery, exploration, 19–21
    (See also Effectance, potential)
Matching hypothesis, 37–39, 42–44
    (See also Attraction prediction rules)
Mate selection, 79
    (See also Attraction)
Mature love, 94
"Me," 11–13, 15–18, 24–25
Meditation (see Transcendental Medita-
    tion technique)
Mental illness/health, 27, 38, 109, 122–123,
    138

Merging, 89
Misattribution of arousal (*see* Attraction,
    theories of)
Moral judgment (Kohlberg test) and pure
    consciousness experience, 15, 117,
    122
Morphogenesis and morphostasis, 81
Motivation:
    and arousal, 20
    and complexity reduction, 20, 22
    and drive theory, 19-20
    and exploration, mastery, 19-21
    and effectance, 21, 24-25
    homeostatic view of, 19-22, 78
    intrinsic, 21
    levels of, 75, 78, 80, 84-86
    to maintain relationships, 78, 84
    optimal level of complexity, 20-21
    psychoanalytic view of, 19-20
    self-expansion view of, 22-27
    traditional view of, 19
    and uncertainty reduction, 20, 22
Mutuality, 28
Mystery, 65

Natural selection, 21
Nature, laws of, 25, 106
Need complementarity, 4, 45-46
Needs, 19
Negative/positive affect and communica-
    tion, 110-115, 132-133, 135
Negentropy, 118
Neuromuscular coordination and pure
    consciousness experience, 15
Neuroticism, 48, 89, 103, 115, 122
Nondifferentiation of self, 89
Norms and social context, 39, 42, 44-48,
    51, 124
    (*See also* Attraction prediction rules)
Novelty, 19-20, 22, 65, 93, 99, 120

Object relations theory, 79
Oceanic experience and Freud, 13
Open marriage, 125
Optimal relationships, 117, 129-138
Other, incorporation of, into self, 27-30
Outcome in exchange theory, 73-74

Pain/pleasure as level of motivation, 75, 78,
    80, 84, 86
Paradigm, 23
Paradigm case, 56

Parsimony, 12
Passion, 3, 79, 95, 134
Passionate love, 5, 27, 58-61, 63, 92, 94
Passive-congenial relationship, 72, 78, 94,
    130
Passivity, 16, 121-122
Perceptual discrimination, 105
Permissive parent, 131
Person, 11, 13
Personal autonomy, 130
Physiological linkage, 111, 132
Pleasure/pain as level of motivation, 75, 78,
    80, 84, 86
Positive/negative affect and communication,
    110-115, 132-133, 135
Positive regard, 131
Possession of Other, 27, 135
Poverty/wealth, 42, 123, 138
Power, 50
    feeling of, 65
    (*See also* Effectance, potential)
Pragma love, 58
Pragmatic flexibility, 130
Preconditions for attraction, 46-53
    (*See also* Attraction prediction rules)
Predictability/uncertainty, 93, 95, 131, 133
Prediction rules (*see* Attraction prediction
    rules)
Prisoners and meditation, 124
Profit/success as level of motivation, 75, 78,
    80, 84, 86
Projection, 79
Propinquity, 36, 42, 44-49
Prosocial behavior, 29
Psychoanalysis, 4, 19-20
    (*See also* Relationship, theories of,
        psychodynamic)
Psychodynamic theory for decline in
    satisfaction, 94
Punishment, 111-112
    relief from, 65-67
Pure consciousness experience, 16
    description of, 13-14, 23, 25, 89
    effects of, on boredom, 105-108
    as "I," 16-18, 25, 106
    and optimal relationships, 136
    and passivity, 121-124, 126
    reports of, 13-15, 25, 101
    research on, 7, 13-16, 103-104
    (*See also* Individual differences)
    and solutions to problems, 107, 114,
        117, 121
    techniques for experiencing, 14
    Vedic psychology and, 7, 13-14

Rational Emotive Therapy (RET), 108
Reciprocal liking (being liked), 36-37, 42,
    46-50
    (*See also* Attraction prediction rules)
Reflection, 30, 76
Relationships:
    maintenance forces of, 83-85
    maintenance of, and self-expansion,
        85-88
    motives to be in, 84
    optimal, 117, 129-138
    prevalence of, 71-72
    problem in, 109-127
        alternatives as, 83-87, 94, 110,
            124-127, 138
        boredom as, 91-109, 117, 137
        change as, 109, 117-122, 138
        incompatibility as, 109, 114-117
        poor communication and other skills
            as, 94, 109-114
        poor health in other as, 109, 122-
            123, 138
    satisfaction in, 4, 102, 110, 115, 129
        decline in, 91-94, 96
    and self-expansion, 28-29
    social influences on, 84-85
    theories of: equity, 73-74, 76, 87-88
        exchange, or social exchange, 73-77,
            83-84, 86-87, 134-135, 137
        psychodynamic, 79-81, 83-86, 110,
            115, 134-135
        reward, 115, 134-135
        role, and symbolic interaction, 77-78,
            83, 86-88, 134-135, 137
        systems, 81-83, 86, 115, 134-135
    types of, 84-86
    close, 5
    devitalized, 72, 78
    communal, 76
    conflict-habituated, 72, 77-78
    exchange, 76
    immature, 81
    intrinsic, 72, 86, 94, 96-97, 99, 130
    neurotic, 81
    passive-congenial, 72, 78, 94, 130
    total, 72, 77-78, 94, 99, 130-131
    utilitarian, 130
    vital, 72, 94, 130
    (*See also* Love, types of)
Relaxation, 15, 107
Releaser mechanisms, 11, 62
Relief from punishment, 65-67
Religion, 96, 124, 130, 138
Resolving conflict, 137

Resources, exchange, 42
Respect, 52, 138
Reward gradients, 25, 93
Reward theory, 41-42, 44-45, 81
Right brain, 103
Rigidity-chaos dimension (of a system),
    82-83
Role, 12
    conflict of, 77-78
    consensus of, 77-78
    expectations of, 77
    fit of, 49, 131
    organismic involvement in, 77-78
    reciprocal, 78
    (*See also* Symbolic interactionists)
Role Repertory Test (REP), 46
Role theory:
    for decline in satisfaction, 94
    and symbolic interaction, 77-78, 83,
        86-88, 134-135, 137
Romantic love, 5, 30, 56-59, 95
    (*See also* Love; Attraction)

Sacrifice in marriage, 122
Salvation, 80, 84, 96, 134, 138
Satisfaction:
    with life, 106, 138
    in relationships, 4, 91-94, 96, 102, 110,
        115, 129
    (*See also* Happiness)
Schemata, 9-11, 89, 93, 109, 114
Secondary reinforcement, 25, 93
Security, 42
Self, 9-18
    actual, 9-12
    as agent, 10-12
    as cognitive structure, 10, 12, 24
    concept of, 9-10, 16-17, 19, 23-24, 28
    development of, 95
    (*See also* States of consciousness)
    esteem of, 9, 11, 88, 100, 103, 119, 122
    as experiencer, 12, 16-17
    and "I," 11-13, 15-18, 24-25, 106
    individual, 17
    integrity of, 89
    and lifespace, 11
    loss of, 88-91
    and "me," 11-13, 15-18, 24-25
    nondifferentiation of, 89
    as person, 11, 13
    personality psychologists' view of, 9,
        11
    as process, 11

Self (*Cont.*):
  schema of, 9–11
  symbolic interactionist view of, 9, 11
  theory of, 23–24
  universal, 17
  Western description of, 9–13
  wholeness of, 24
Self-actualization, 12, 29, 103, 107–108, 124, 133–138
Self-expansion, 5, 9, 18, 22–30, 74, 81, 85–90, 94, 97–101, 122, 138
  and alternatives, 125–127
  and attraction: defining, 52–53
    predicting, 45–52
    strong, theories of, 66–67
  and boredom, 91, 117
  capacity for, 26
  and coping with change, 119–122
  and deexpansion and de-integration, 25–26, 85–87, 97
  and external stressors, 123–124
  and incompatibility, 116–117
  individual differences in, 22, 26, 86
  and integration, 22–25, 88, 90, 94
  and integrating reward and Gestalt theories, 45
  internal source of, 101
  and losing self, 88–91
  and maintenance of relationships, 85–88
  motivation for, view of, 22–27
  and optimal relationships, 136–138
  and skills training, 114
Senility, 122
Sex-relevant schemata, 114
Sexual dissatisfaction, 109
Shared experience, 98, 105
Shared interests, 96
Simplicity, 43
Skills training, 112–114
Social context and attraction, 39, 42, 44–48, 51
Social exchange theory, 73–77, 83–84, 86–87, 94, 134–135, 137
Social support networks, 29, 119
Specific cues in attraction, 62–63, 66, 67
Spending time together, 130–131
States of consciousness, 16, 17
Status, 42
Stimulation, 22
Stimulus-Value-Role theory, 49
Storge love, 58
Strain, 119
Stress, 22–24, 29, 89, 113, 118–121, 123–124

course on management of, 119, 120
  (*See also* Change; Coping)
Sublimation, 79
Success, 26
  as level of motivation, 75, 78, 80, 84
Superego, 81, 83
Support, emotional, 42
Survival, 21, 22, 29
Symbolic interactionists, 9, 11, 94
  (*See also* Role)
Syntaxic modes, 13
System properties:
  differentiation, 82
  disengaged-enmeshed dimension, 82
  flexibility, 82–83, 138
  morphogenesis, 81
  morphostasis, 81
  rigidity-chaos dimension, 82–83
Systems theory, 81–83, 86, 115, 134–135
  for decline in satisfaction, 94

Tension reduction, 84
Thematic Apperception Test, 63
Tissue needs, 20
Tolerance, 105, 116, 123
Torrance Test of Creativity, 103
Total relationship, 72, 77–78, 94, 99, 130–131
Transcendental experiences, 34
  (*See also* Pure consciousness experience)
Transcendence as level of motivation, 75, 78, 80, 84
Transcendental Meditation (TM) technique, 13–15, 23, 89, 103–107, 121, 124, 126, 136
  techniques other than, 15
"Transcenders," 103
Transference, 79, 94, 109, 115–116, 134
Trust, 42, 105, 130
Two-component theory (*see* Attraction, theories of)

Uncertainty theory, 95
Uncertainty/complexity uncertainty reduction, 20, 22
Uncertainty/predictability, 93, 95, 131, 133
Unconscious, 79, 88, 99, 111, 115, 134
Unconscious contract, 79
Undifferentiated ego mass, 89
Unemployment as relationship stressor, 123
Union, 27, 29
Unity conscious, 17, 18, 136

Upanishads, 7, 16
Utilitarian relationship, 130

Vedic psychology, 3, 6-7, 13, 16-18,
    23, 85, 91, 103, 121-122, 124, 136
    (*See also* Eastern psychology)
Violence, family, 110
Vital relationship, 72, 94, 130

"We" feeling, 76
Wealth/poverty, 42, 123, 138
Well-being, 99, 101, 113, 138
    (*See also* Happiness)
Wholeness, 24, 84, 104
Working together, 96

Yielding, 50